IMAGES
of America

AROUND MAYSVILLE

ON THE COVER: The photograph of this political barbecue on a farm in Mason County was dated April 22, 1916. A note on the back says, "The 3 kettles held 500 gallons each." An advertising stamp on the back says, "From Dr. J.A. Dodson, Dentist, 206 Court St. Maysville, Ky." Crowds of people are in the background. Local historian David Cartmell says the two cauldrons used here were once placed in front of Maysville High School. (Courtesy of the author.)

IMAGES of America

AROUND MAYSVILLE

Tom Roberson

ARCADIA PUBLISHING

ISBN 9781-4671-6235-7

Published by Arcadia Publishing
Charleston, South Carolina

Printed in the United States of America

Library of Congress Control Number: 2024952313

For all general information, please contact Arcadia Publishing:
Telephone 843-853-2070
Fax 843-853-0044
E-mail sales@arcadiapublishing.com

Visit us on the Internet at www.arcadiapublishing.com

Contents

Acknowledgments		6
Introduction		7
1.	Maysville, Kentucky	9
2.	Mason County, Kentucky	41
3.	Bracken County, Kentucky	57
4.	Fleming County, Kentucky	63
5.	Lewis County, Kentucky	75
6.	Robertson County, Kentucky	87
7.	Adams County, Ohio	95
8.	Brown County, Ohio	113

Acknowledgments

I would like to dedicate this book to three friends of mine who have passed away: Don Skillman, who was a huge postcard dealer; Steven D. Poynter, an original picker from Maysville; and Tommy Conway, a fellow collector from Mason County. All three gentlemen helped expand my collection, which started in the mid-1980s. This hobby started as collecting views of my hometown but quickly grew to the general area on both sides of the river and connecting counties around Maysville. I have made some lifelong friends over the years who have bought, traded, or sold cards to me, including Bill Feldman, John Henderson, Darrell Maines, Roger Richter, Terry Sissell, and Richard Stracke, who continues to sell me so many good quality postcards from the northern Kentucky and Ohio areas. I would also like to thank my wife, Libby, who has been beside me on this project and puts up with the many hours I spend handling my collection and trying to catalog and organize every card, not to mention the time I spend on the road searching for that one card that I do not have! I am thankful that my mother took so many photographs of Maysville in the 1940s through the 1960s with her 35mm camera. Many of the photographs she had developed as slides. I had the slides digitized, and to my surprise, I was thrilled to see the results of her hobby. Some of those photographs around Maysville are in this book. Thanks go to Libby's cousin Peter Levy, who helped me with technology so my photographs would meet the requirements of Arcadia Publishing. Thanks to Arcadia Publishing for taking a chance on an idea I had after realizing an Images of America book on the Maysville area had not been published. A very special thanks goes to Tommy and Wanda Conway of Mayslick, Kentucky, who were caretakers of part of my collection for a period of years; otherwise, this project would not have been possible. Unless otherwise noted, all images appear courtesy of the author. Note that most photographs in this book are real-photo postcards.

Introduction

Maysville, originally named Limestone in 1787, was one of the first established towns along the Ohio River when the early pioneers like Daniel Boone, Simon Kenton, and George Rogers Clark first arrived in this wilderness area in the 1770s. There were no villages or homes here, and Simon Kenton established the first settlement in 1775. The landing place was called Limestone. The only cleared road was from the bison or buffalo herds that cleared paths from Blue Lick Springs. This route was named Buffalo Trace, or Route 68 in later years, or Lexington Pike, as it was mainly a route connecting Maysville and Lexington, Kentucky. Today, Route 68 runs southwest to Paducah, Kentucky. Simon Kenton and John May are credited with laying out the town, and the town's name was changed to Maysville. In 1833, it was made a city. The original county seat was in Washington, Kentucky, about four miles away, but in 1848, the county seat was moved to Maysville due to a large fire in Washington, the expanded growth along the Ohio River area, and the ports with flatboats bringing in goods and supplies. This area that had been the Indian territory for hunting was now being overrun by settlers from the northeastern states. People upriver were hearing about this new fertile unsettled area and began coming down the Ohio on flatboats from Virginia, Pennsylvania, New Jersey, Maryland, and other northeastern states. *The Frontiersman* by Allan Eckert describes this area in detail when the early settlers arrived and the struggles they dealt with to occupy this land they called Kaintucke.

Among other settlers that came to this area was a cousin of Daniel Boone, Jacob Boone, who ran a tavern on Front Street. Jacob and his wife, Mary Boone, are buried in the frontier cemetery behind the Kentucky Gateway Museum Center in the city of Maysville. Daniel and Rebecca Boone operated a tavern in Maysville from 1786 to 1789.

Just downriver from Maysville was a community called South Ripley that was very important to the abolitionists who lived in this area and helped the slaves cross the Ohio with signals from the Rankin House on the hill above Ripley, Ohio. Harriet Beecher Stowe visited Maysville in 1833 and went to a slave auction at nearby Washington, Kentucky, at the courthouse for Mason County. When she experienced seeing a slave being sold there, she was inspired to write about it in *Uncle Tom's Cabin*.

When all the new riverboat traffic started increasing on the Ohio River in 1811, Maysville became an exporter of wrought iron, bourbon, hemp, and tobacco, and more and more people began to settle in the town. By the 1830s, the population had grown to over 3,000. The railroad through Maysville started in 1850, and that brought even more growth.

Pres. Ulysses S. Grant was born April 27, 1822, downriver about 40 miles from Maysville at Point Pleasant, Ohio. Grant, at the age of 14, attended the Maysville Seminary Academy located at 109 West Fourth Street for about one year. While there, he lived in a home on Front Street with his aunt, a widow of Grant's uncle, Peter, who is buried in the frontier graveyard behind the Kentucky Gateway Museum Center in Maysville. One of the postcards in this book shows the home he lived in on Front Street while in Maysville. Upon leaving Maysville, Grant attended John Rankin's Academy about 10 miles downriver from Maysville at Ripley, Ohio.

There have been many other notable people who were born in Maysville or called it their home. Most notable are probably Rosemary Clooney and her sister Betty, who were singers, and brother Nick, who was a television news personality in Cincinnati, Ohio, and the father of George Clooney. Heather French Henry, who also called Maysville home, was Miss America of 2000.

With no floodwall or protection from the rising Ohio River due to rains, Maysville was damaged by the flood of 1907 at 50.1 feet, the flood of 1913 at 62.2 feet, and especially the flood of 1937 when the water level rose to 75.2 feet, which was more than 25 feet above flood stage. This flood severely damaged most of the homes and businesses on Front Street. It became obvious that a floodwall was needed to protect the city. In 1949, that project began, and it was completed in 1956.

Growing up in Maysville in the 1950s and 1960s and riding my bicycle from one end of town to the other or walking to the many schools we had in our local communities, I knew the business structures, the homes, and even the cracks and raised concrete from tree roots in the sidewalks. I also knew many of the people who lived there or at least their names, connecting the name with a home, business, or portion of the town where they lived. Maysville, in my childhood, was mainly confined to a few miles of flat land along the river, surrounded by what some call the eight hills. As the town grew and Washington was annexed, Maysville began to spread out to the hills above the town, where back then, there was only the Maysville Country Club golf course, one subdivision on Route 68, and some very nice homes on Jersey Ridge Road that ran along the golf course. The farmlands of my childhood were seeing many new homes and businesses springing up everywhere. Some of the businesses in the historic downtown buildings relocated, but some stayed, and today, as you walk the streets, there are many new shops, bars, restaurants, and other businesses. These old buildings and the architecture were precious because they held so much history, and many of the structures are being preserved, including the Russell Theatre in the heart of town. The Kentucky Gateway Museum Center is a must-see as you walk the town.

Postcards were a very good source of communication, and the golden age of postcards was between 1905 to 1915 and ended with World War I. A postcard cost one penny, and a stamp cost a penny, so anyone could afford to send a message.

Rather than having my collection in binders or boxes, where I am not able to share them with many people, I decided to team up with Arcadia Publishing so others can enjoy the scenes from this special historic small-town America.

For those who live in the Maysville area or those who have left, I hope the views in this book will bring back fond memories. When I was in high school, the saying on the police cars was "Valley of Opportunity." Many of us growing up in Maysville with loving families, supportive churches, and the many dedicated teachers received a great foundation for the opportunities to come. I hope this book will interest you and create a sense of appreciation for our relatives and the people who lived in Maysville in the early 1900s. I am thankful and proud to call Maysville my hometown. I hope the photographs and this book are a blessing to you.

One

Maysville, Kentucky

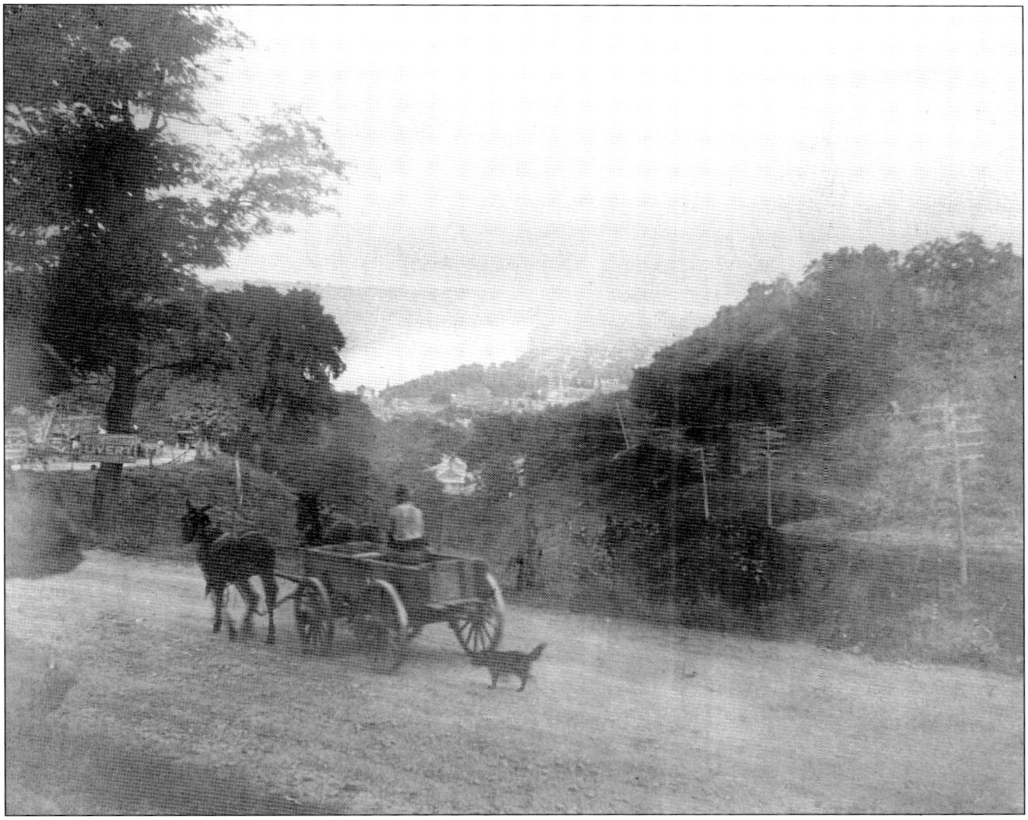

With his faithful dog following, this farmer and his team of horses wind their way down the steep incline of the old Buffalo Trace Road above Smokey Hollow to purchase supplies. As he enters Maysville looking eastward upriver, the promise of a growing town built on a strong foundation of family and close community ties is revealed through the misty "Valley of Opportunity."

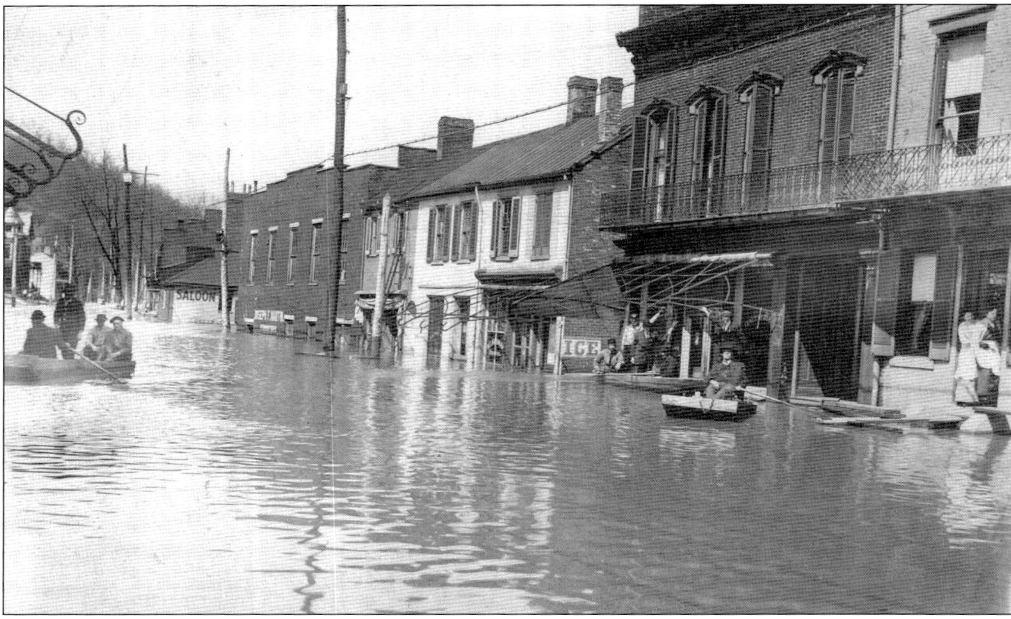

On April 1, 1913, this photograph was taken of the receding floodwaters on West Second Street near Wall Street. On the right corner of Wall Street is the Joseph F. Martin Furniture store, and Caproni Brothers Grocery is just to the right of the ice sign. Notice the ladder that has been set up to go from a flatboat to the second story of a home. Below, on April 1, 1913, the Ohio River floodwaters crested and began to recede. This view is looking east on Second Street just before the intersection of Market Street. Struggling to go on with their lives and make a living despite the devastation brought by the flood, people used flat-bottom boats to get around.

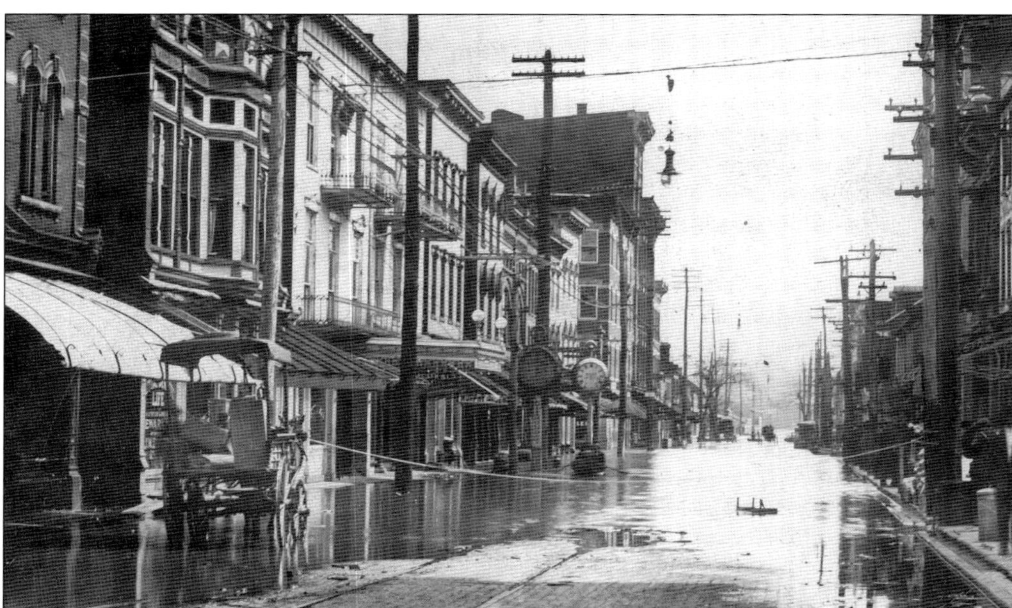

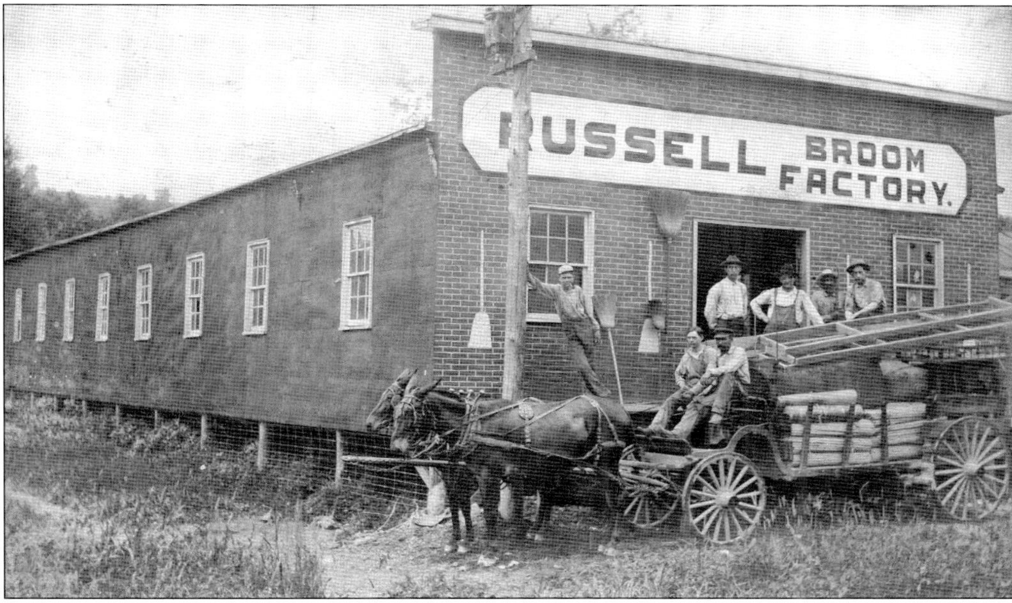

The Russell Broom Factory was established by J. Barbour Russell on July 6, 1907. "J.B.," as he was called, was the son of M.C. Russell, who originally owned the M.C. Russell Wholesale Grocery, which was later turned over to his sons. The new, innovative broom factory had full electric power to run the machines. The company's motto on its advertising cards was "Old fashioned brooms made in the old-fashioned way," and some cards that were handed out showed the factory on the front with quotes and rhymes printed on the back. The business was located on Schubert Avenue, and its quality brooms were shipped to Ohio, Tennessee, Indiana, and West Virginia. The workforce below poses at an unidentified location, showing off their brooms and the iconic herringbone-patterned brick streets.

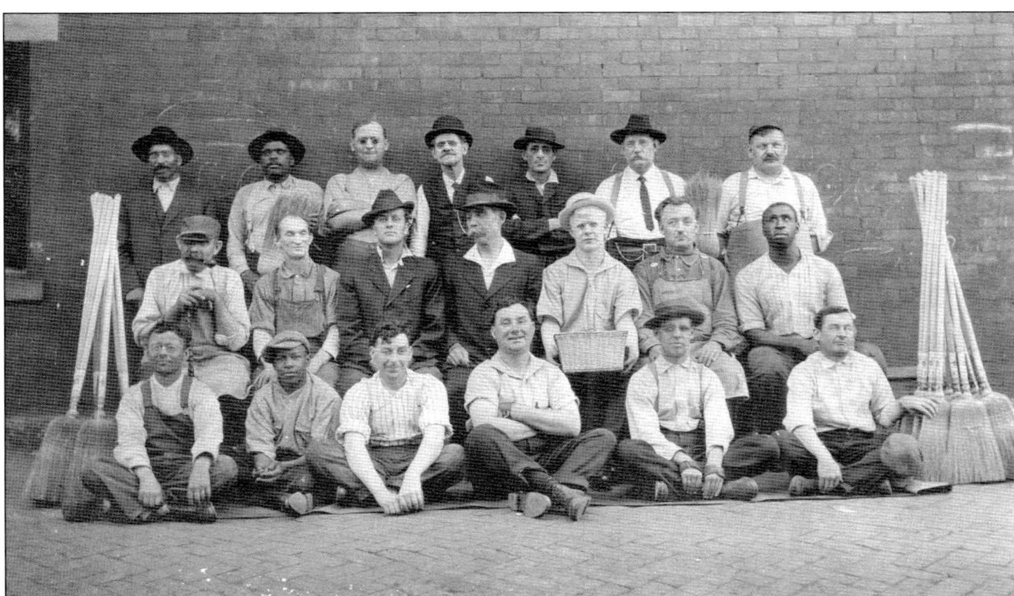

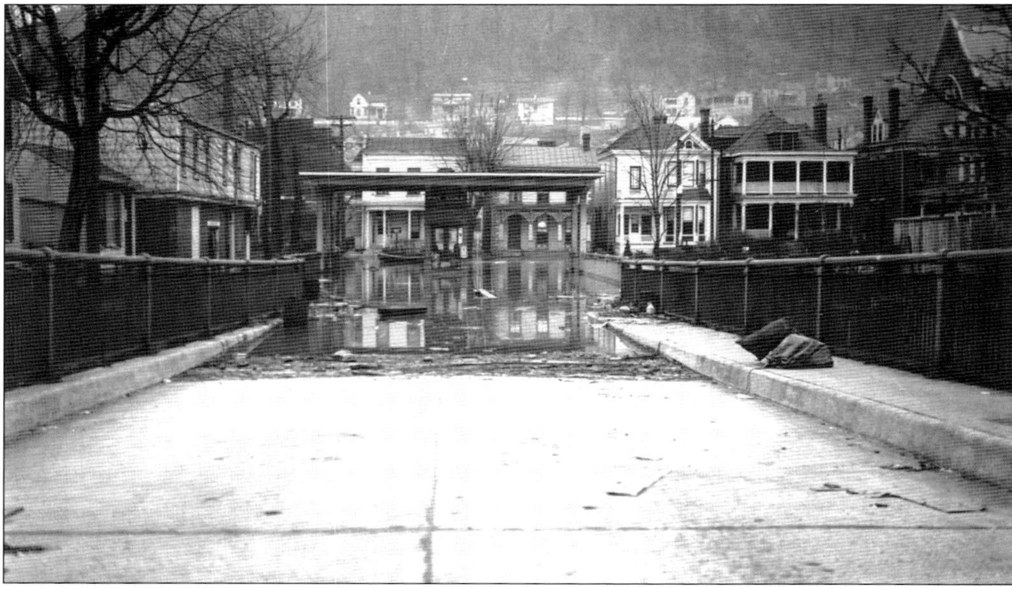

This photograph, dated January 27, 1937, when the worst flood hit Maysville, shows that the Simon Kenton toll bridge station on the Maysville side was underwater. The toll started when the bridge was opened on November 25, 1931, and tolls were collected to purchase bonds. In 1945, the bonds were redeemed to help pay the $1.57 million construction cost, the toll was closed, and the station was removed.

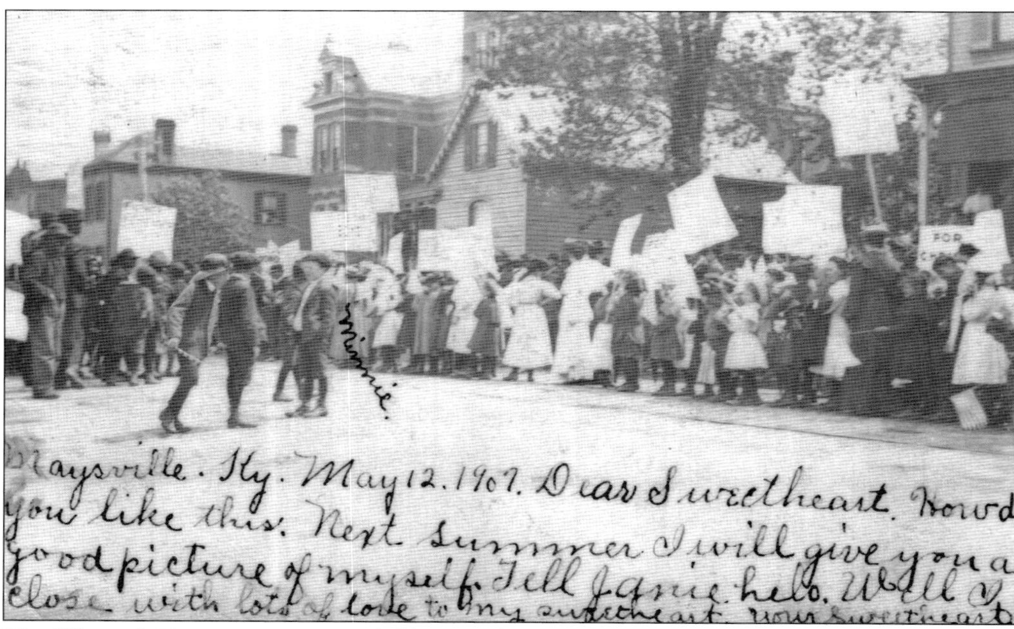

The Women's Temperance Union held a march on Third Street on Sunday, May 12, 1907, and were heading east across from Government Street and the current post office. Homes are located where the Mayfair Court is today. This photograph was sent to Carrie Cunningham in Maysville on May 13, 1907.

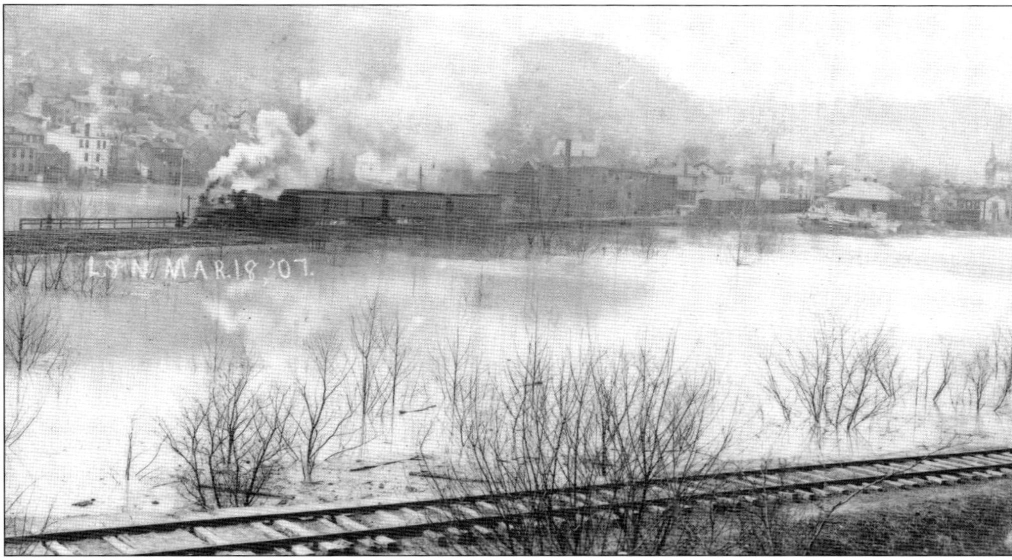

This Louisville & Nashville Railroad (L&N) passenger train crossing Limestone Creek pulls away from the L&N depot located at the intersection of Third and Bridge Streets as the water from the 1907 flood nearly covers the tracks. The Maysville City Mill building can be seen in the distance, just behind the train cars. Today, a new building housing the public library is located on this site.

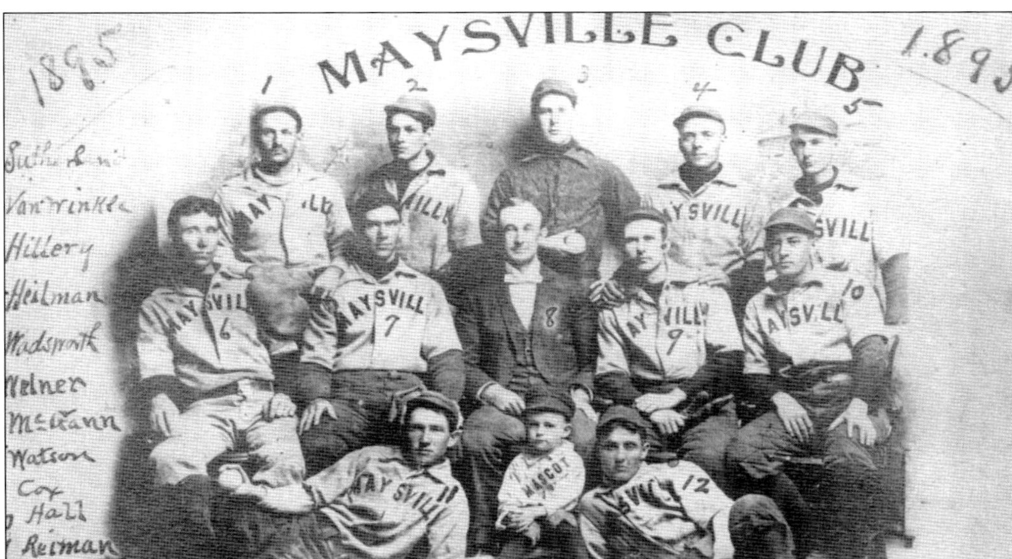

This 1895 photograph of the Maysville Club baseball team lists the last names of the players: (1) Sutherland, (2) Vanwinkle, (3) Hillery, (4) Heilman, (5) Wadsworth, (6) Welner, (7) McGann, (8) Watson, (9) Cox, (10) Hall, (11) Reiman, and (12) Tenley. The young mascot is not identified, but the manager at the time was Watson. Maysville had minor baseball teams from 1894 to 1923, and in 1910, Casey Stengel played for the Maysville Rivermen. There is an article online about a game played against Ashland dated June 1, 1895.

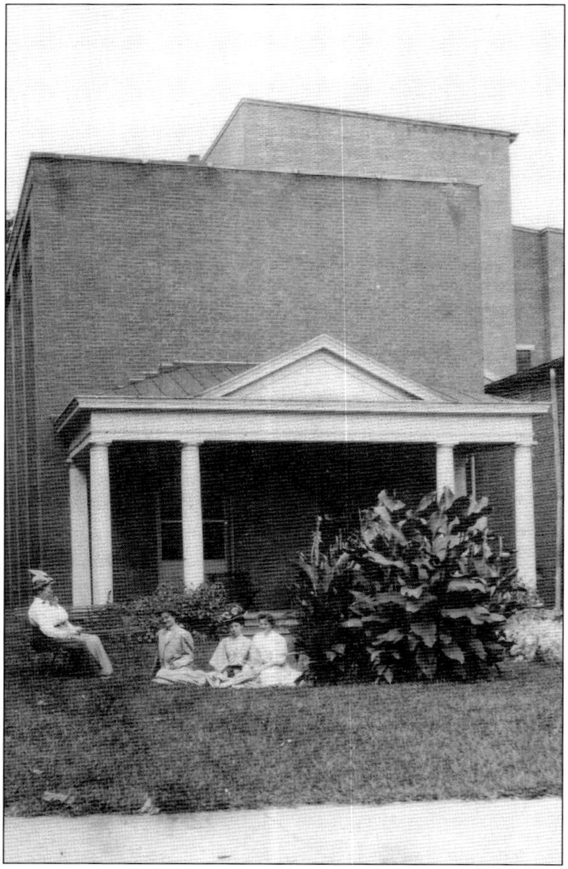

Five ladies dressed in typical Edwardian attire relax in the front yard of the Maysville Public Library as it looked when completed in 1880. In 1973, a new front wing was added with windows and double doors. This library is connected to and is part of the Gateway Museum in Maysville today. Prior to 1907, this photograph was sent to Carrie Cunningham, Maysville, from S. Straus at the New York store.

Located on West Second Street, the Washington Opera House and Fire Company No. 1 shared a two-story building. An advertisement for Snyder's Catsup and Herald Square Opera is on the fence to the left of the building. The firehouse has been relocated, but the opera house is still a popular venue for the Maysville Players today.

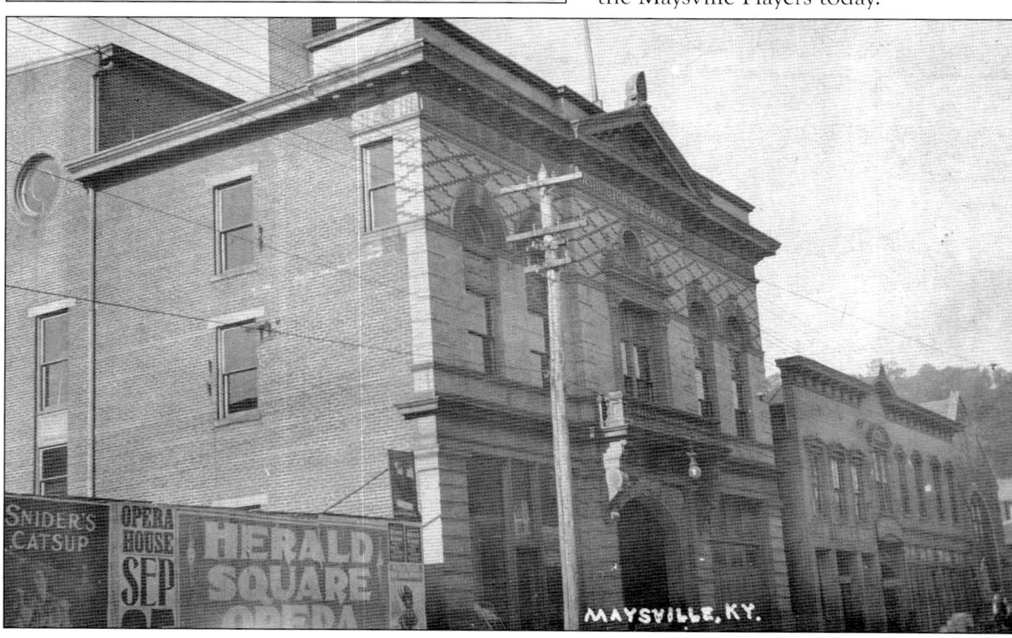

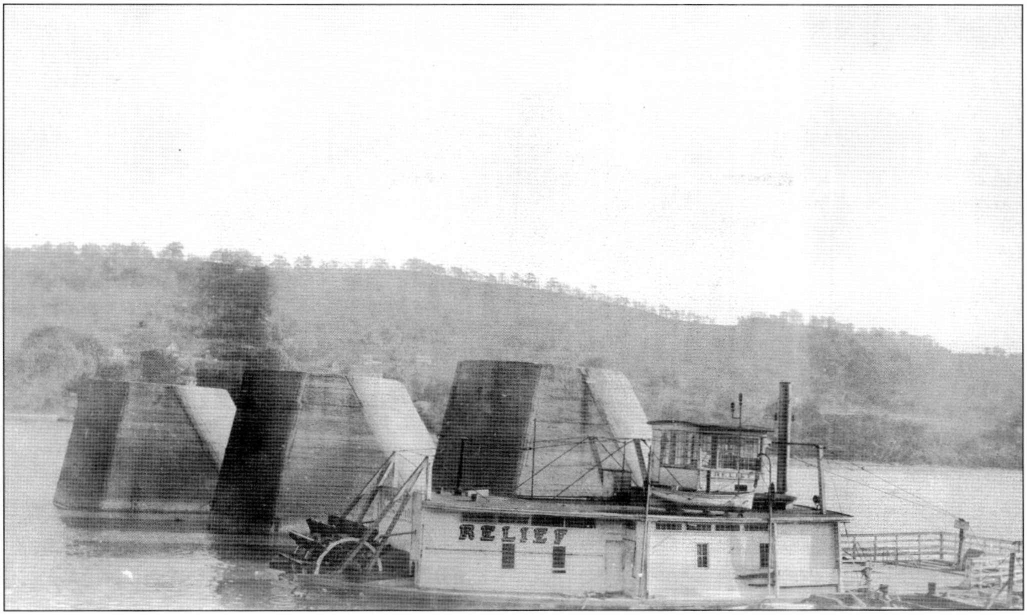

Captain Green owned and ran this *Relief* ferry in the Maysville, Kentucky, area until the 1930s, but when the Simon Kenton bridge was completed, the ferry relocated to the town of Augusta, Kentucky, about 19 miles downstream. The three ice breakers are still there today under the Simon Kenton Bridge, but as the new dams allowed the river level to rise, only a small portion of the breakers is exposed today.

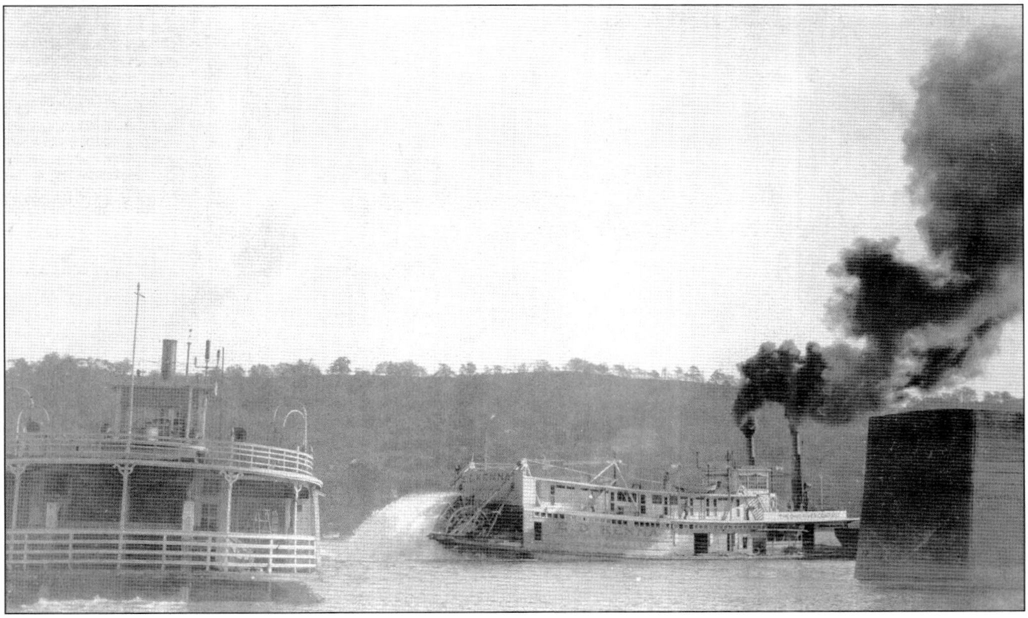

The steamer towboat *E.D. Kenna* is hidden behind the ice breakers in the previous photograph showing the *Relief*. The photographer was able to quickly capture this image before it was out of site. This towboat was built in July 1926 in Charlestown, West Virginia, and was used mostly on the Ohio River until it was dismantled in 1953.

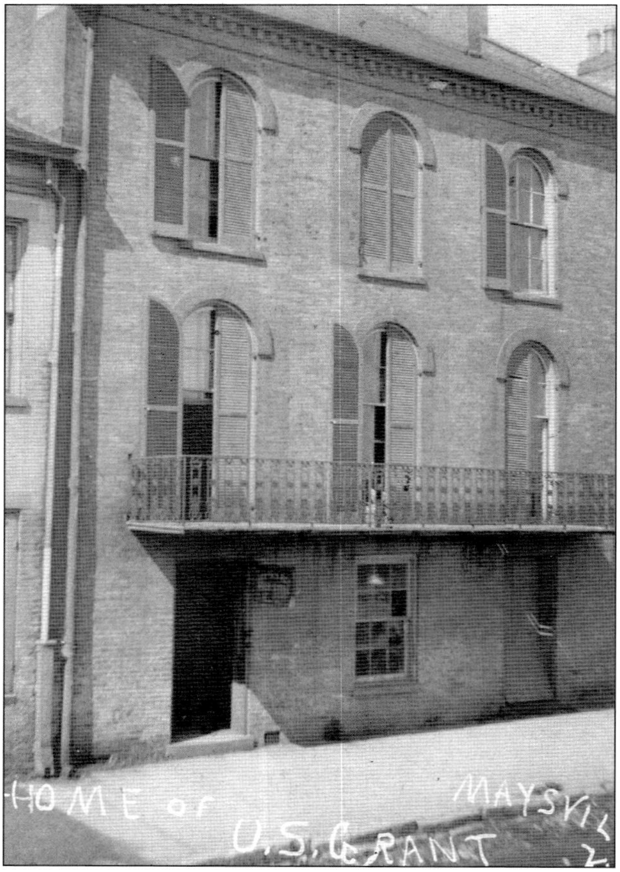

Taken around 1906, the photograph on the left is of the home on Front Street where Ulysses S. Grant lived with his aunt while attending school at the Maysville Academy. His uncle, Peter Grant, originally owned the home, but he died before Grant moved there. After leaving Maysville, Grant later went on to attend John Rankin's school in Ripley, Ohio. Below is the second photograph of the home, with a closer view from an Ohio River boat, showing the river during the flood of 1913. Homes and businesses, seen here along Front Street, were torn down in the 1960s during the urban renewal program, including the largest and tallest building owned by Cooper & Power. What a loss this was from a historical perspective. Only four houses were left, and even the home of U.S. Grant's uncle Peter Grant, second from the left in this photograph, was demolished.

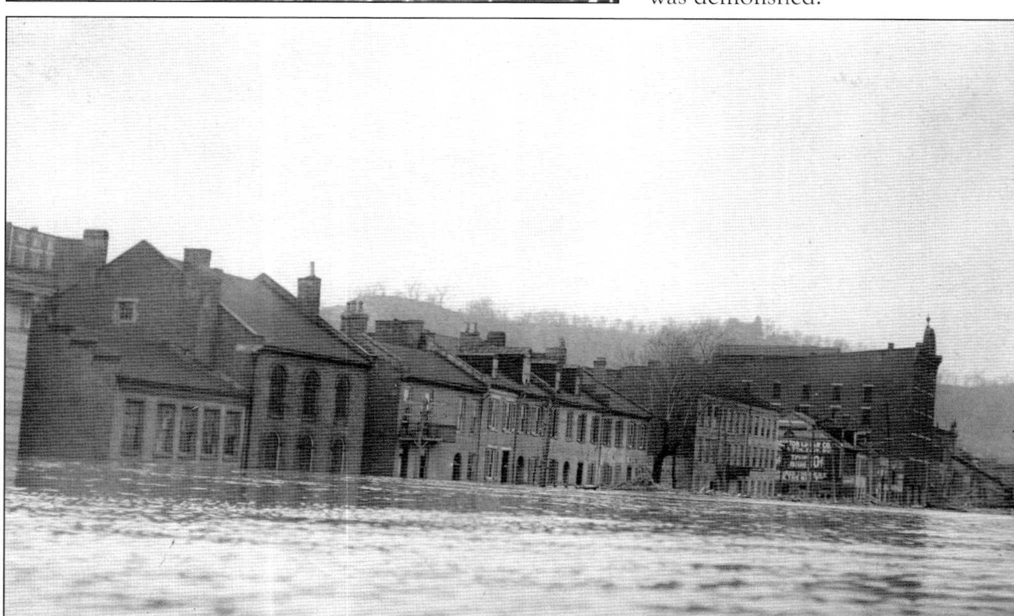

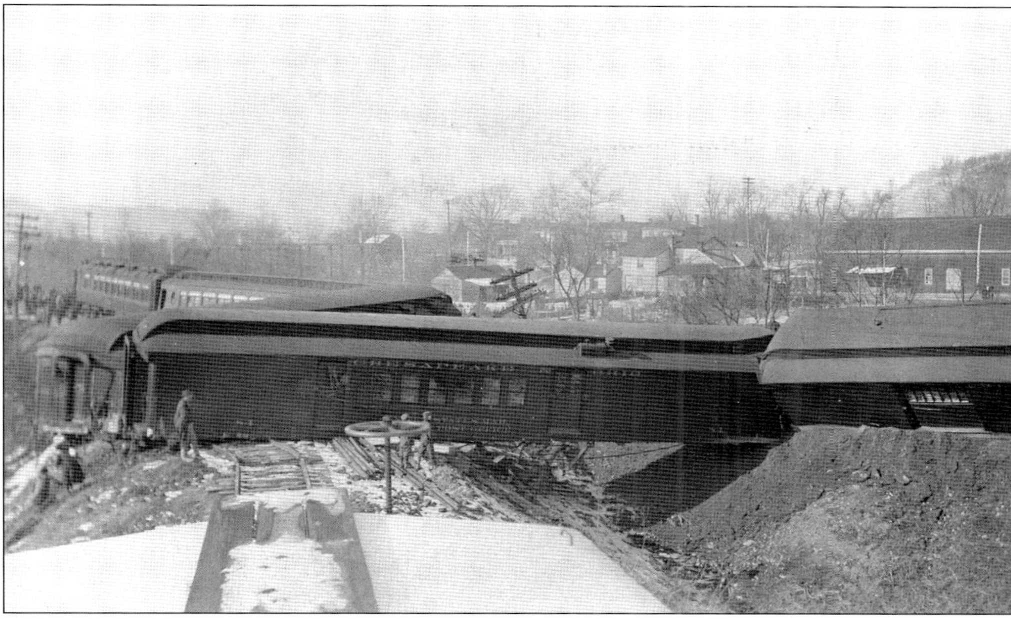

In February 1911, the train wreck of the No. 2 Chesapeake & Ohio Railway (C&O) happened in the early afternoon just after passing the L&N switch near Limestone Creek. Four of the seven cars came off the track and overturned. The train had just left the depot and was only going about 25 miles per hour when the wreck occurred due to a broken switch rod. None of the 200 passengers were seriously injured or killed in the slow-speed accident. Workers moved in and started cleaning up the wreckage, and by the next morning, the tracks were clear. A photographer snapped three other views of this wreckage for preservation.

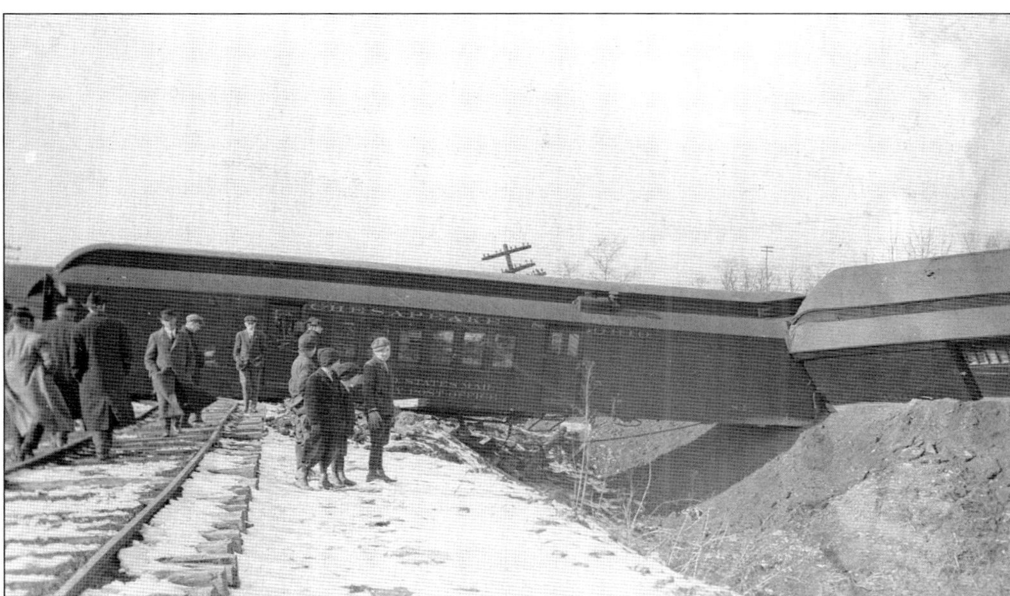

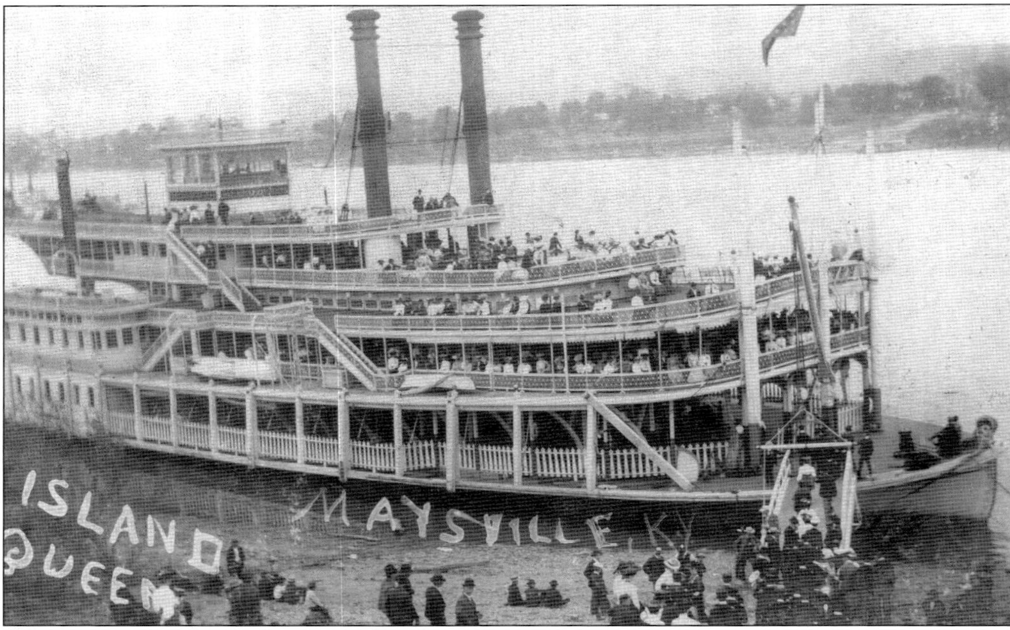

The *Island Queen* left Cincinnati, Ohio, and traveled to Maysville, Kentucky, up the Ohio River to transport people to the Coney Island Amusement Park east of Cincinnati. The park had a variety of entertainment, including a roller coaster, small train rides through the park, picnics, and dancing. The captain would pick up visitors in the morning and return in the evening on this excursion steamer, while calliopes played music for entertainment.

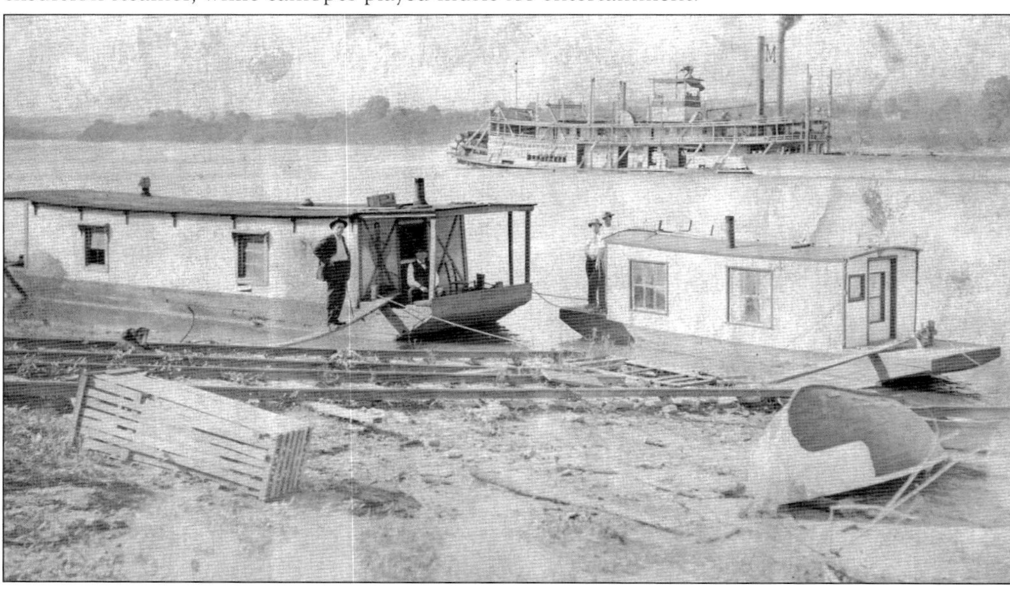

The wharf in Maysville, Kentucky, was a busy place over the years where workers loaded and unloaded supplies and goods of all types for the city businesses, and the rails helped workers transport the products. People up and down the Ohio River living in these shanty boats from the 1850s to the 1950s could dock anywhere. The eastbound steamer in the background is the *Florence Marmet*.

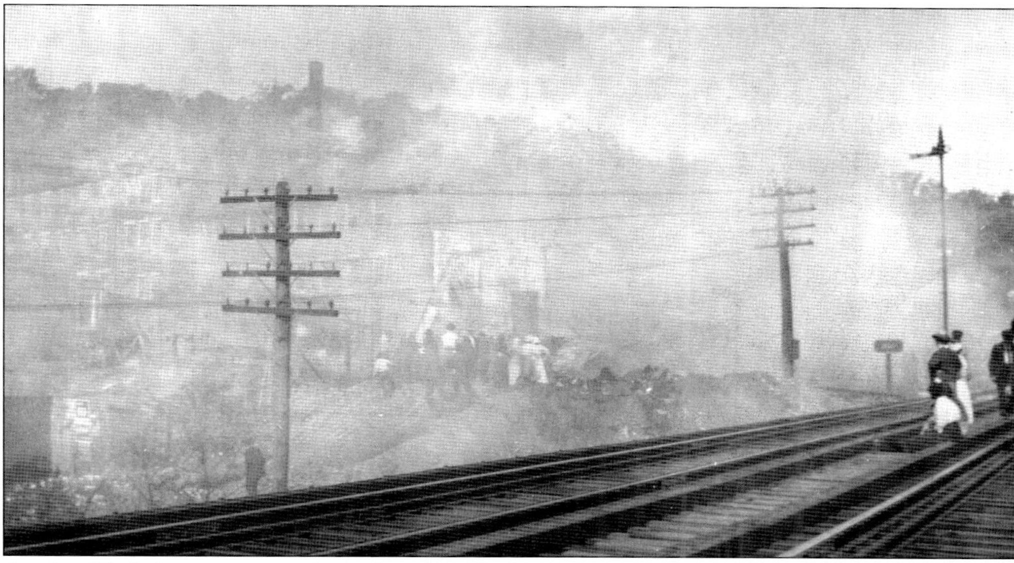

Smoke filled the air as people gathered around watching the smoldering fire that destroyed a portion of the January and Wood Cotton Mill in the west end of Maysville in May 1915. The main factory was not damaged, but the "iron clad" attached building was destroyed. Around 400 bales of cotton were destroyed, and many others got wet from the water used to put out the fires.

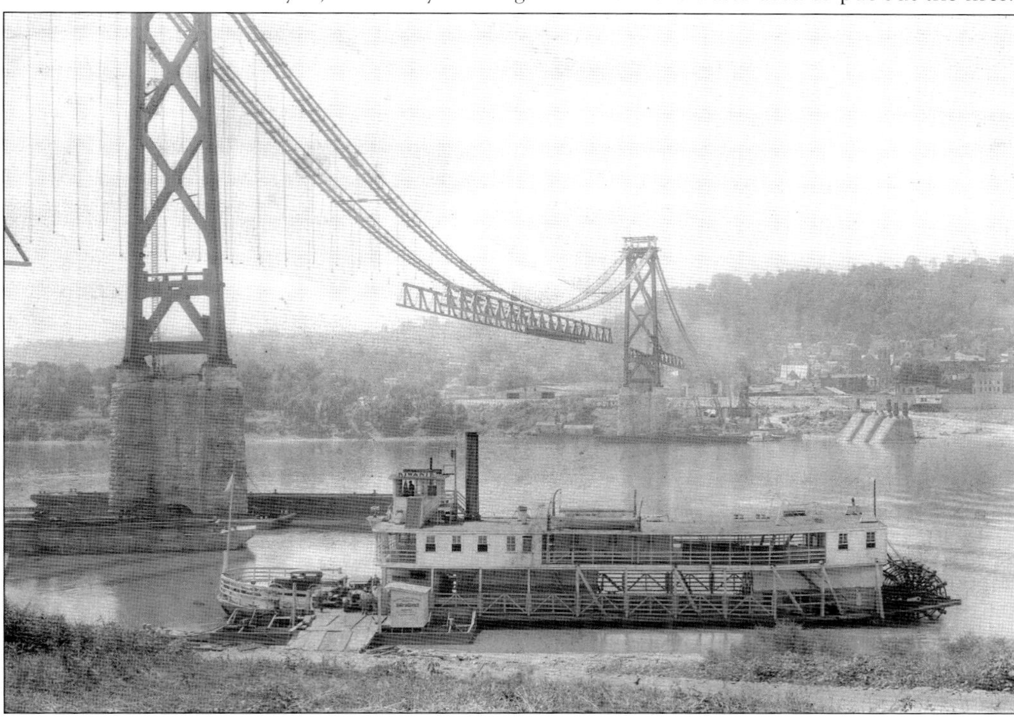

The center section of the Simon Kenton Bridge is in place between the upright supports as the *Laurance* ferry continues to transport cars, people, and livestock back and forth across the Ohio River between Maysville, Kentucky, and Aberdeen, Ohio. This business would shortly come to an end when the bridge was completed on November 31, 1931.

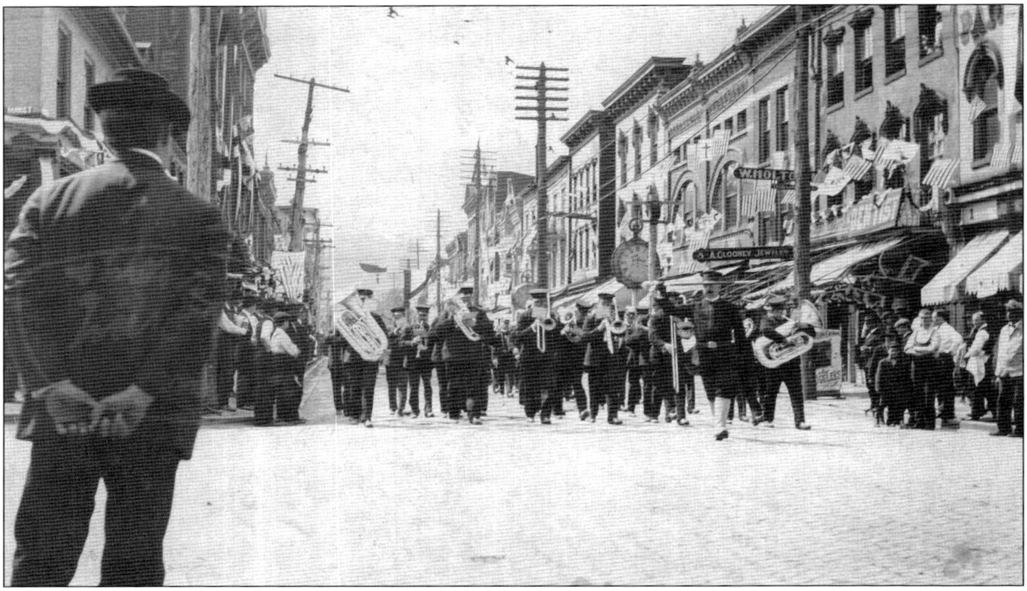

John Phillip Sousa was the conductor of the Marine Band from 1879 until 1892. He resigned to create his own civilian marching band and traveled around the world with them. With the Marine baton he was given at retirement, Sousa leads his band through the streets of Maysville as they head east on Second Street preparing to make a turn south on Market Street.

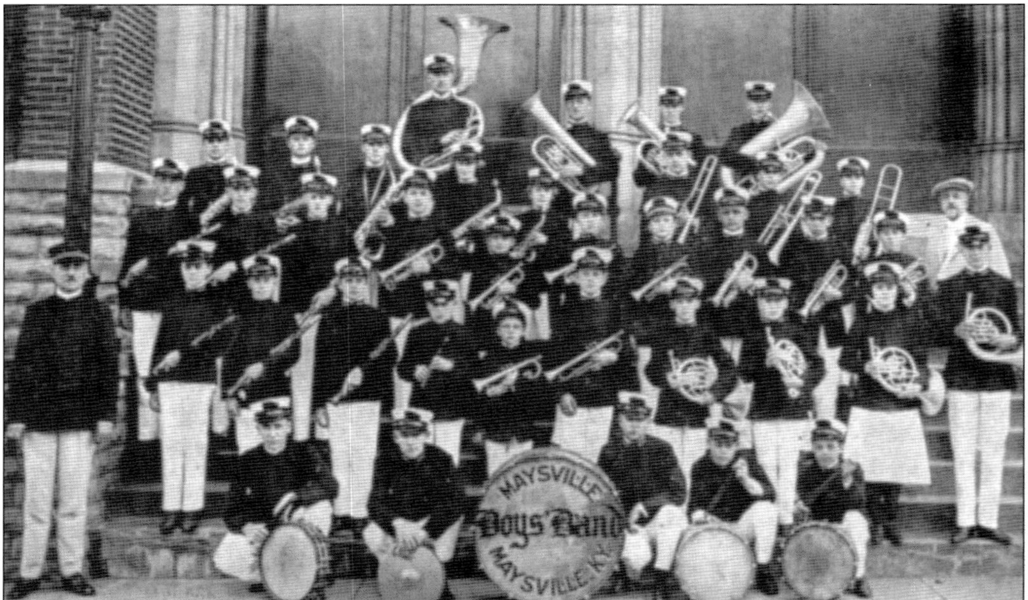

The Million Dollar Band from the Blue Grass of Old Kentucky was organized in February 1919. The progressive citizens of Maysville, Kentucky, paid all expenses to educate these boys. George D. Barnard was the director; Dr. P.G. Smoot was the physician; and Col. J. Barbour Russell of M.C. Russell Company was the manager, seen on the right in the white suit.

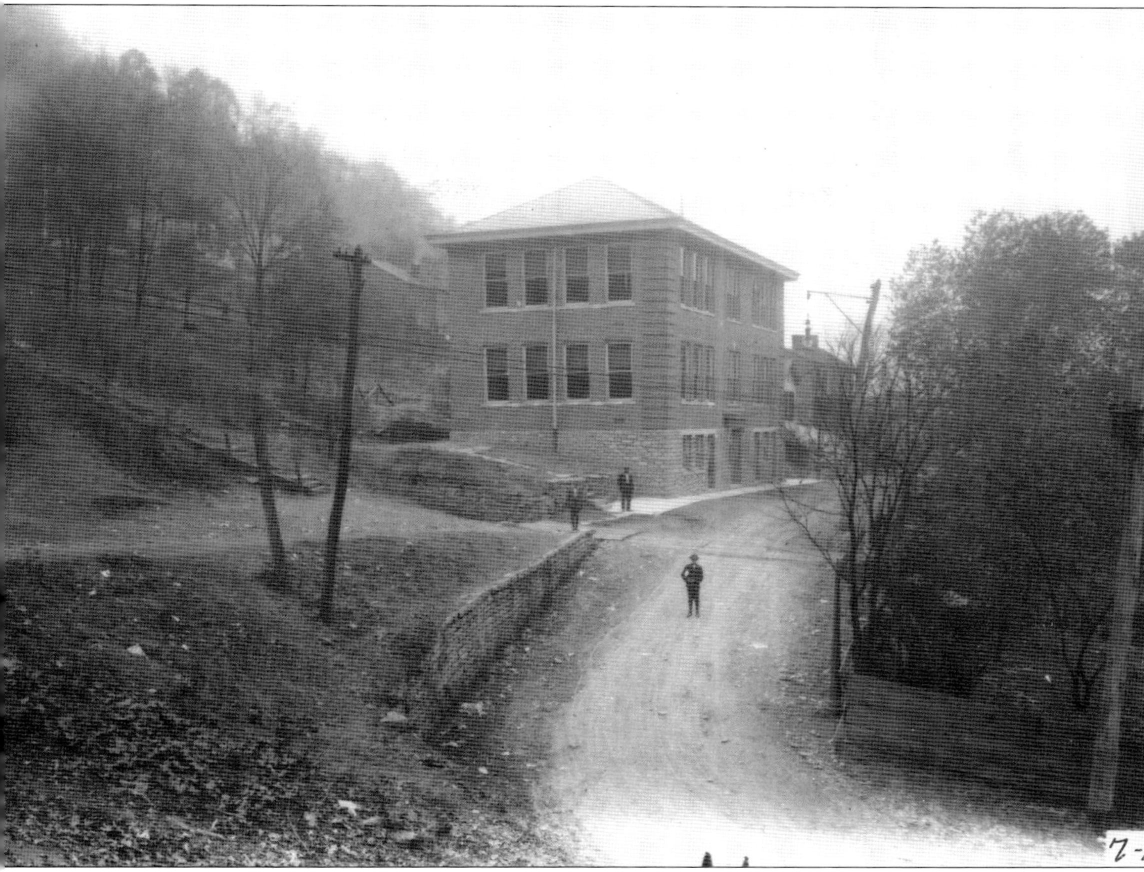

The principal at the new Maysville Black school was Prof. William H. Humphrey, and the school was located on Fifth Street near the old Hayswood Hospital. The first-through-third-grade teacher was Letitia Henderson. Taken by a Kraemer Art photographer who traveled in many rural areas during the postcard era, this photograph was developed from a glass plate.

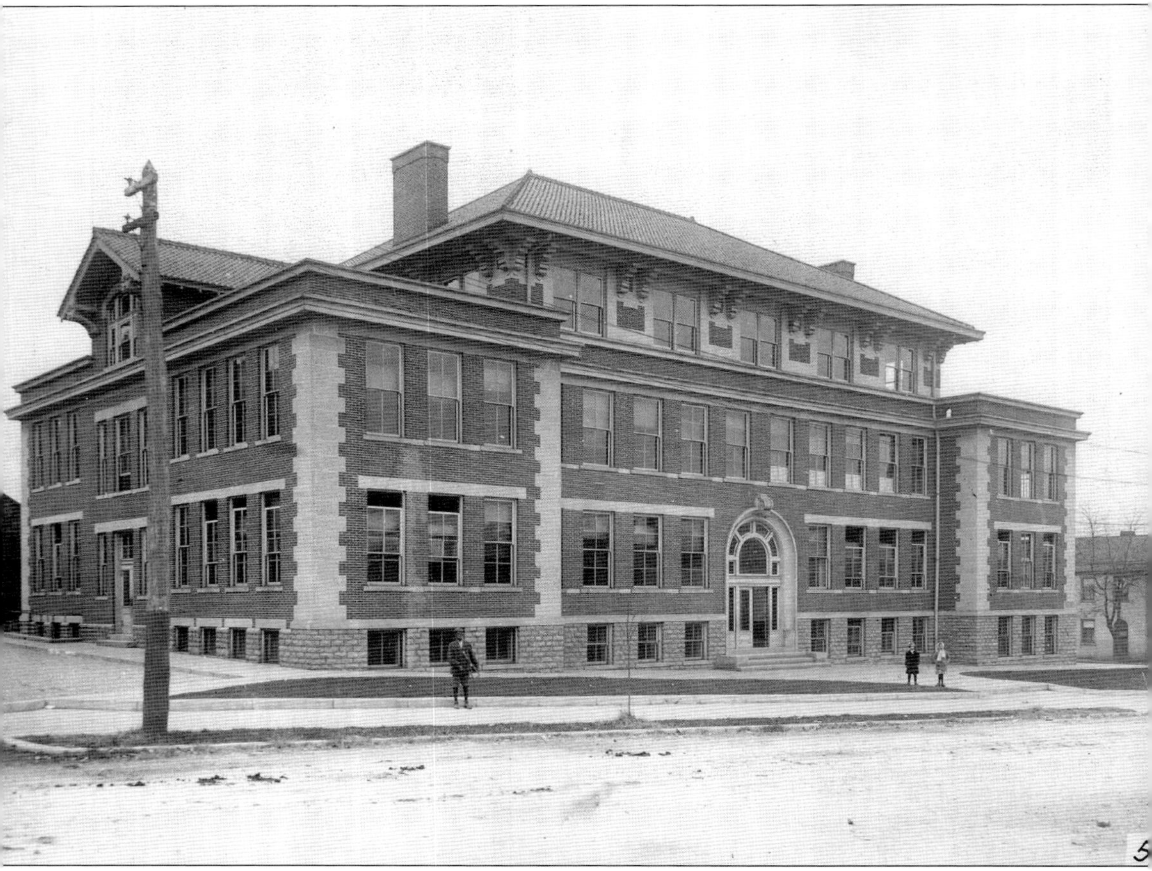

This view taken from across Limestone Street is of the old Maysville High School. The cornerstone for building this school was laid on May 14, 1908, and was placed on the northeast corner of the first floor. The stone foundation lower level was already completed at that time. The celebration included a parade and a large crowd to watch the dedication.

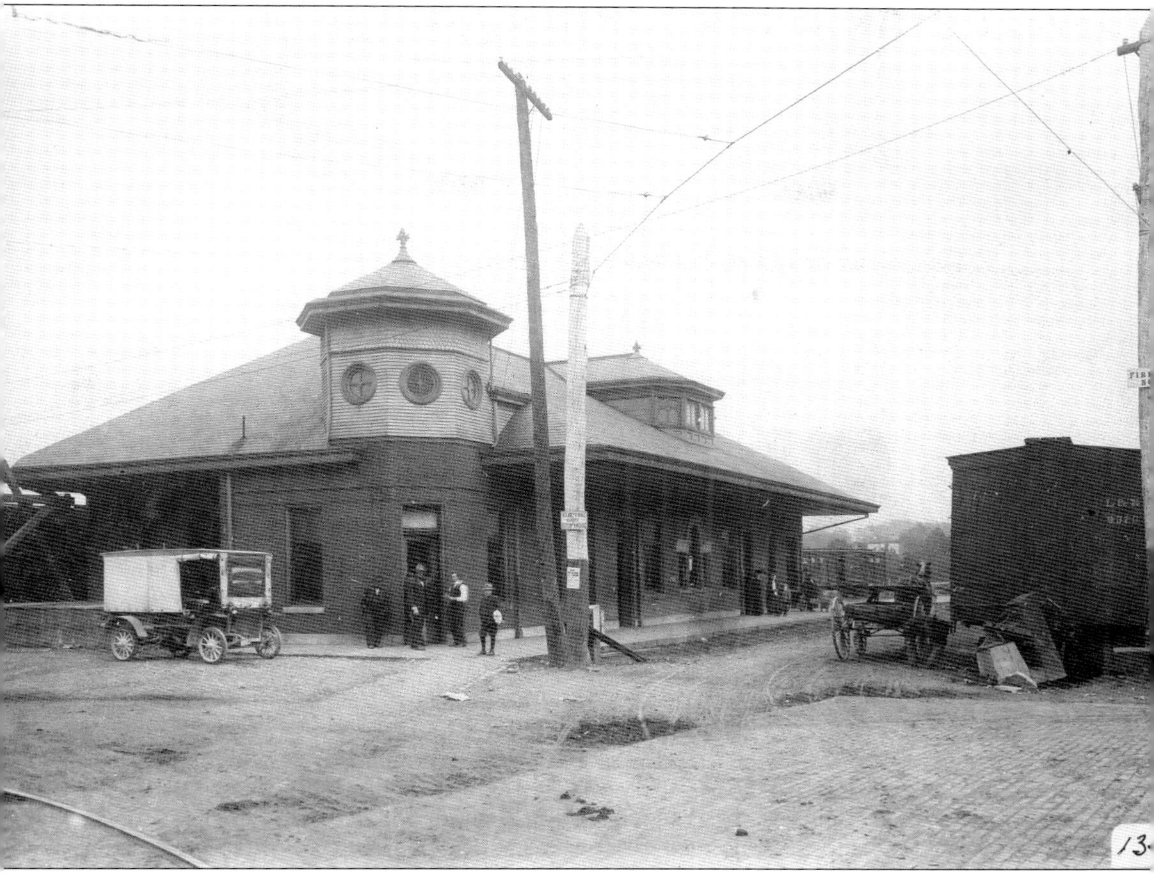

The original L&N depot was located at the intersection of Third and Bridge Streets. Over the years, this original old depot has been used as a firehouse and police station and is currently the Maysville Chamber of Commerce. In September 1939, a new L&N depot was opened near the viaduct, 1,200 feet to the southeast.

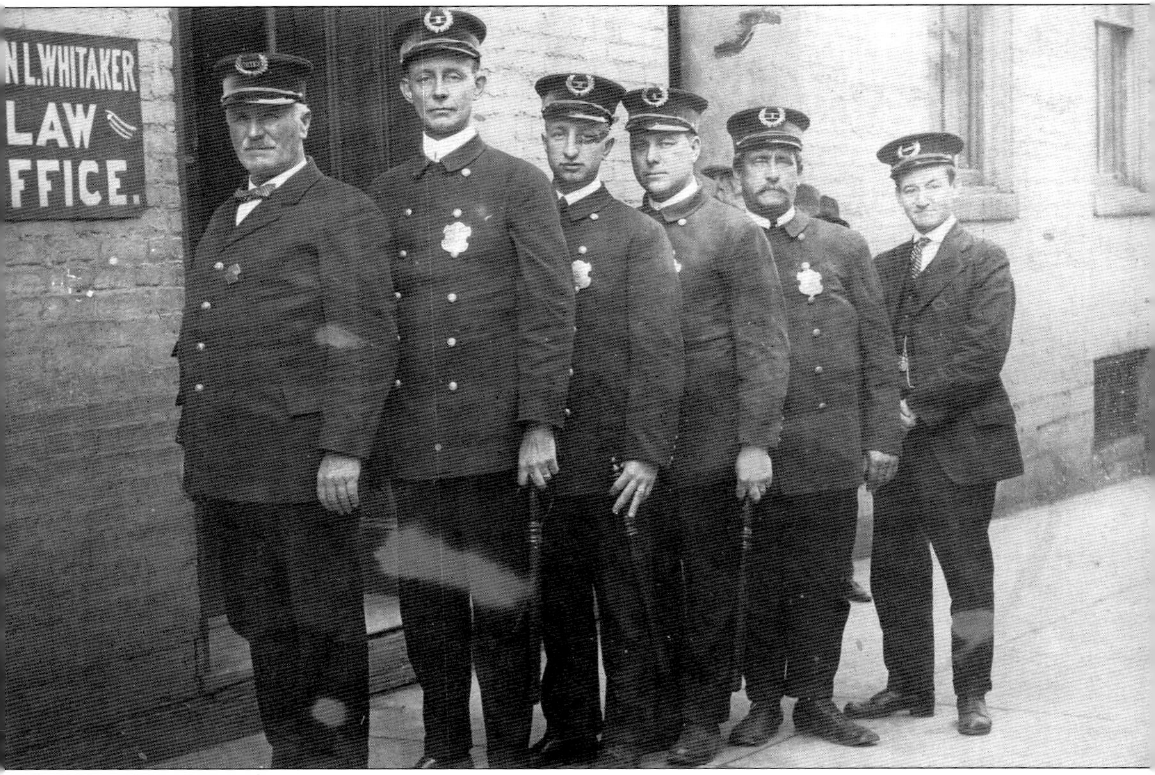

This is a real-photo postcard of the Maysville police officers on Court Street near the courthouse walkway. Harry Ort, who joined the force in July 1899, was elected as the police chief in 1905 and reelected in 1909. This is the period that this photograph was taken. The law office sign was for attorney John L. Witaker, who was the police judge.

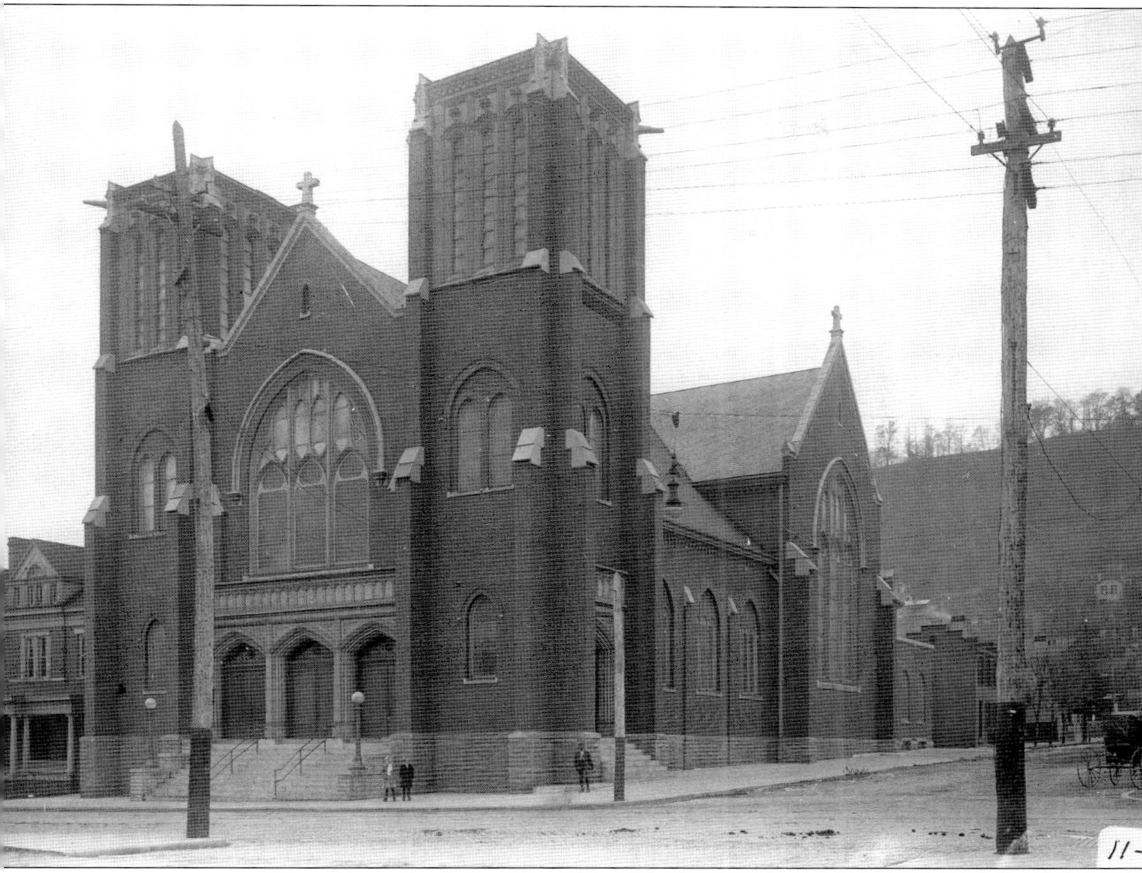

St. Patrick's Church is located on the corner of Third and Limestone Streets. This photograph was taken shortly after the completion of the church that was overseen by Fr. P.M. Jones at a cost of about $100,000. The original church that faced Limestone Street was demolished to complete the new church design. Many famous people have attended church here. This is another photograph developed from a Kraemer Art glass plate.

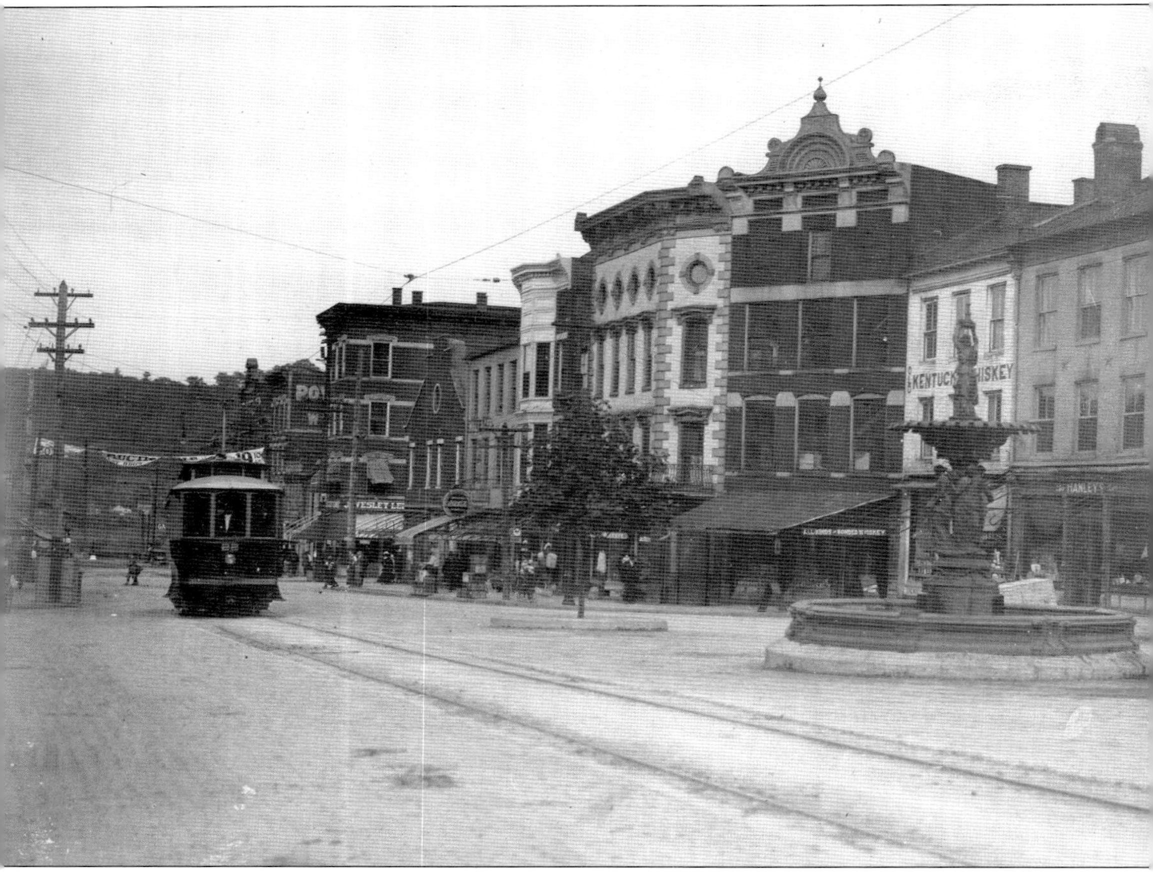

Taken from the southwest side of Second Street looking north, this photograph shows trolley No. 22 coming up the grade on Market Street. This street is still mostly brick today, and although the businesses have changed, most of the buildings remain. This photograph was taken by a photographer from Kraemer Art in Cincinnati, Ohio, and developed from a glass plate.

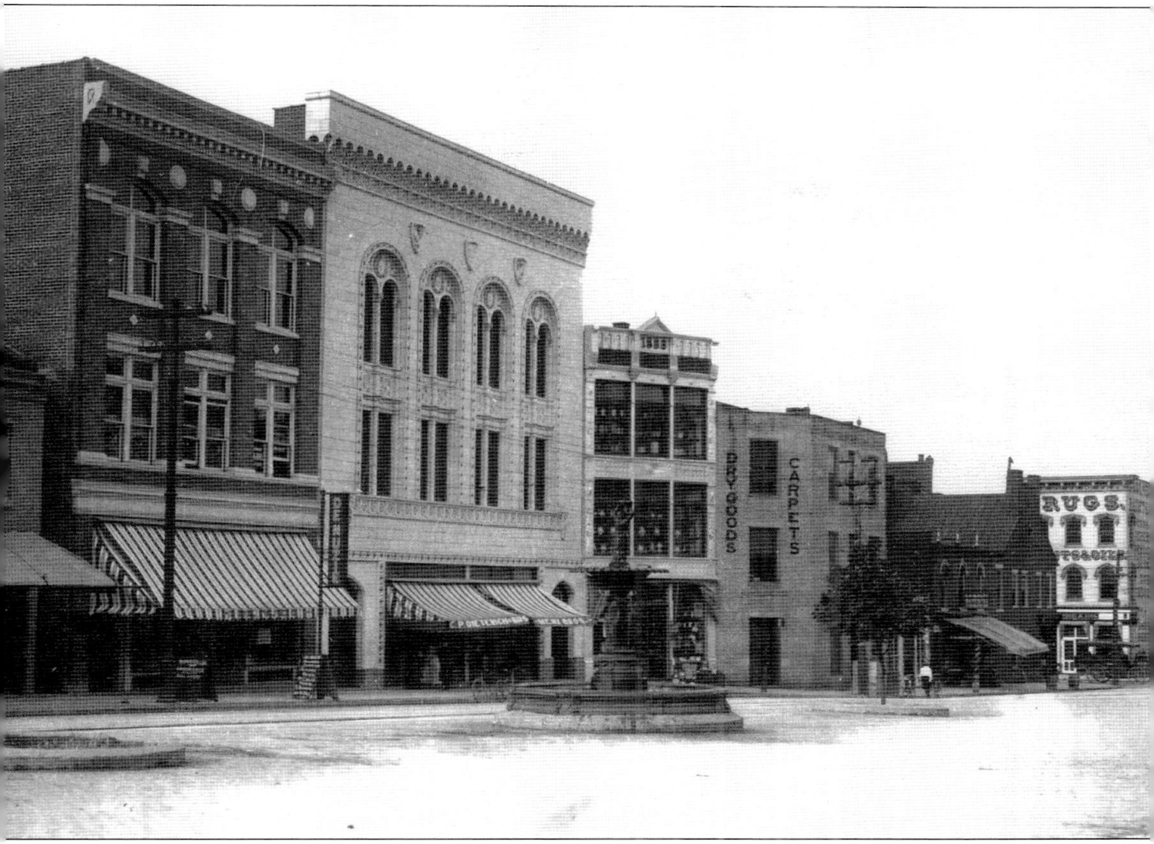

This view of the west side of Market Street looking down toward Second Street reveals buildings that are still being used today. This photograph illustrates where the fountain was located back in the early 1900s. The De Nuzie Bookstore, shown here, published many postcard views during the postcard era and beyond.

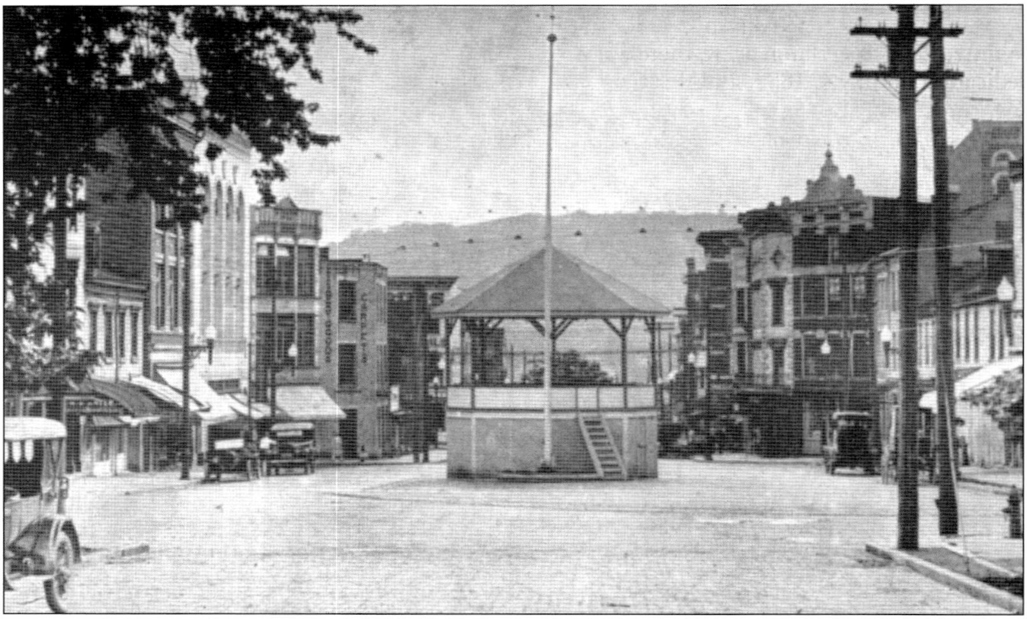

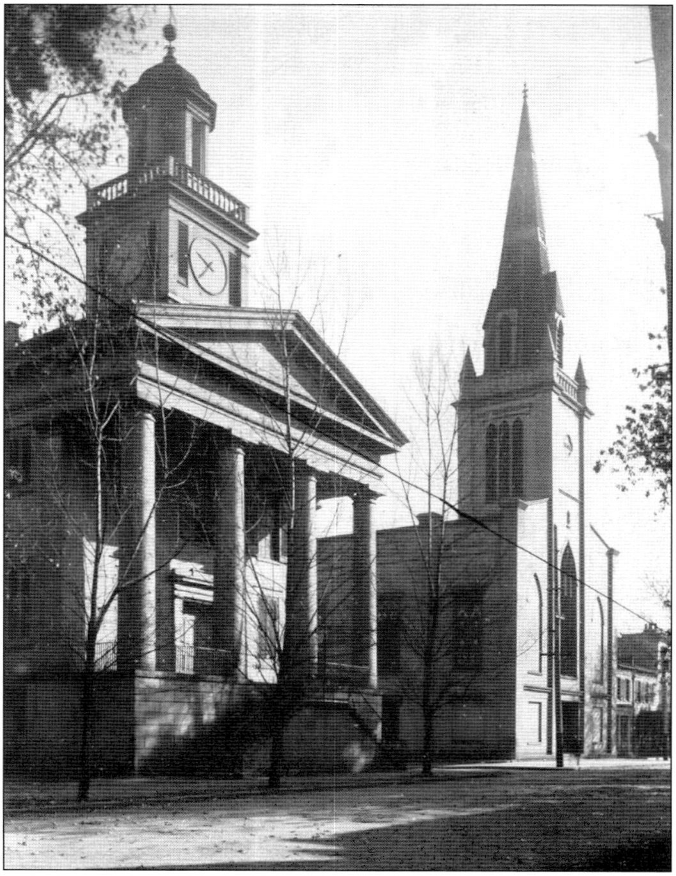

This photograph was taken looking north on Market Street at the Boy's Band Stand, where young musicians would entertain the locals with their instruments. Other names for this group of young men playing their brass instruments were the Pride of Maysville and the Million Dollar Band. The band was founded and managed by James Barbour Russell. This is an Auburn Postcard Mfg. Co. card from Auburn, Indiana.

The historic Mason County Courthouse and Presbyterian church are separated by Court Street looking towards the New Orleans-style townhouses named Mechanic's Row. This courthouse was built between 1844 and 1846 as court business was relocated from the original Mason County Courthouse in nearby Washington in 1848. The Presbyterian church was built in 1850, and towers over everything else in this location.

To honor the men from Mason County who volunteered in the Union army, there was a dedication on July 4, 1887, and this GAR (Grand Army of the Republic) Monument, standing 42 feet in height, was dedicated in front of a crowd of about 15,000. It was placed on land donated by the Maysville Cemetery and stands tall on the right when one enters the cemetery.

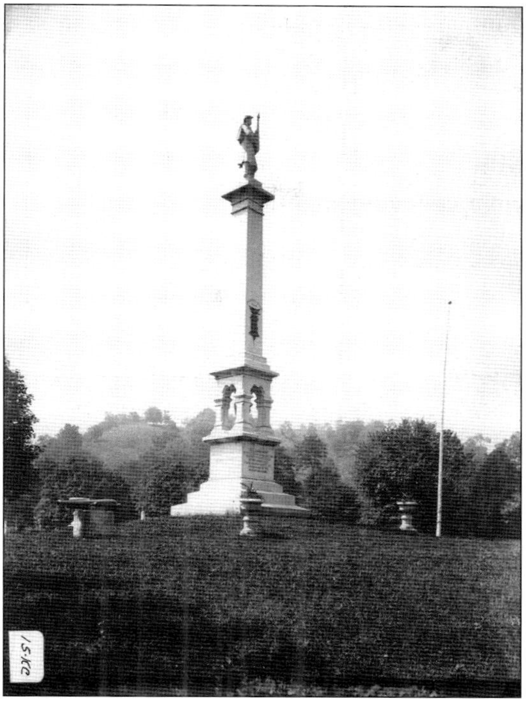

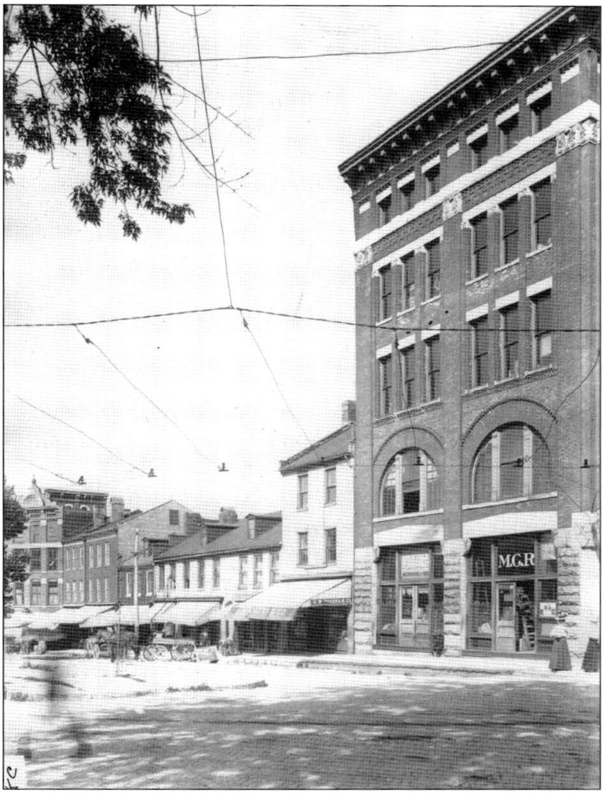

Among the many successful businesses on the eastern side of Market Street were M.C. Russell's and G.W. Rogers Whiskey Store located next to Russell's. Two men are opening the steel plates on the sidewalk to expose the chutes to unload the barrels of whisky from the wagon. This print was developed from a glass-plate photograph taken by one of the Kraemer Art photographers of Cincinnati, Ohio.

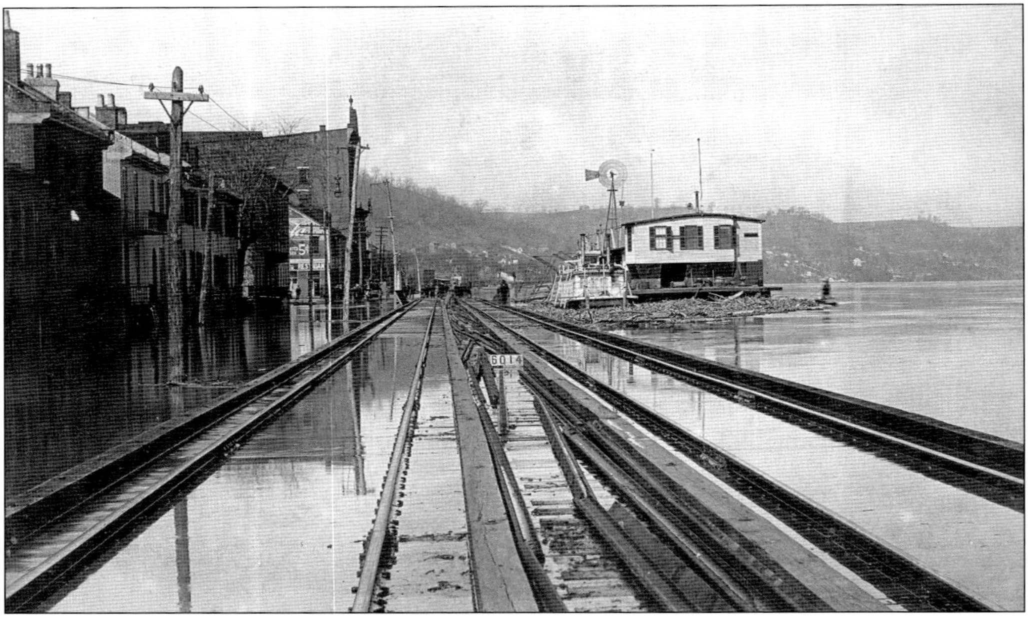

With train tracks barely above water, this is a typical flood scene along Front Street. A wharf boat is tied off in front of the Cooper and Power Building protecting a small tug snuggled on the inner side, but debris still gathers from the dangerous rising river where almost anything could be picked up.

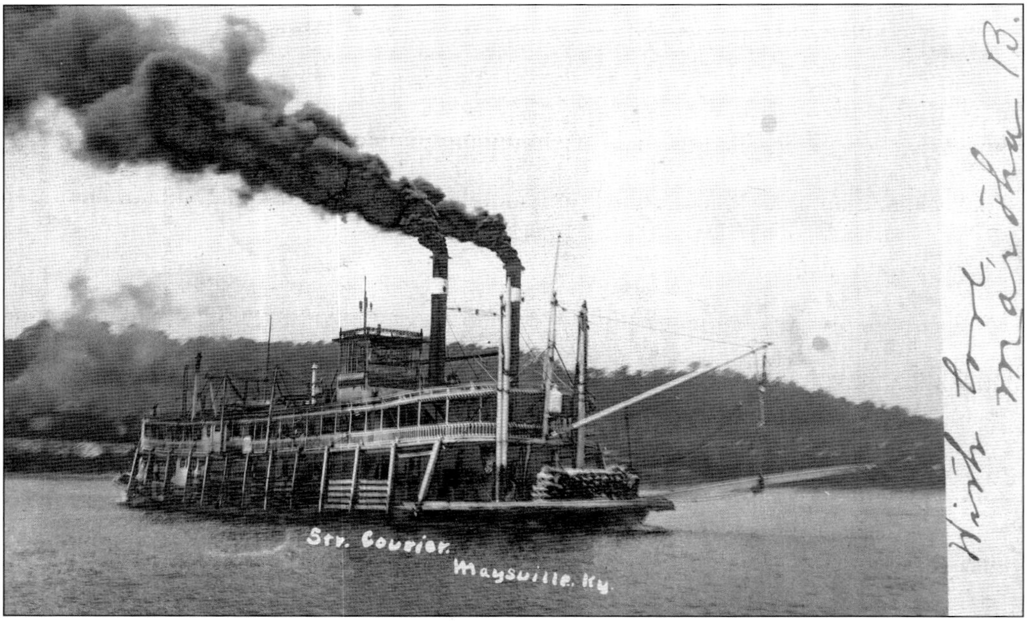

The steamer *Courier* was an Ohio River US Mail Packet boat that hauled cargo, passengers, and of course, the mail. These were dangerous vessels used in the 19th and 20th centuries because many of the steam boilers exploded, causing many deaths over the years. They did provide a great service to many towns along the waterways, but trains and automobiles soon changed the need for service.

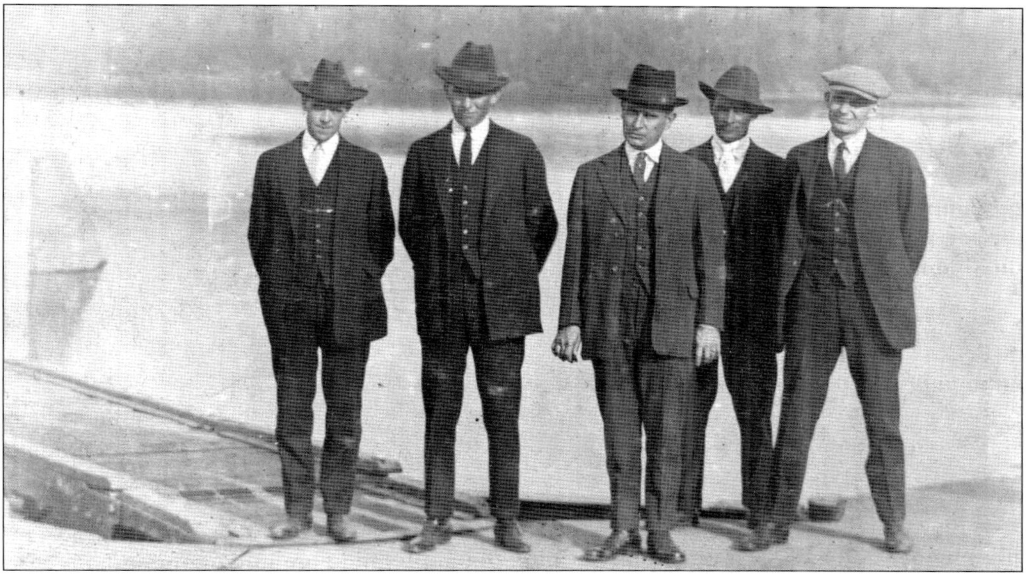

These local men are standing on the wharf area near a hinged walkway used to board the Ohio River steamers that traveled by Maysville. One of the concrete icebreakers can be seen to the left of these gentlemen. During the winter, ice flows down the Ohio, and many steamers docked behind the three breakers to prevent damage to the hull.

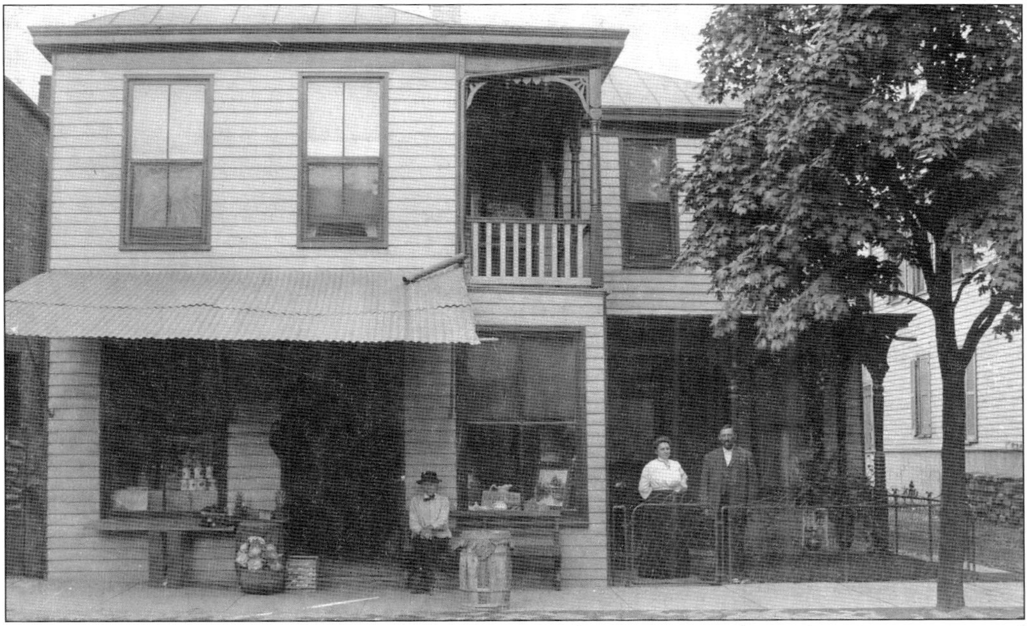

Joe and Betty Trisler stand in front of their home and grocery store, located at 617 East Second Street in Maysville. With the bow tie on, Hayes Storer is sitting on the bench in front of the grocery where he worked for the Trislers. A sign in the front window advertises framed pictures for $1.50.

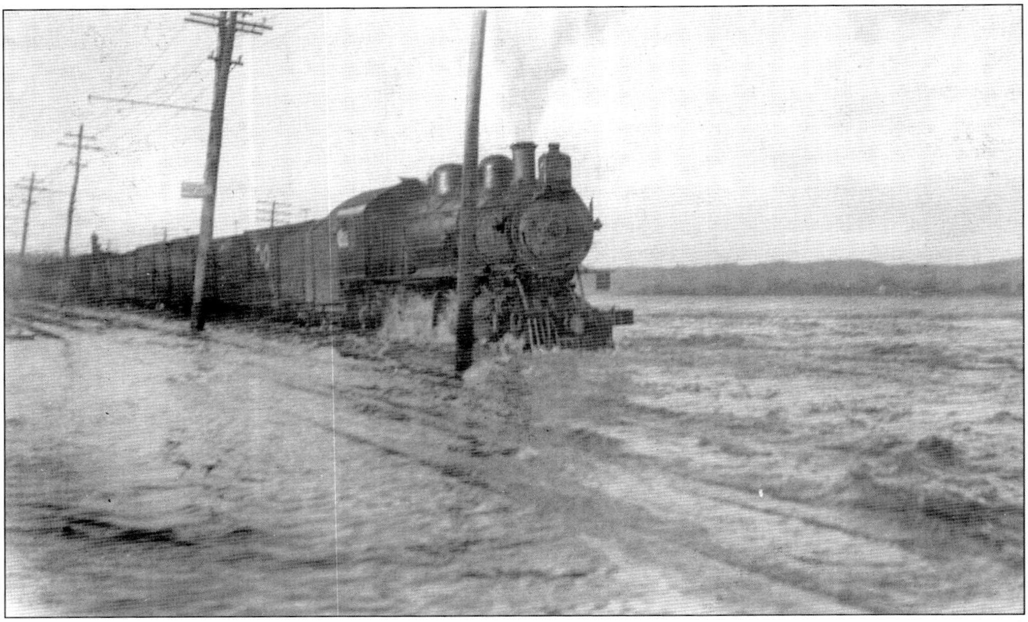

As the conductor keeps an eye on the depth of the water ahead, the train makes its way eastward along Front Street, as the river waters move swiftly downstream. Documentation on the back of this photograph states that the C&O encounters flooding of the Ohio River at Maysville, Kentucky, in March 1907.

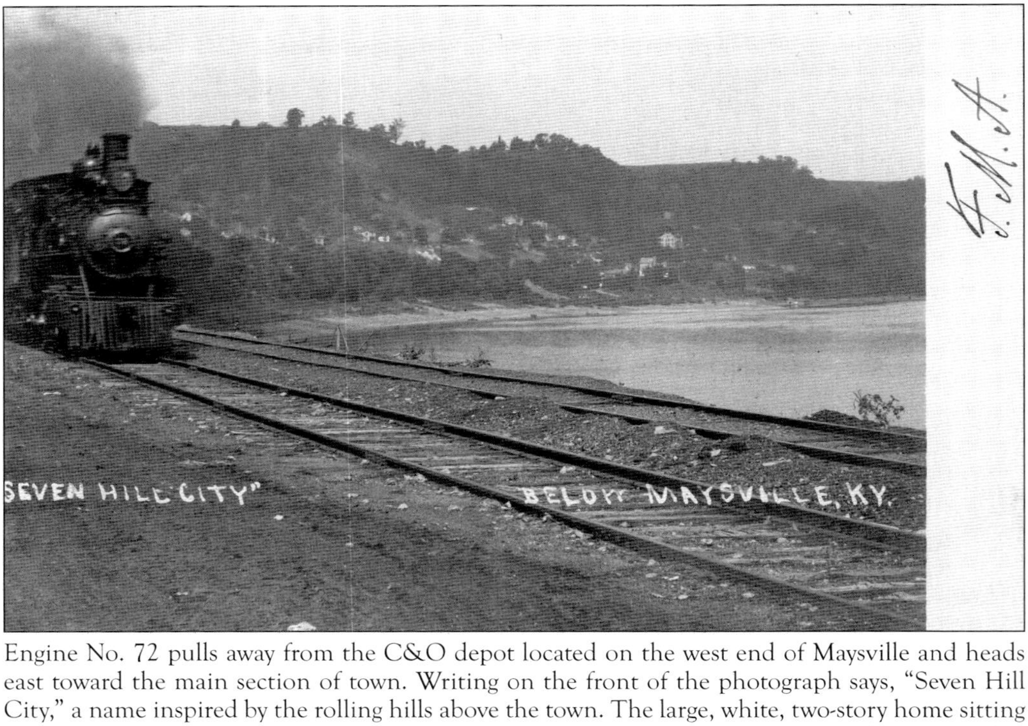

Engine No. 72 pulls away from the C&O depot located on the west end of Maysville and heads east toward the main section of town. Writing on the front of the photograph says, "Seven Hill City," a name inspired by the rolling hills above the town. The large, white, two-story home sitting halfway up the hill in the distance is the Old Pogue Distillery, still producing great bourbon today.

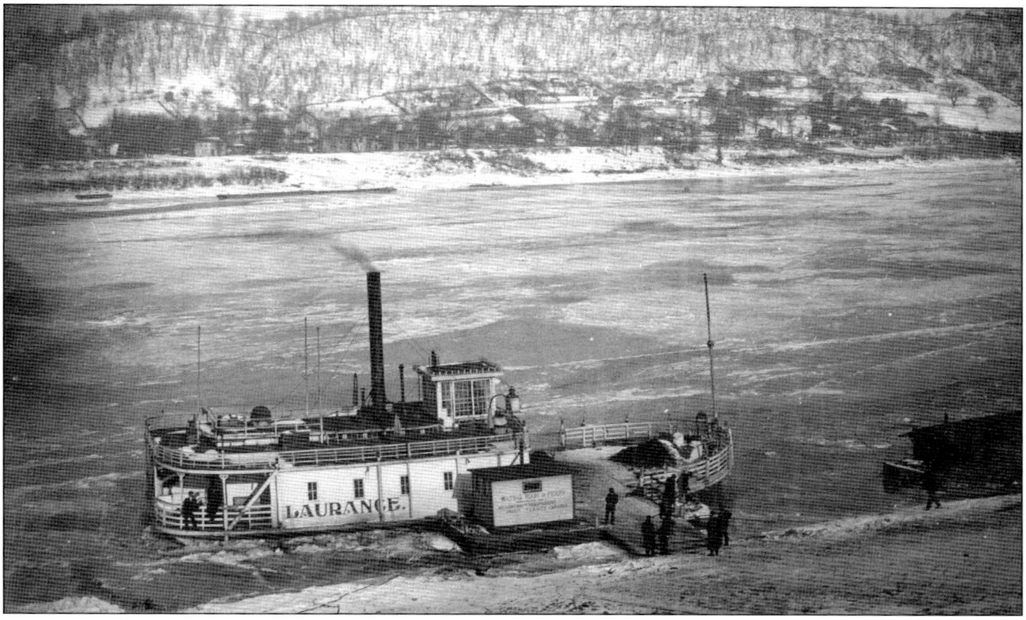

Icy waters float down the Ohio River past the shore and the homes near Aberdeen, Ohio. The ferry *Laurance* awaits passengers from the Maysville side of the river to navigate through the ice. Ferries were the only method of transportation across the river in the days prior to the Simon Kenton Bridge completion in 1931.

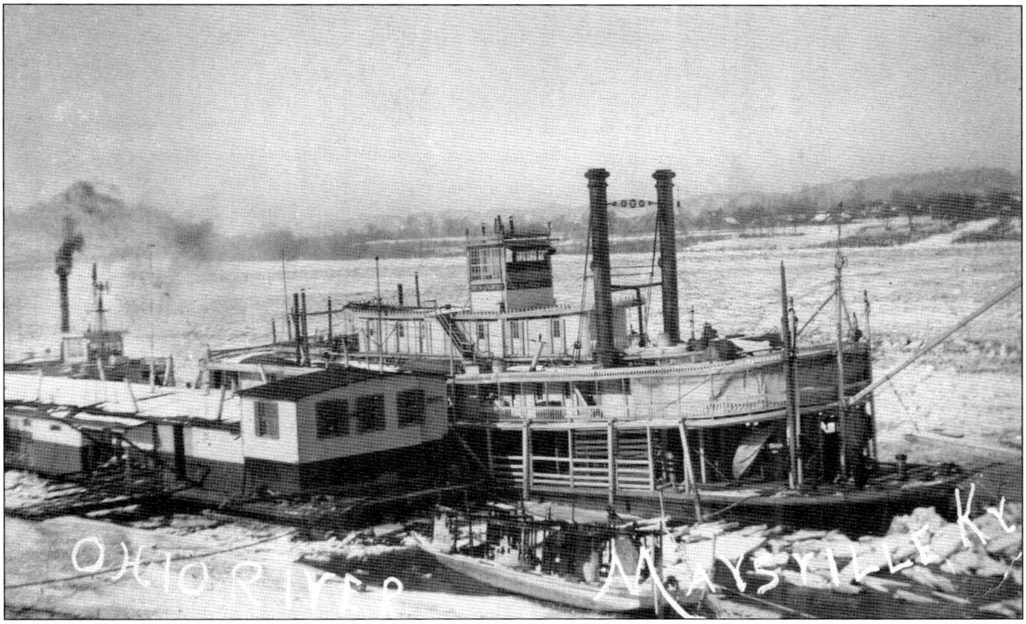

Packet steamer *Big Kanawha*, built in Madison, Indiana, in 1887, is docked behind the ice breakers at the wharf boat on the Ohio River at Maysville. In 1905, shortly after this photograph was taken, the packet boat encountered moving ice and sank. A closer look shows a shanty boat that has burned down to the hull. The ship's bell wound up at the Trinity Church in Point Pleasant, West Virginia.

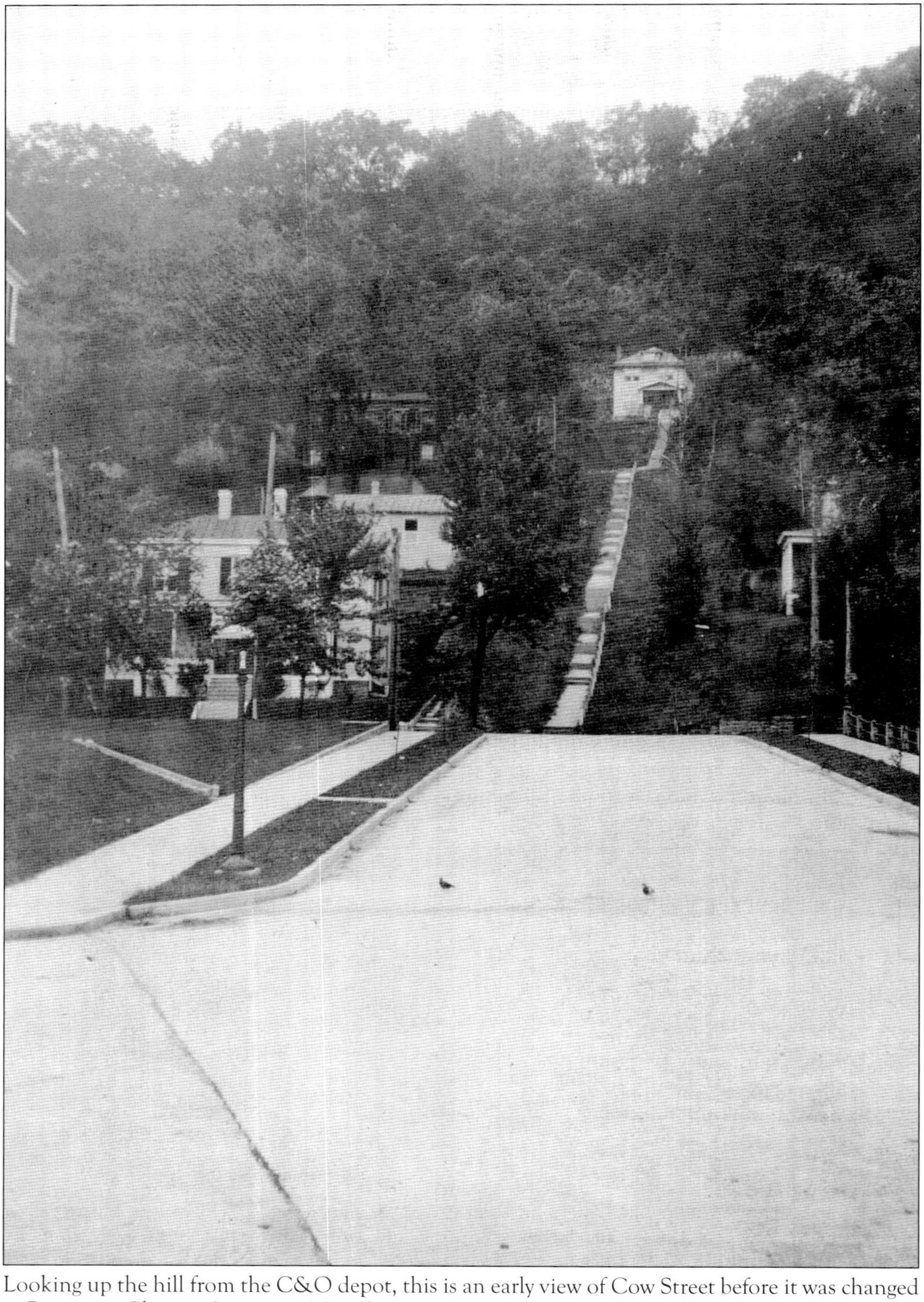

Looking up the hill from the C&O depot, this is an early view of Cow Street before it was changed to Rosemary Clooney Street in 1953. The steps from West Second Street lead up to a home located on Third Street that is no longer there today.

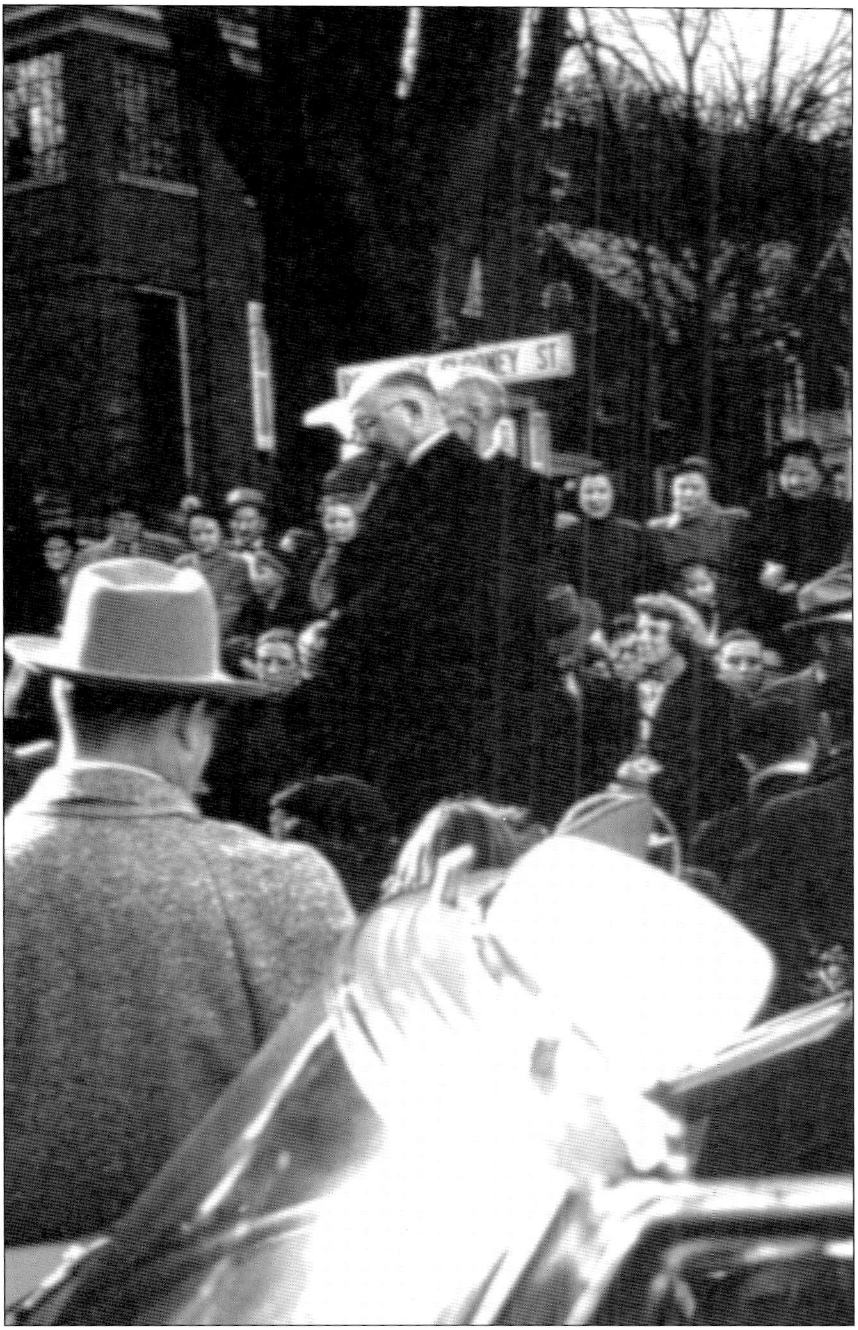

A parade was held through Maysville, and then the street sign was changed from Cow Street to Rosemary Clooney Street. Clooney can be seen in this photograph just above the car sun visors where the street sign has been changed. Later that evening, Clooney attended the premiere of *The Stars are Singing* at the Russell Theatre, where Clooney starred in the movie. The movie was released by Paramount Pictures on March 11, 1953. (This photograph was taken by Virginia F. Roberson, who attended the ceremonies.)

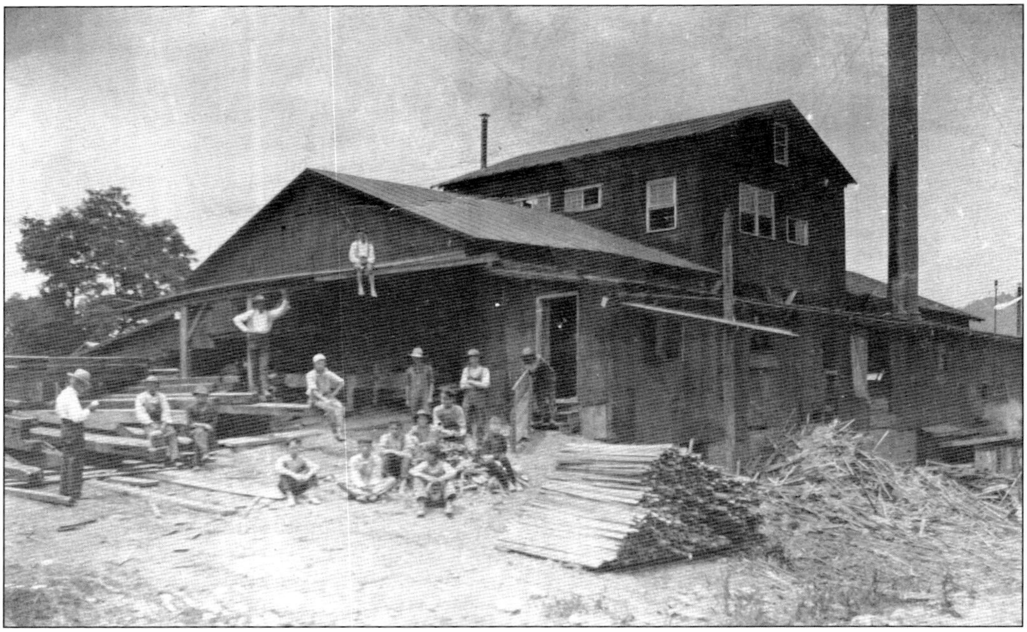

Other workers join Vic, a noted worker at this sawmill, who took a break to have this photograph taken on October 5, 1909. The Collins & Rudy Saw Mill, the Ohio River Lumber Company, and the W.B. Matthews Company all supplied the Maysville area with most of their building products in the early 20th century. At one time, logging on the Ohio River came to the mills in Maysville.

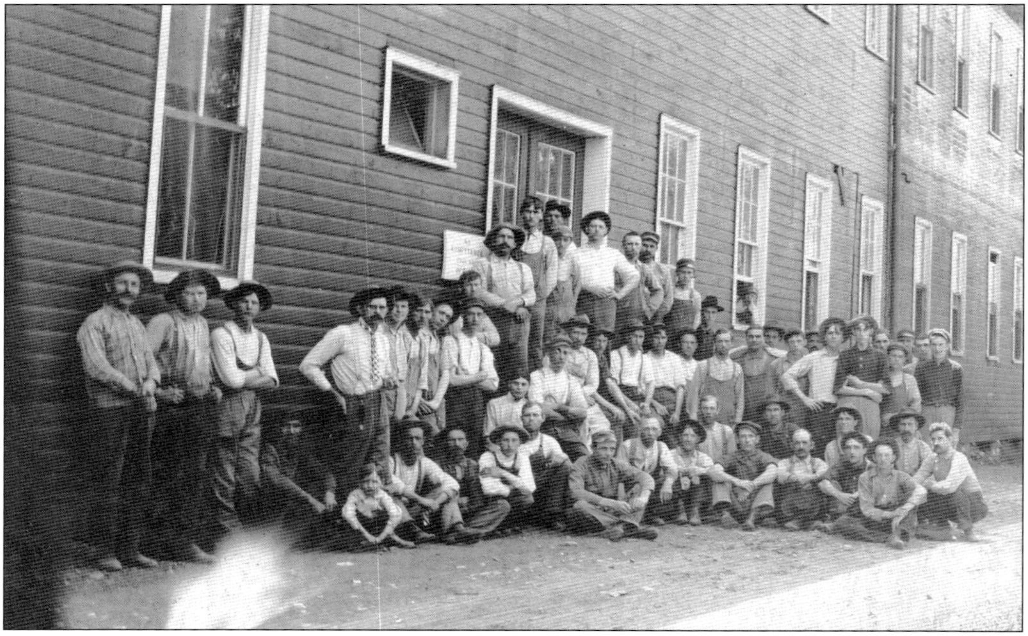

At the time this photograph was taken in 1908, this was the Ohio Valley Pulley Works. In 1911, the Browning family, who bought most of the stock, changed the name to Browning's. Some of the workforce is pictured here near the intersection of Main Street and Chester Street in Maysville's east end. The photograph is dated August 10, 1908, and was sent to Lola Payne in Aberdeen, Ohio.

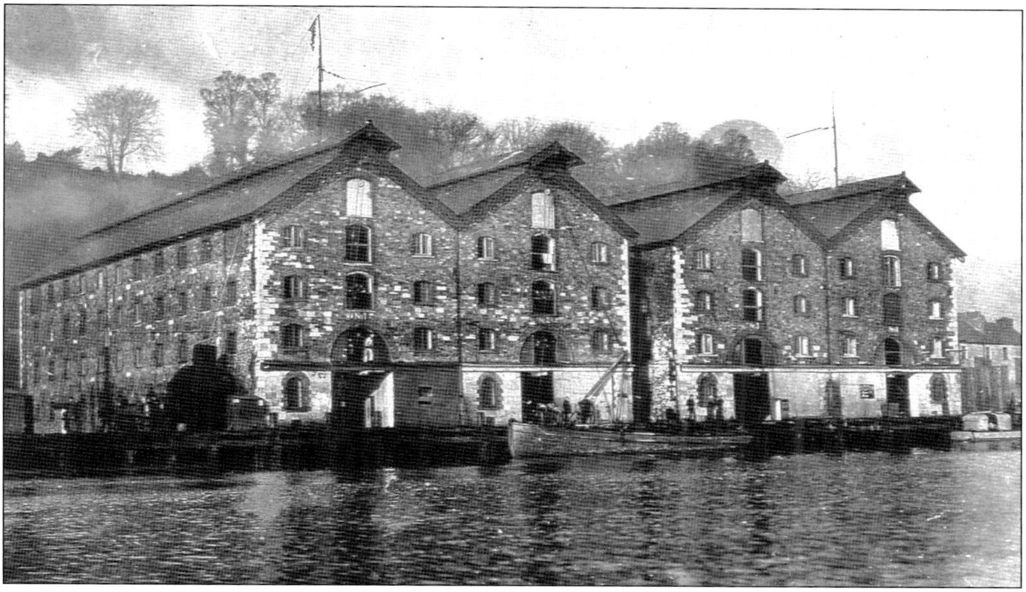

Henry Edgar Pogue I registered and established the Pogue Distillery in 1876 in the state of Kentucky and located the business in the west end of Maysville, Kentucky. The warehouses were located near the Ohio River where many name brands were labeled, and the Pogue bourbons were shipped throughout the United States and world. The distillery continues to be operated by the family today, producing fine bourbons.

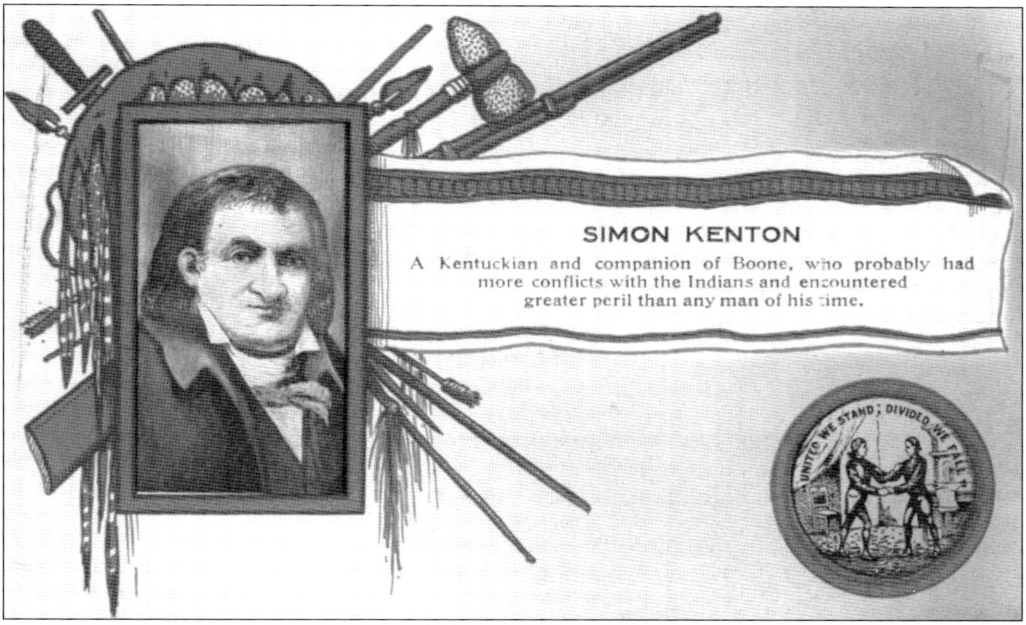

Born April 3, 1755, in Virginia, Simon Kenton was, without a doubt, one of the greatest and bravest men of his time, and he personally knew many of the great men of that period. Kenton grew to love the outdoors and relocated from his native Virginia downriver into the Ohio River Valley, where he helped establish the early village of Limestone, later named Maysville. Kenton died April 29, 1836, and is buried in Urbana, Ohio.

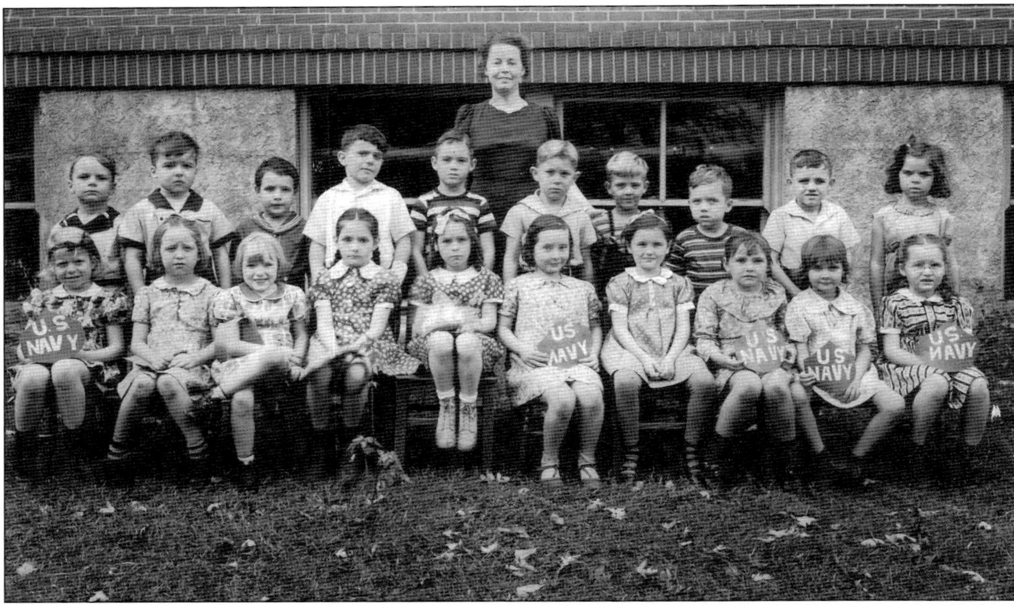

It seems that Sixth Ward School was a forgotten school, as postcard photographers did not produce many images of the school. Sixth Ward was in the east end of the town of Maysville and located on Broadway Street. Many children made lifelong memories at this school during their first through fourth grades. Script was taught, and one was expected to write in between the three lines. First grade for many in the 1950s usually followed kindergarten at Helen Smoot's home in Deerfield Village. Below, the school entrance can be seen here behind this class photograph. The single-pane glass windows were big and heavy with weights and ropes to help them go up and down more easily. The ropes often broke, so the teachers had to operate them. These two photographs date back to a period from around 1939 to 1944.

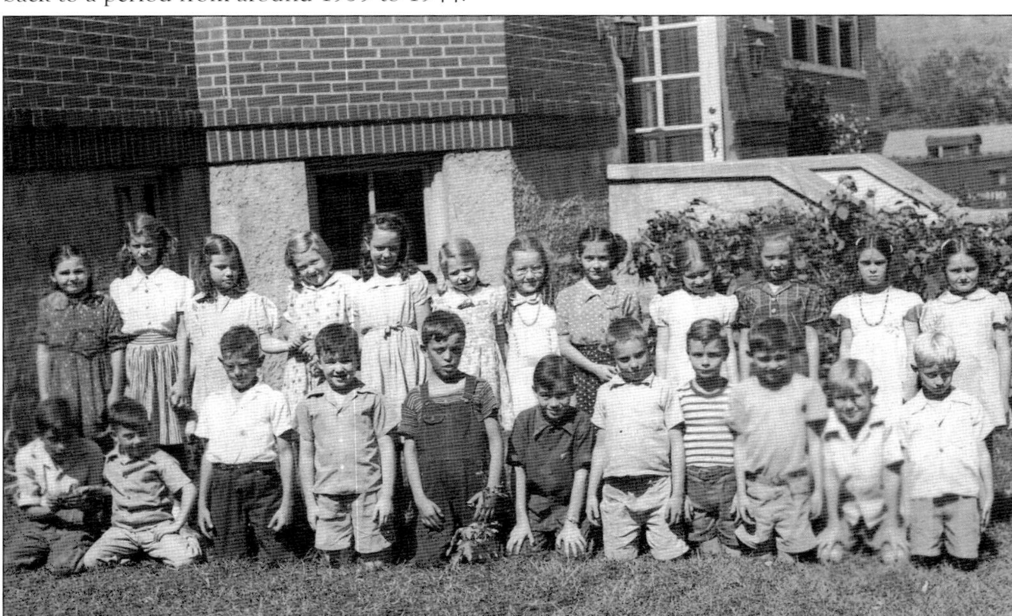

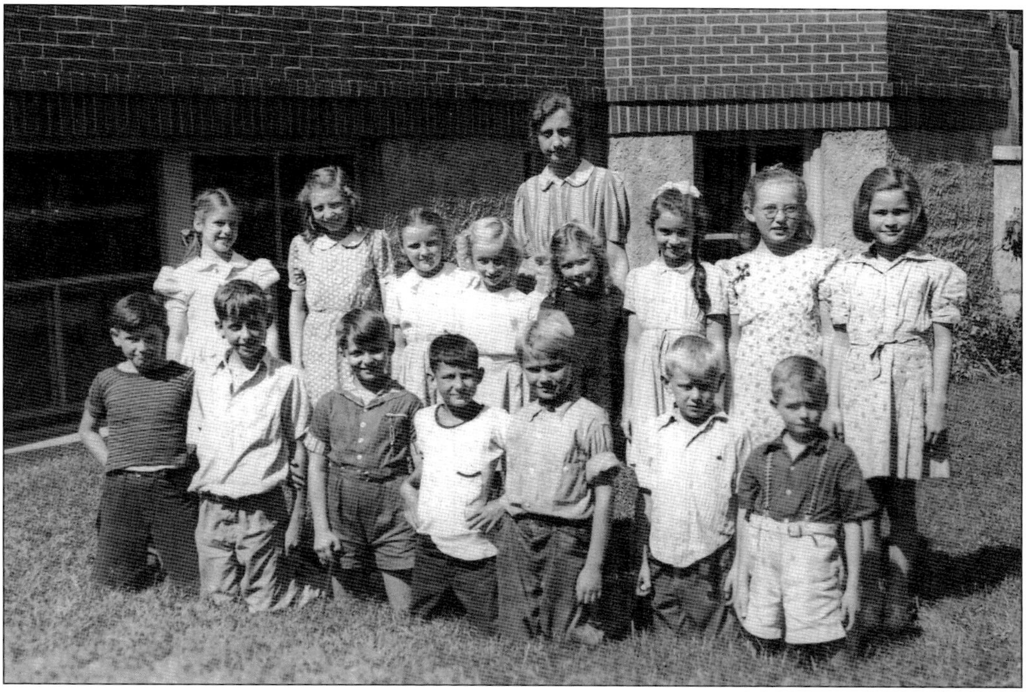

This photograph was taken just left of the entrance doors of Sixth Ward School, where these children and their teacher pose for a class photograph in the early 1940s. There was no air-conditioning, and the heat came from a steam boiler in the basement. The music class was just to the left, where one learned how to play a tonette and dance the minuet as in the days of George Washington.

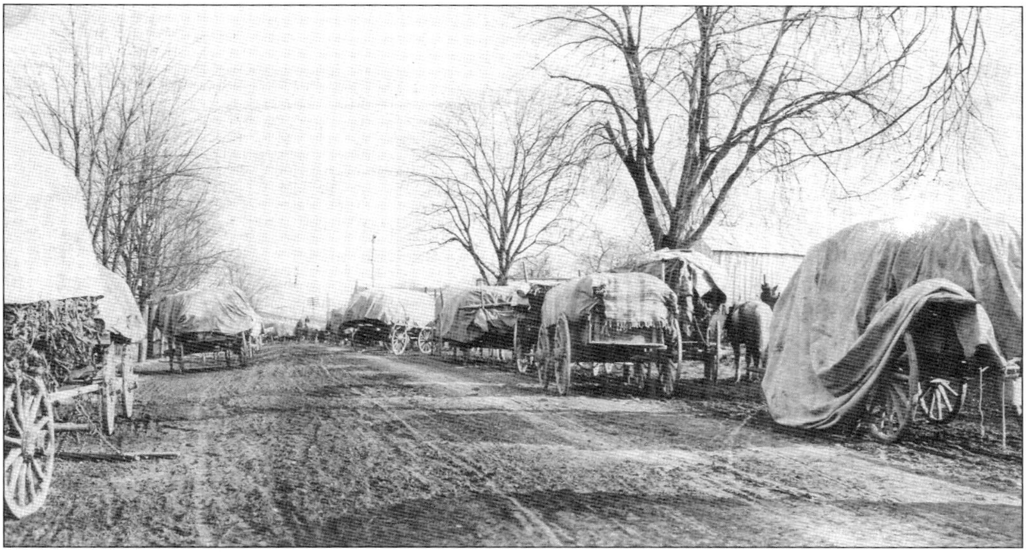

Years ago, growing up in the Ohio Valley meant being in the center of the "World's Finest Tobacco Market," where the call letters on the local radio station are advertised, even today, as WFTM by Standard Tobacco. Many of the smaller towns had their own tobacco warehouse until Maysville expanded and built warehouses along the streets of Forest Avenue, where these wagons wait for their crops to be unloaded.

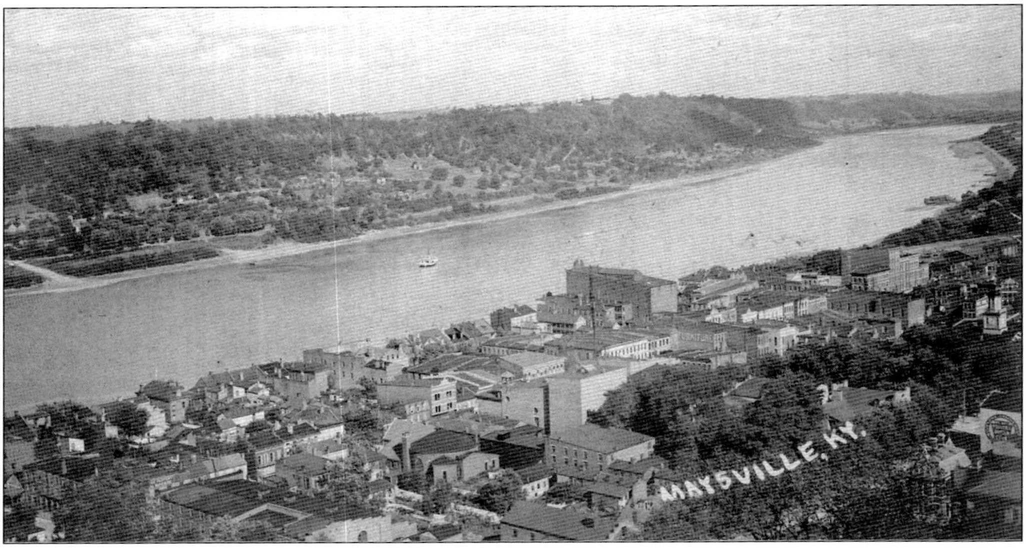

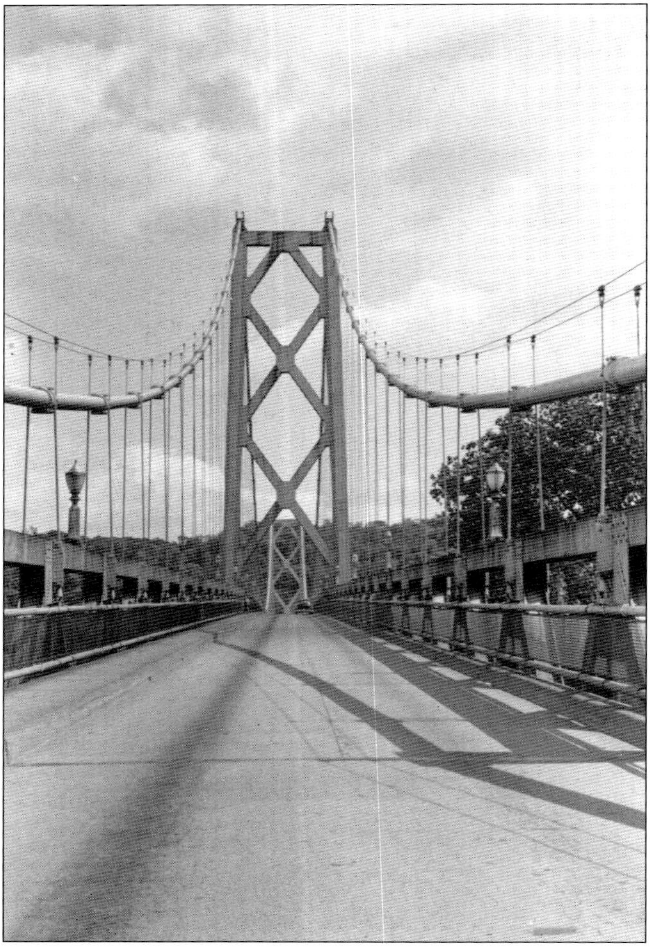

When reflecting on the town prior to the completion of the Simon Kenton Bridge, one must consider how this bridge helped connect people and products on both sides of the Ohio River in this community. Even though the ferries did their job, having the bridge and the improvements in automobiles and trucks made everyone's life so much better.

The famous Simon Kenton Memorial Bridge, which has connected Maysville, Kentucky, to Aberdeen, Ohio, since 1931, has allowed this community to expand. The bridge is a landmark, and those who have had a chance to visit this area can see why, especially if they had an opportunity to eat at Caproni's one evening and see the bridge lit up.

Two

MASON COUNTY, KENTUCKY

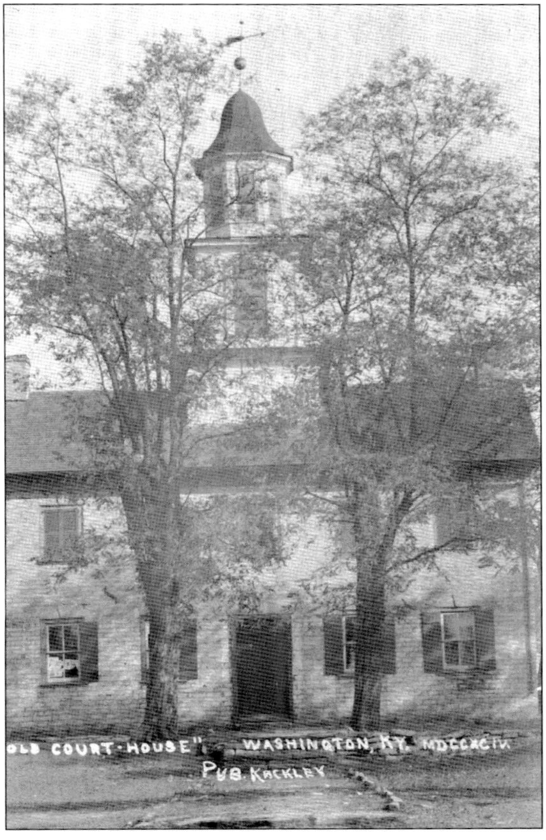

The first courthouse in Mason County, Kentucky, was constructed in 1794 and located in Washington about four miles south of Maysville. The limestone courthouse was built by Lewis Craig who was also a Baptist minister. This is the courthouse where Uncle Tom (of *Uncle Tom's Cabin*) stood to be sold into slavery. This photograph was published by Kackley in Maysville.

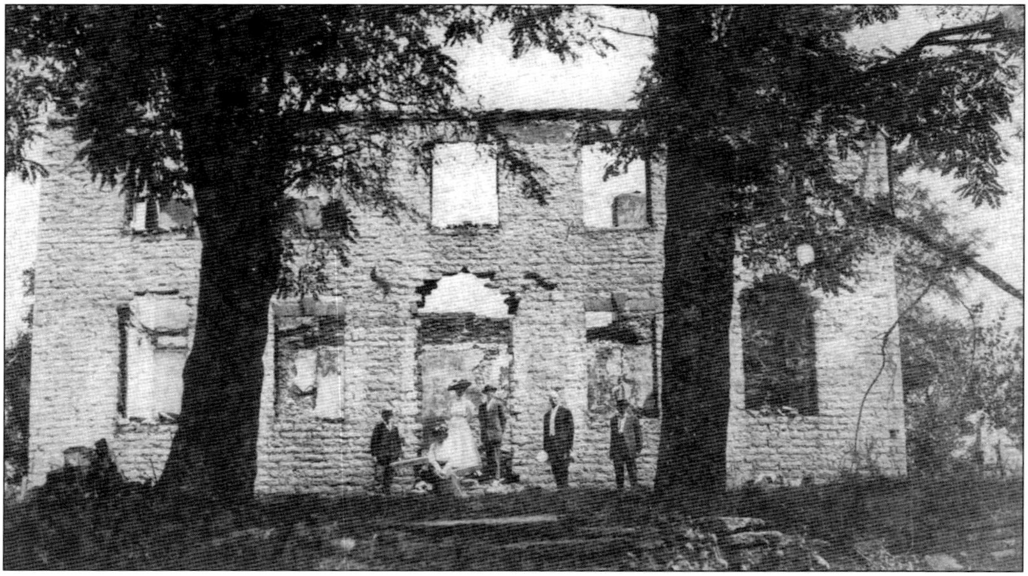

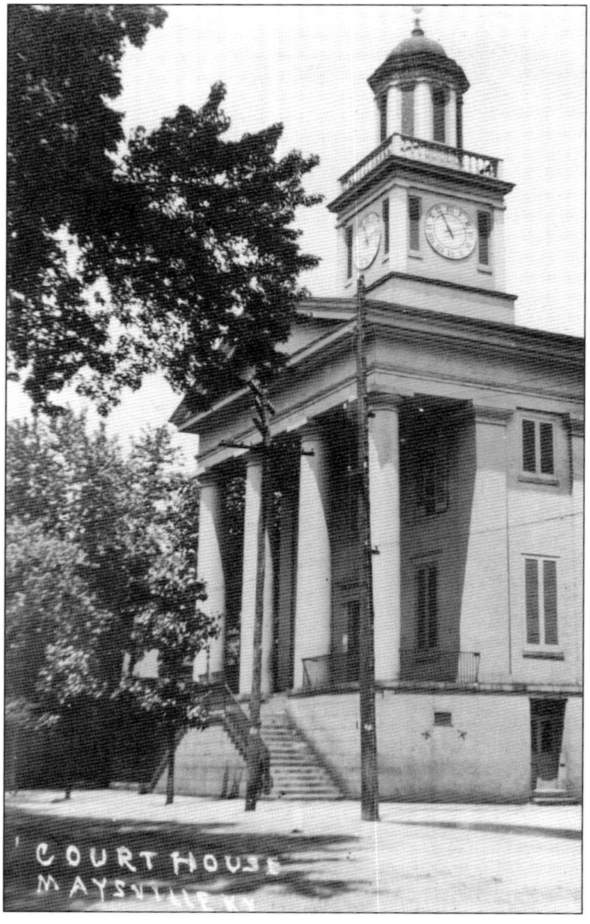

When court business ceased in the original Mason County Courthouse in Washington in 1847, it was used as a school and then as an academy conducted by Rev. Robert McMurdy. On August 13, 1909, lightning struck the old courthouse, resulting in a fire that destroyed everything except the outer stone walls.

Following a vote by the residents of Mason County, the courthouse was moved to Maysville, in part due to the population growth. This courthouse is located on Third Street at Stanley Reed Court and was built between 1844 and 1846. A newer courthouse has been built on Third Street, but some business is still done at this historic one.

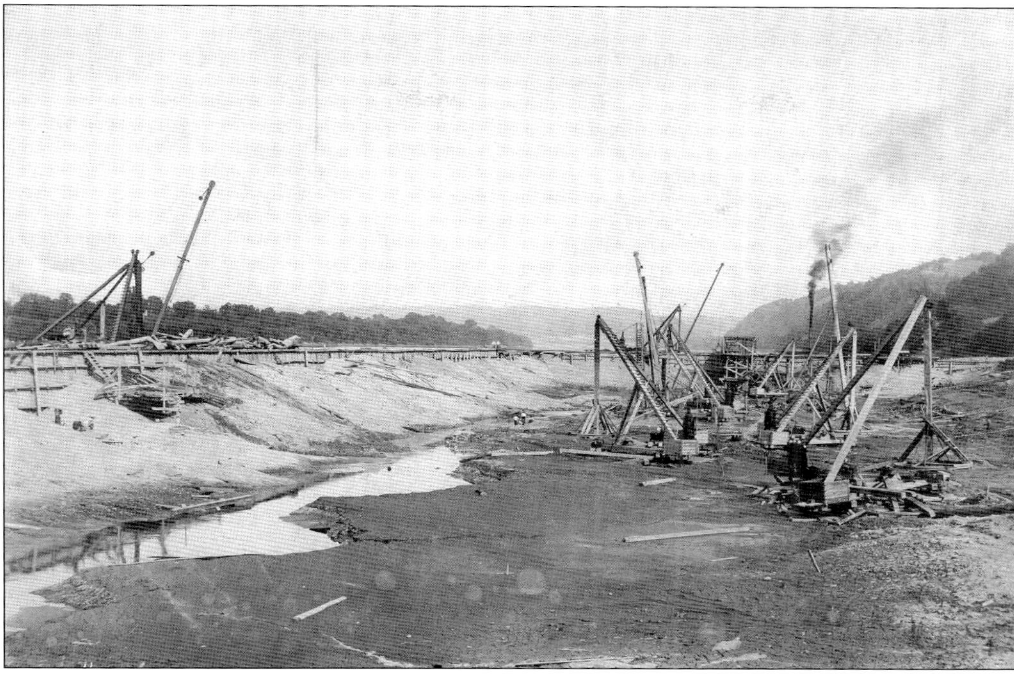

The building site of Lock and Dam No. 33 was located just upriver a few miles from Maysville. Part of the Ohio River has been diverted where the equipment is being used, and forms are in place to pour the concrete walls. In the distance, one can see the town of Springdale, Kentucky, which was later purchased by the Dravo Corporation to build a limestone quarry, so the town ceased to exist. This photograph is dated August 1, 1915. Below, the newly established 20th-century company, Bates and Rogers Construction Company, based in Chicago, Illinois, was awarded the contract to build Lock and Dam No. 33 and was known for new construction methods using steel and concrete. The *Frank Tyler* tug is seen docked against the company's workboat, while men are building the hull framework for a steamboat to be used during this construction project.

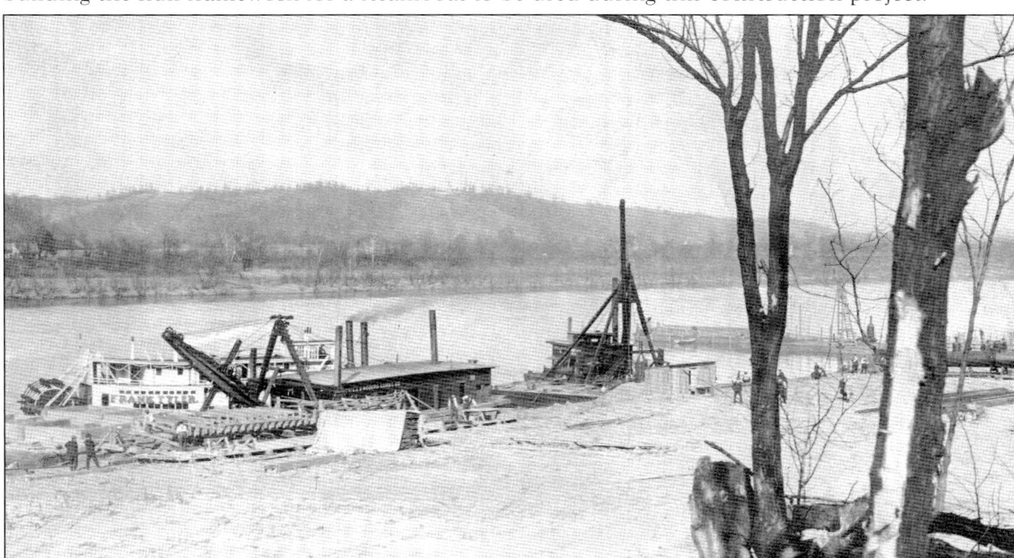

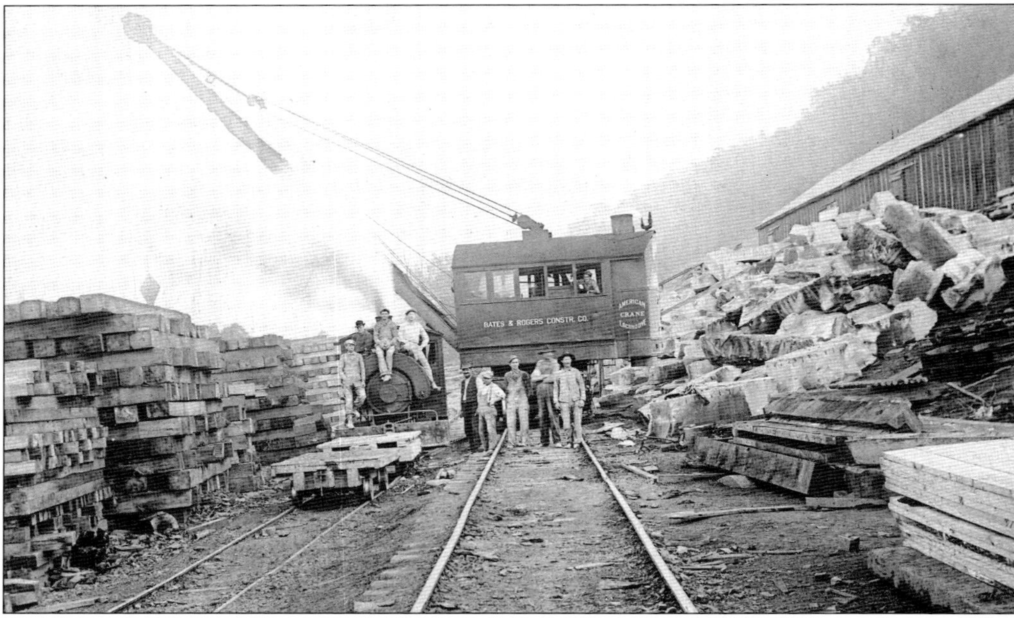

Just below the train tracks of the C&O Railway, the Bates and Rogers workers were busy laying out their own tracks with the help of this American Crane locomotive and the small train locomotive. The large timbers were used to lay out the on-site train tracks to move the materials to the Ohio River Lock and Dam No. 33 site. Workers pose for this photograph taken on August 1, 1915. Below, the group of men sitting near the lock gates appears to have on their Sunday best for this photograph. People continue to this day to visit and watch the operations that take place when a riverboat is locked through the dams from one level of water to another.

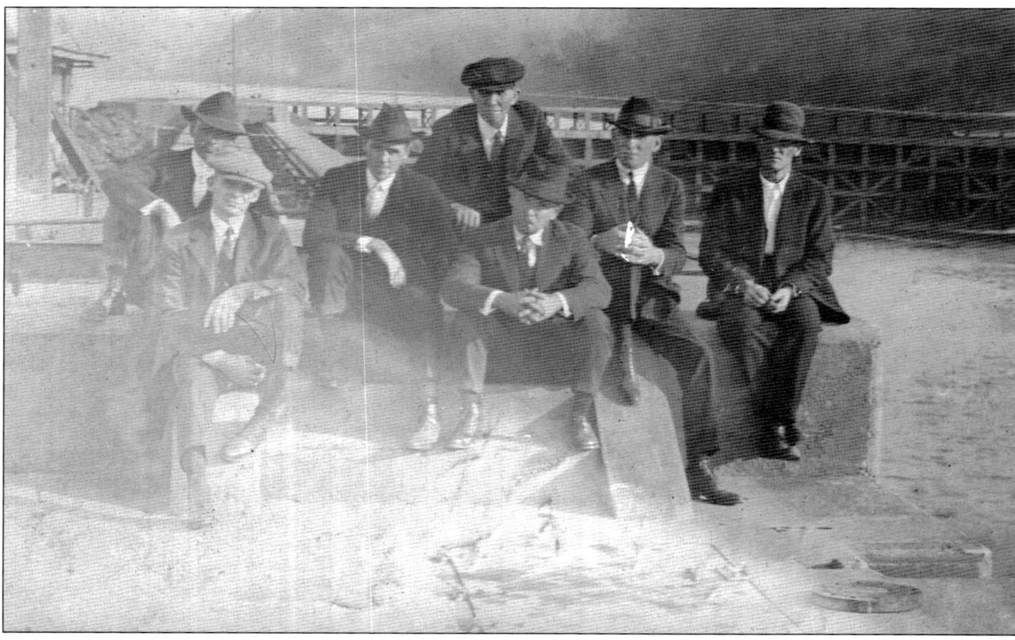

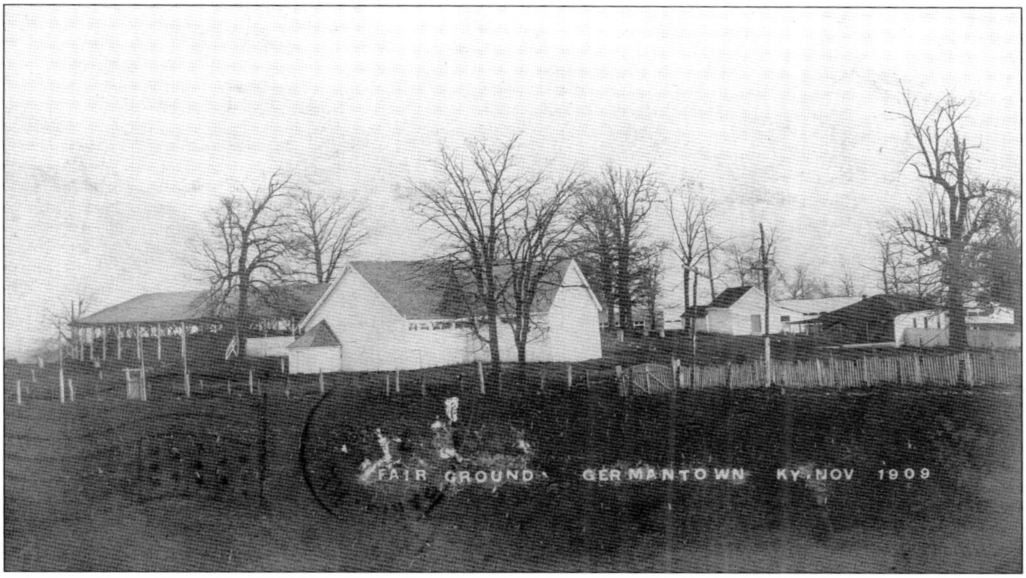

The first Germantown Fair started in 1854 and, like many county fairs in Kentucky, provided an important gathering place for people to come together from all over this rural county to compete and have a good time. This view is dated December 4, 1909, and has a note on the back from Maggie Lea in Germantown to Amanda Carr in Paris, Kentucky.

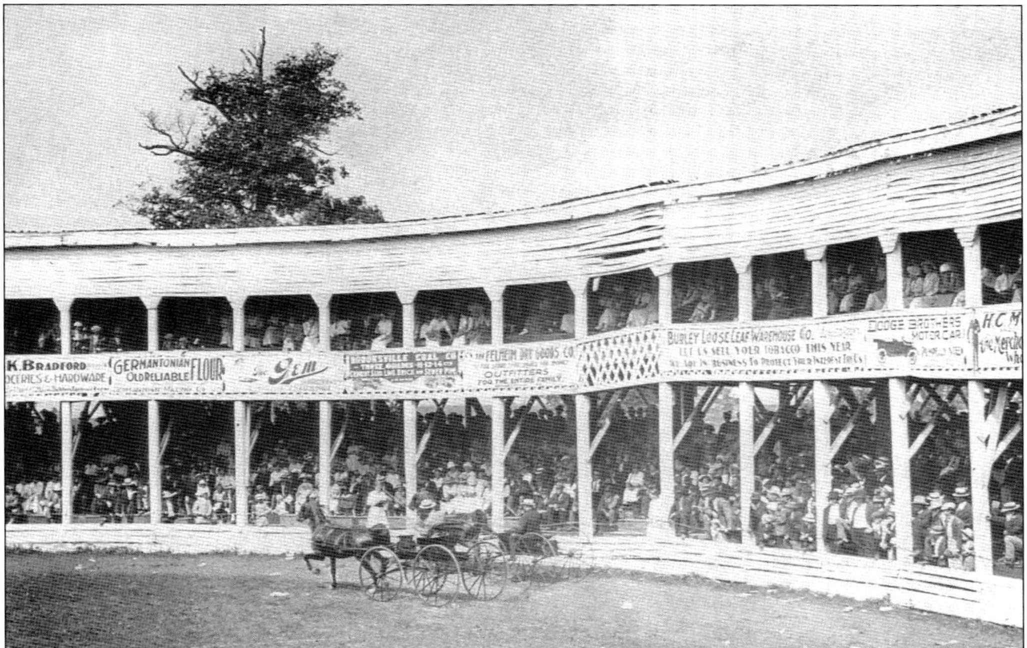

The Germantown Fair, held in Mason County, Kentucky, was the largest fair in this area and drew in people from at least five surrounding counties. The fair was located off Route 10 west of Maysville before entering Germantown and still draws a crowd there today The first president of the fair was Anthony Kilgore. Local advertising banners separate the first and second floors of the newly whitewashed grandstands.

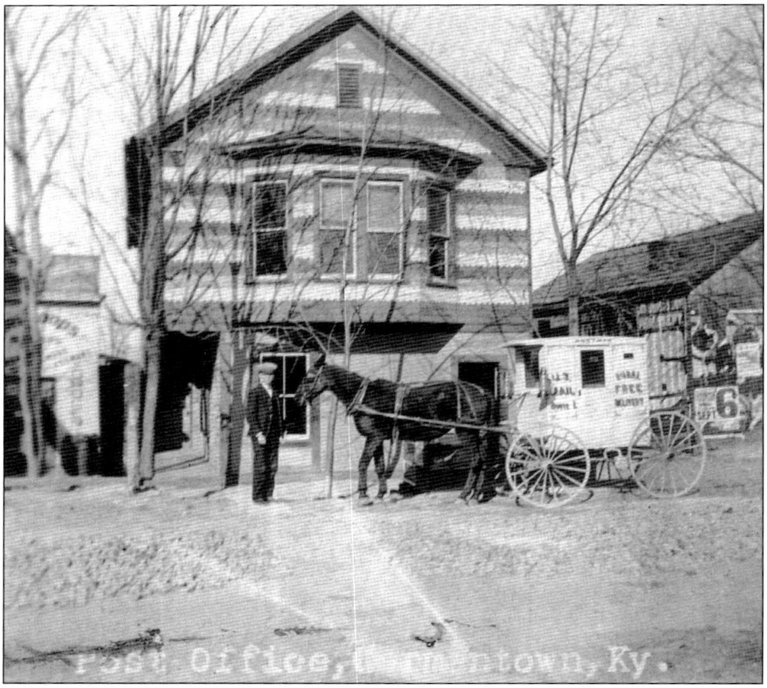

A typical rural route postal carrier stands for a photograph with his trusty horse in front of the Germantown Post Office. Germantown is split between Mason and Bracken Counties, so prior to this more permanent location, mail was delivered where the elected postmaster's business might have been located. This photograph, sent to Ethel Pollock and dated March 2, 1908, was taken by D.W. Short, Westerville, Ohio.

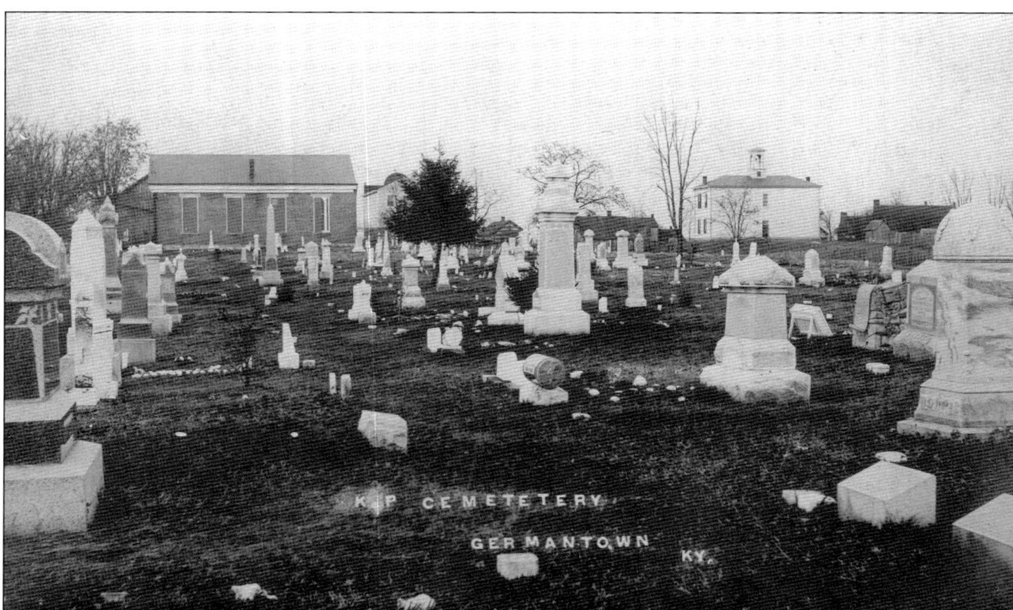

One photograph identifies this as the Knights of Pythias Cemetery (K&P), and another image of the same view, dated March 30, 1910, names it the Maple Grove Cemetery, with a note from a pastor or speaker by the name of E.R. Overley. The cemetery is located in the town near Highway 10 on Bridgeville Road in Germantown, Kentucky.

The Baptist church in Mayslick, Kentucky, has a long history dating back to the founding of Mayslick. A great article by John A. Ulrich about the overall history is available online. The congregation continues to have services in the church today. This photograph was published by Dan T. Fischer, Jeweler & Optician, Flemingsburg, Kentucky, and dates to around 1907 to 1910.

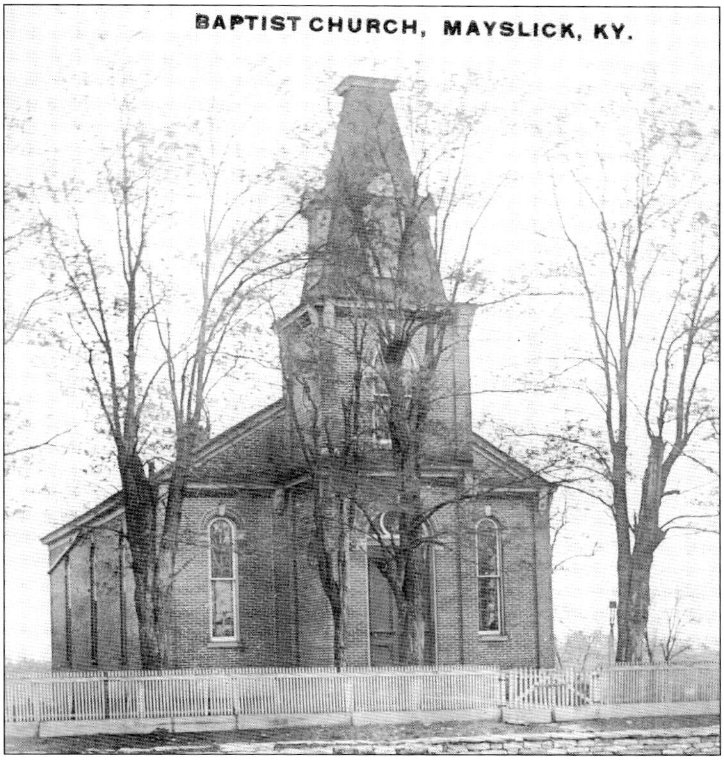

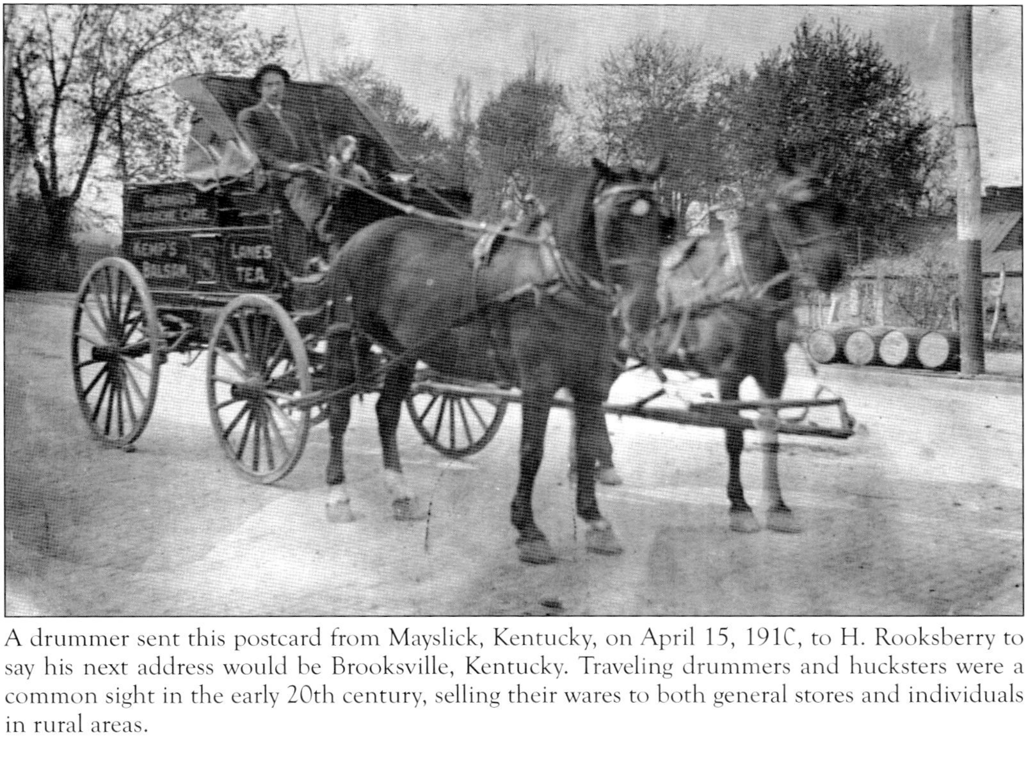

A drummer sent this postcard from Mayslick, Kentucky, on April 15, 1910, to H. Rooksberry to say his next address would be Brooksville, Kentucky. Traveling drummers and hucksters were a common sight in the early 20th century, selling their wares to both general stores and individuals in rural areas.

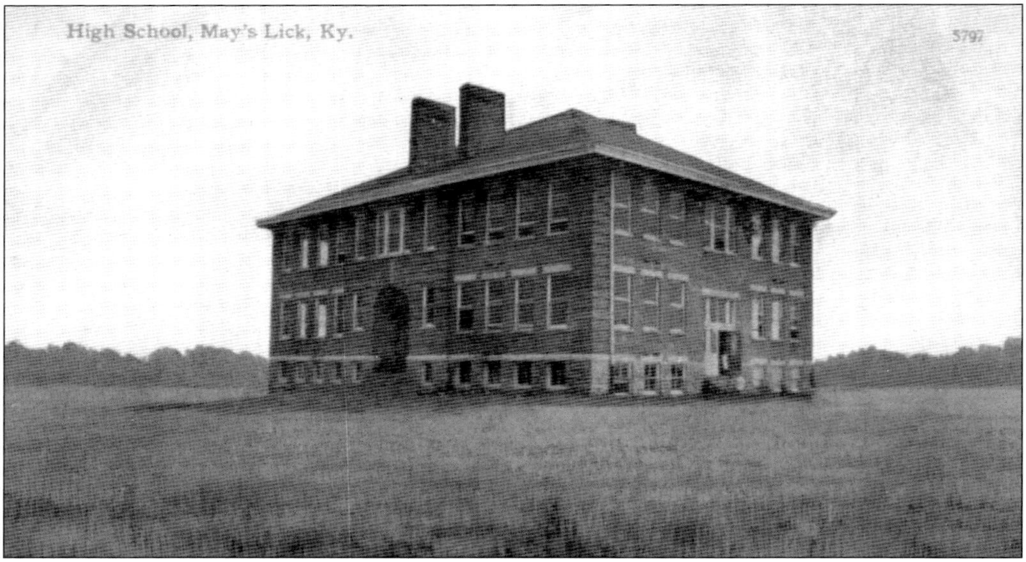

Construction of the Mayslick Consolidated School began in 1909 and was completed for $37,500. This school was the first consolidated school in Mason County when it added the students from the Arthuranna one-room school that was destroyed by a flood in 1910. The school building was placed in the National Register of Historic Places in 1982. This postcard was published by Art Mfg. Co., Zanesville, Ohio, card No. 5797, and dated August 14, 1911.

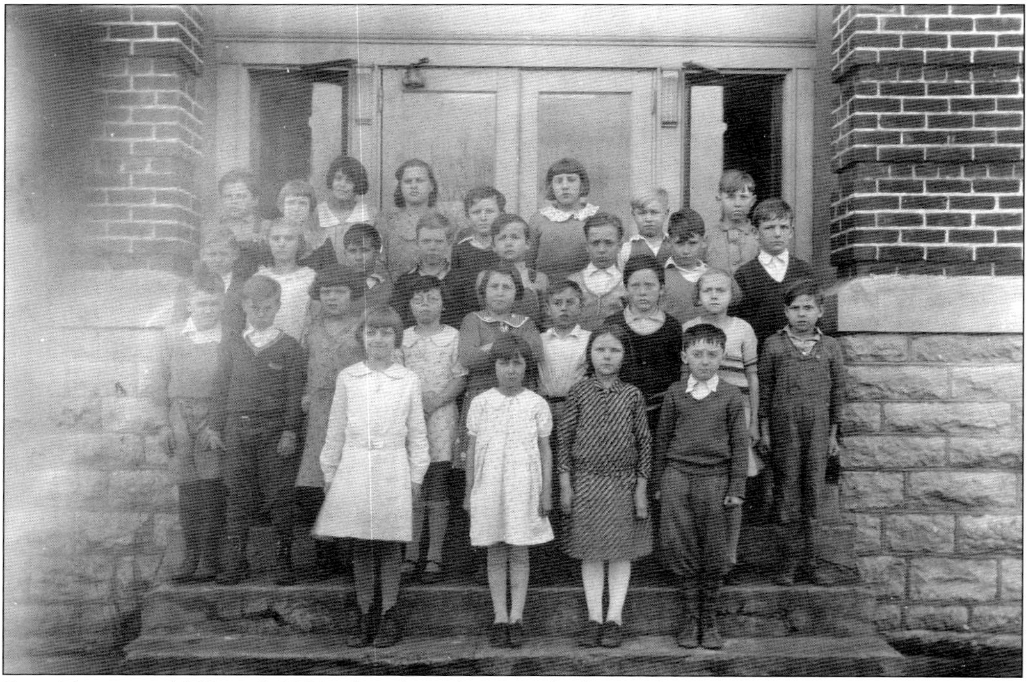

Dated between 1930 and 1932, this class photograph shows children standing at the entrance of the Mayslick Consolidated School. Unfortunately, only a portion of the beautiful quoins of the brickwork arch above the front door can be seen. The original school was built by the construction company of Douglas McCowell. In modern times, the old school was renovated to make apartments.

This 1934 group photograph is also from the Mayslick Consolidated School. The names written on the back are the teacher, Kathryn Clark, from Mount Olivet, and students Lucian Taylor, Ruby Dean, Glen Crawford, Johnie, Cecil Gifford, Etna Cox, Earl, Robert, William Roberson Jr., Junior Morgan, Frank, and Gus Roberson.

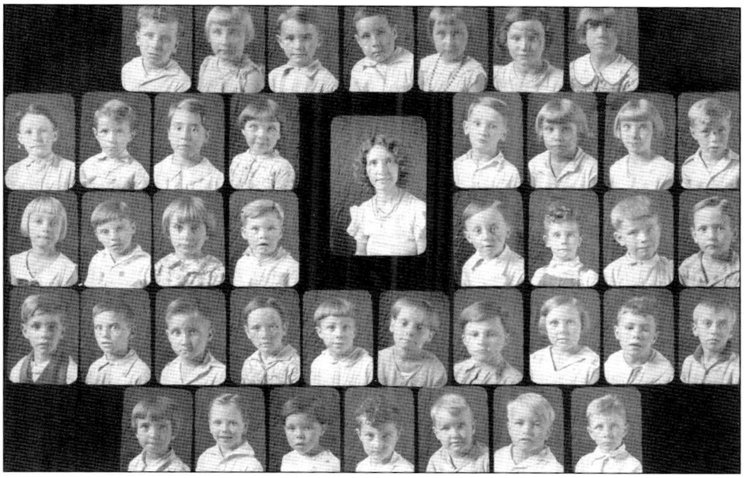

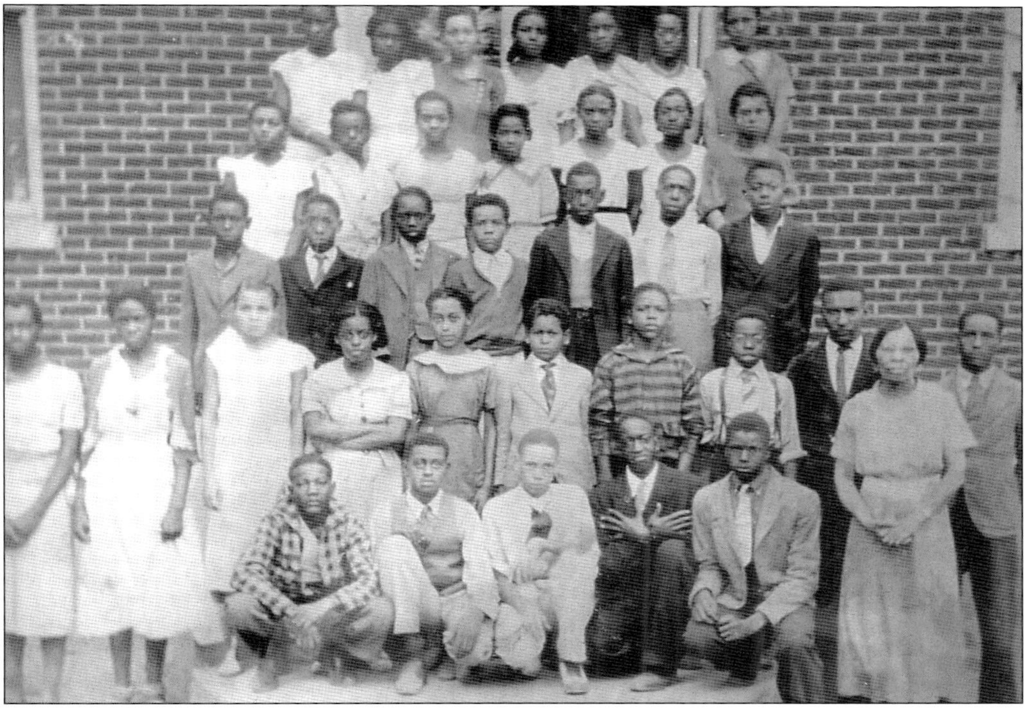

These students gather in front of the Rosenwald Mayslick Negro School in Mayslick, Kentucky. This brick school was one of 3,537 schools built between 1917 and 1932 with the help of local citizens, Booker T. Washington, and Julius Rosenwald. This was the first Black consolidated school in Mason County. Placed in the National Register of Historic Places, this school is in the process of being restored. The school closed in 1961. (This photograph is courtesy of Cheryl French and the Mayslick Community Development Corporation.)

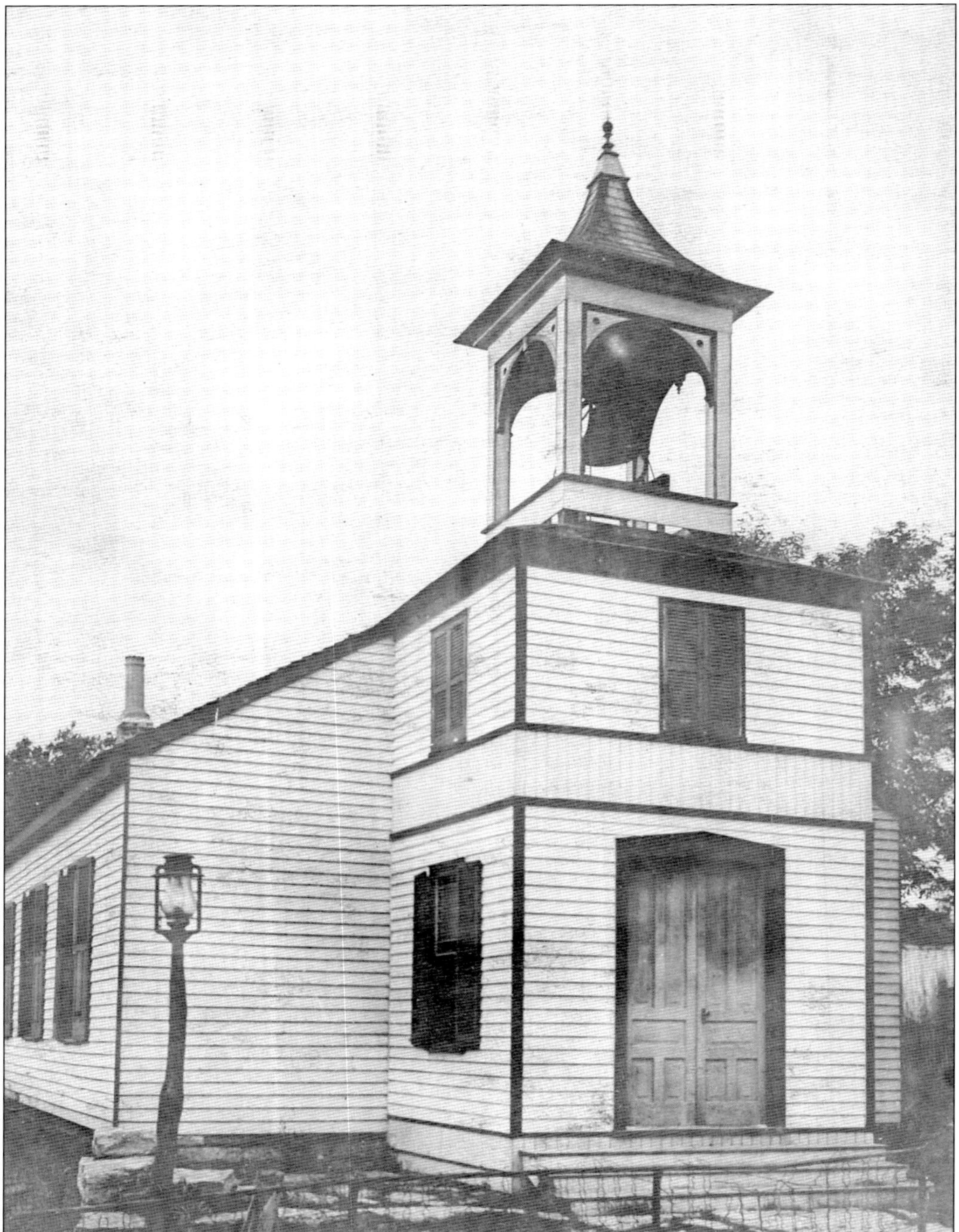

In the 1876 Mason County Atlas showing Helena, Kentucky, there was only one church, and that was the wood-frame Methodist church shown here. This photograph was dated after 1907, and a fire destroyed the church sometime afterward. A new stone Methodist church was built and has a cornerstone dated 1914; it was dedicated on June 27, 1915. This photograph was published by Dan T. Fischer, Jeweler & Optician, Flemingsburg, Kentucky.

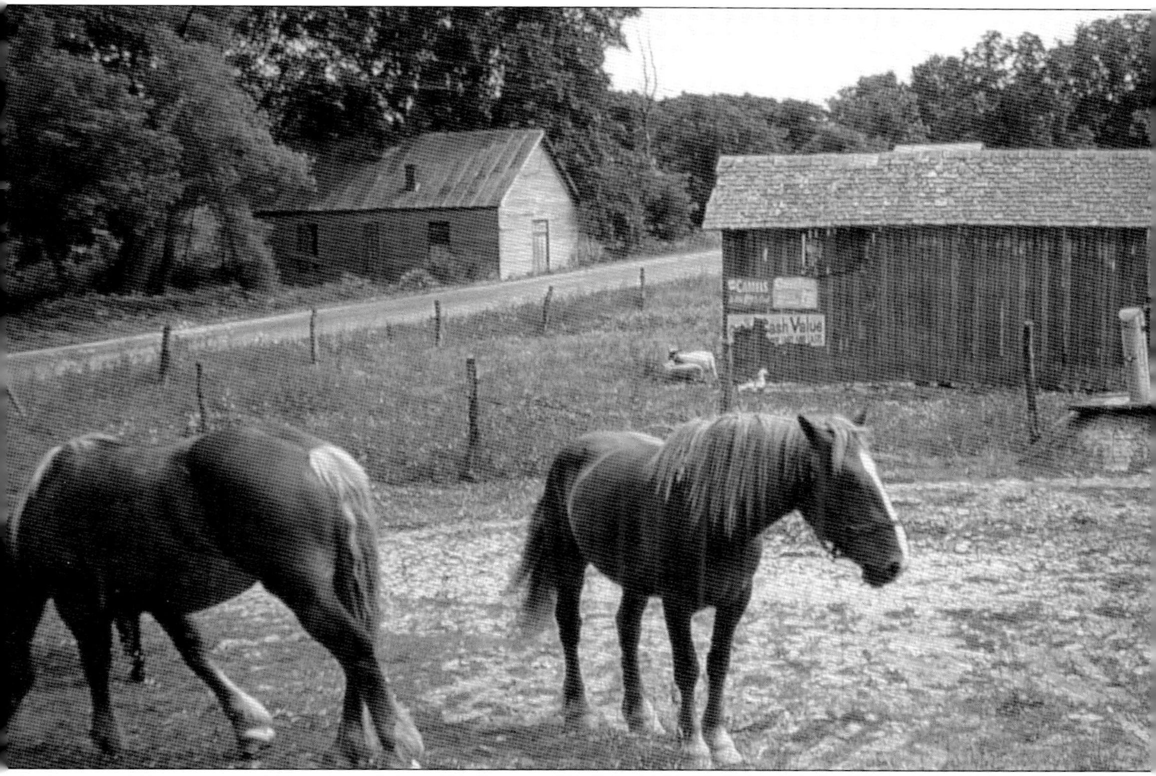

Taken in 1950, this photograph shows a typical rural farm in Mason County, Kentucky, between Helena and Johnson Junction in Fleming County. Across the road is an old Black church that is long gone today. According to Cheryl French of Maysville, the name of the church was Mount Zion, and there was also a Black school just down the road towards Helena during this time period.

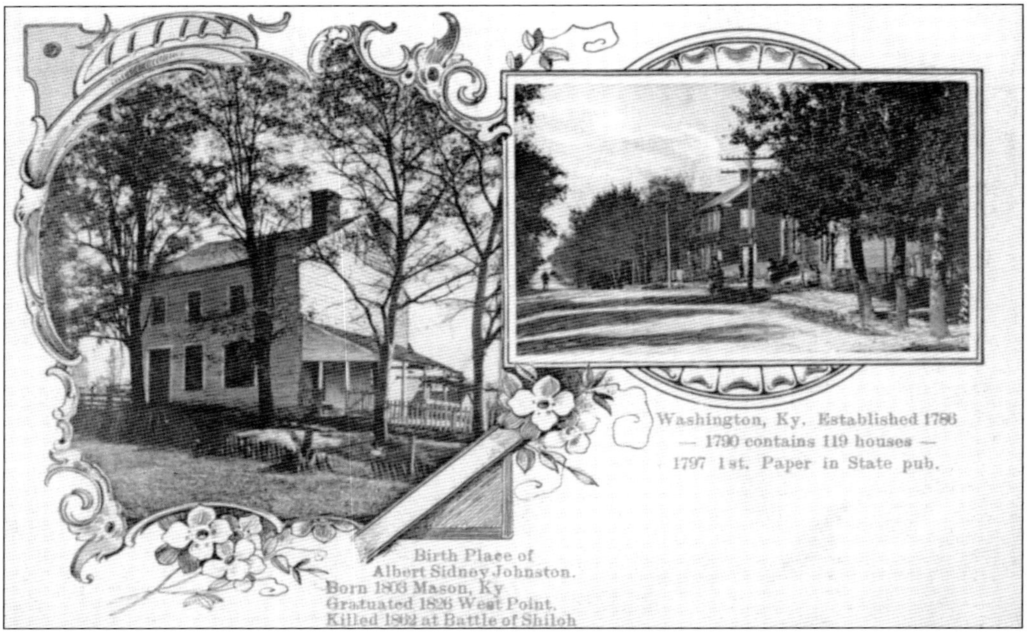

Gen. Albert Sidney Johnston was born in Washington, Kentucky, and was the youngest son of Dr. John and Abigail Johnston, who moved to Washington from Connecticut. General Johnston had a 34-year military career before he was killed on April 6, 1862, at Shiloh, one of the earliest battles of the Civil War. Washington continues to be a very historical place to visit, especially during some of the annual town festivals.

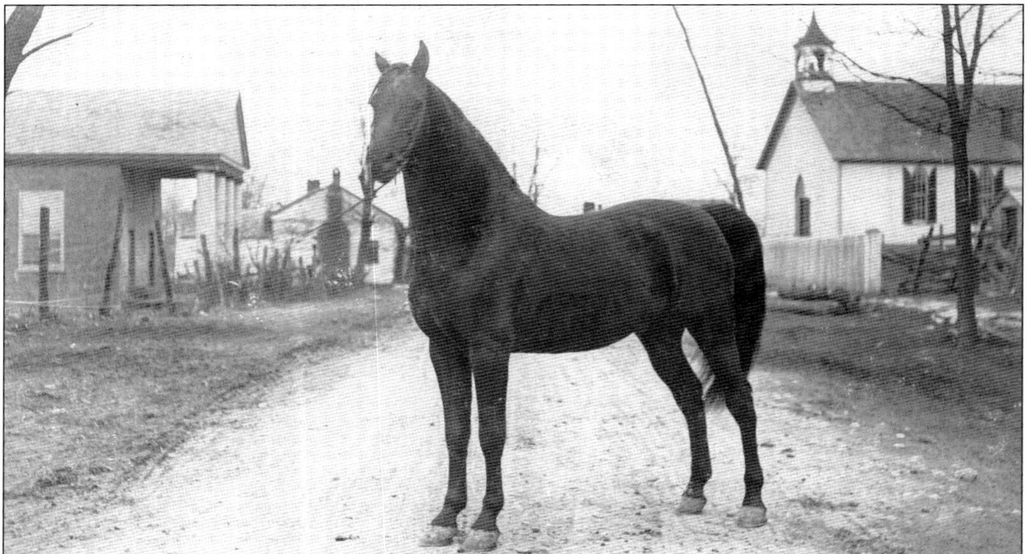

This horse seems to pose in the middle of Main Street in Minerva, Kentucky, which was settled in 1792 by Lewis Craig. In the background on the left is the original brick Baptist church, incorporated on January 31, 1844, where meetings were held until 1900. On the right side is the Minerva United Methodist Church, which today has a glass transom with the dates 1836 to 1894 above the current church door.

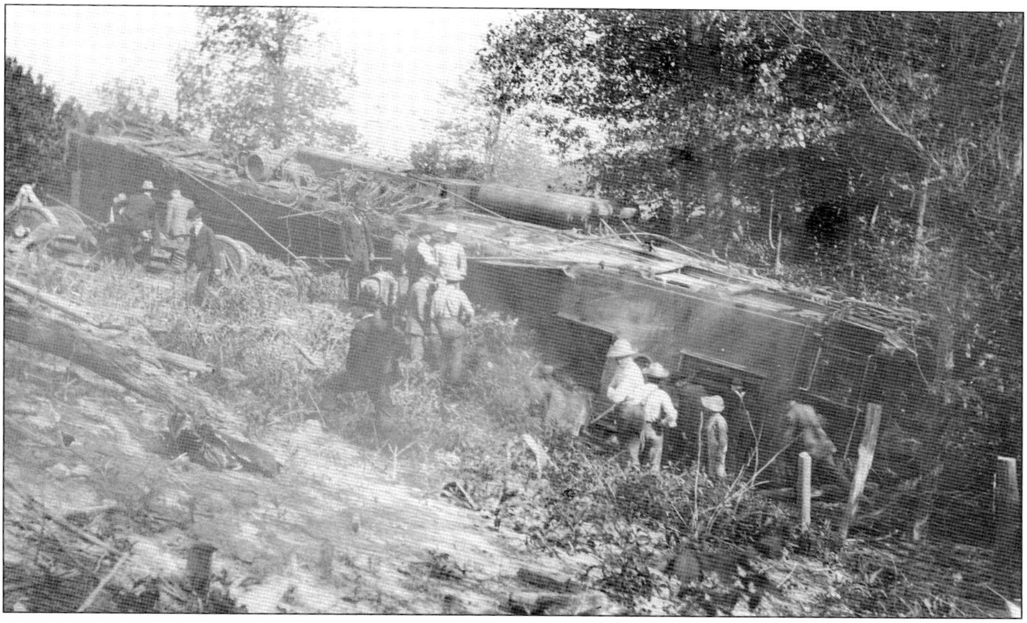

On May 22, 1907, in the early afternoon, a C&O sleeper car and observation coach jumped the tracks near Lawrence Creek, six miles west of Maysville, and went down a steep embankment where even the train car wheels were ripped off in the wreckage. One lady passenger was killed, and numerous others were injured. As seen below, when word got to Maysville about the train wreck, volunteers, including multiple doctors, rushed to the site on another train car on the tracks above. The injured were taken to the New Central Hotel in Maysville to be treated, and some had life-threatening injuries.

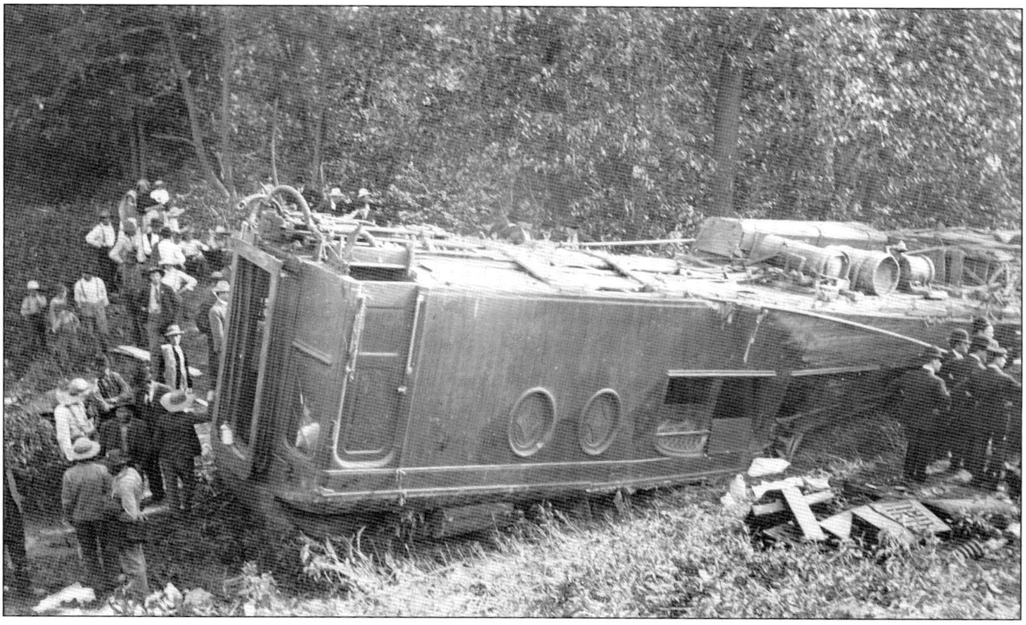

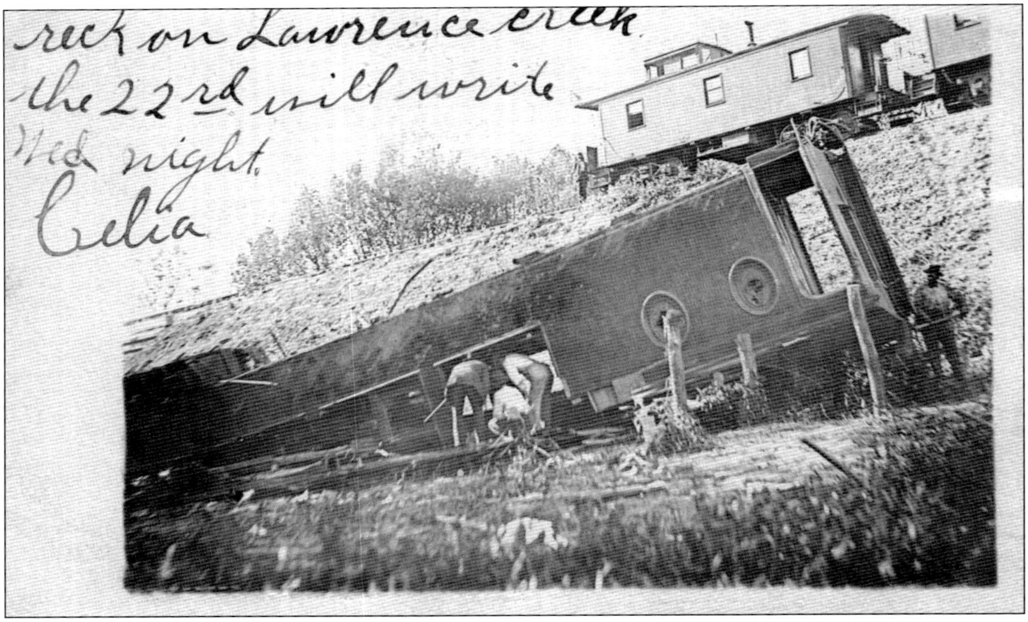

Here is another view of the damage this sleeper car suffered as it left the tracks near Lawrence Creek. It does appear that many folks showed up to help with the injured and assist with the cleanup. According to his YouTube upload, Mark Humphries of Maysville recently found pieces of the wreckage at the site with his metal detector.

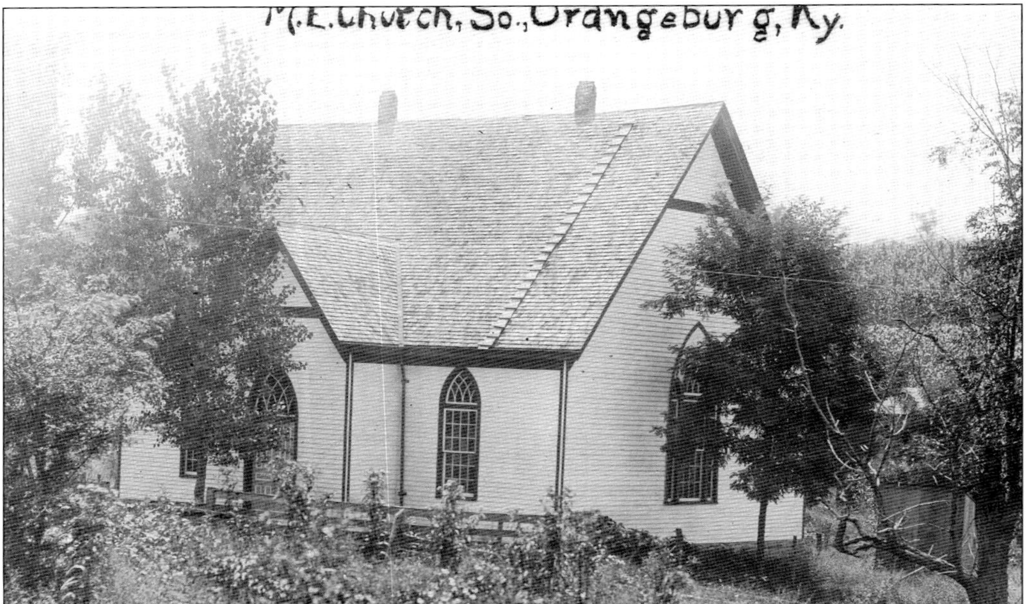

ME Church South of Orangeburg, Kentucky, still holds church services here today, although the appearance has changed. The church is located on Highway 1234 on the right as one comes into Orangeburg from the AA Highway. This photograph was sent to Lula Raymond in Ewing, Kentucky, from her grandson Howard on August 23, 1910.

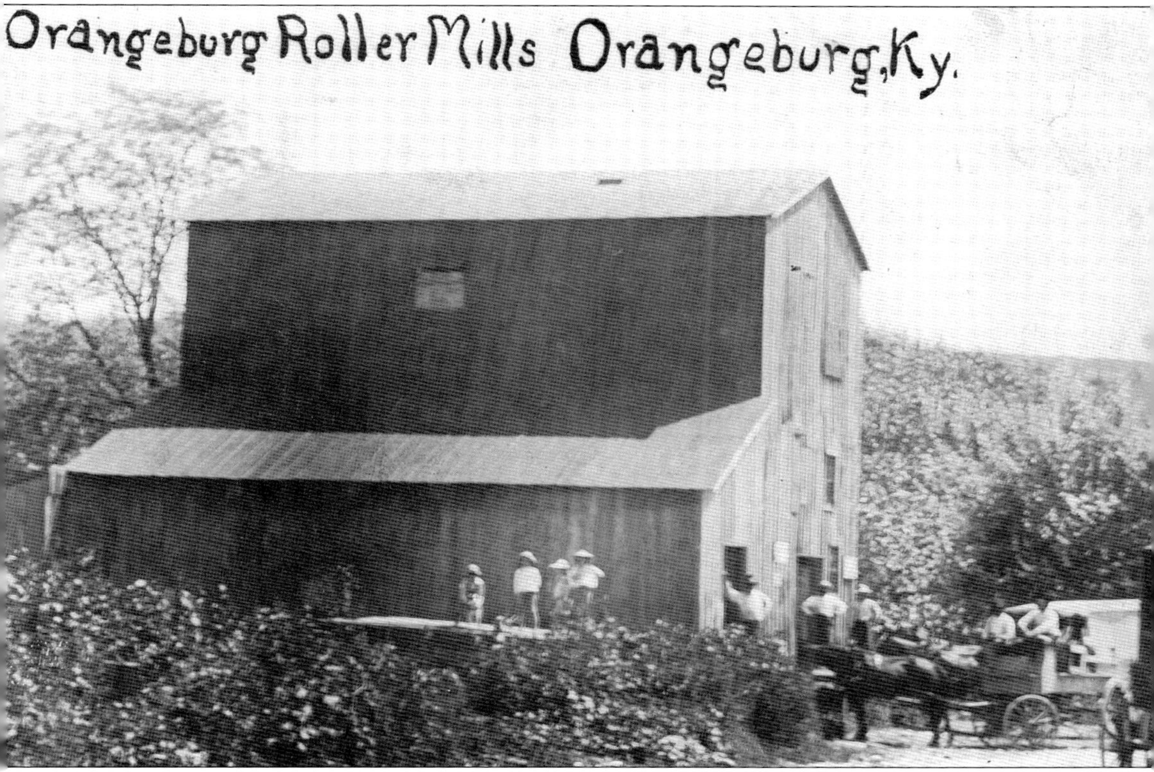

According to Dean McCord, the Orangeburg Roller Mill was located behind the Christian Church in Orangeburg, Kentucky, on property owned by Charlie Kennan, on the left before reaching Stonelick Creek. This mill was not powered by water but had one engine that powered the machinery. The building was torn down at least 20 years ago. This photograph is postmarked from Springdale on October 20, 1909.

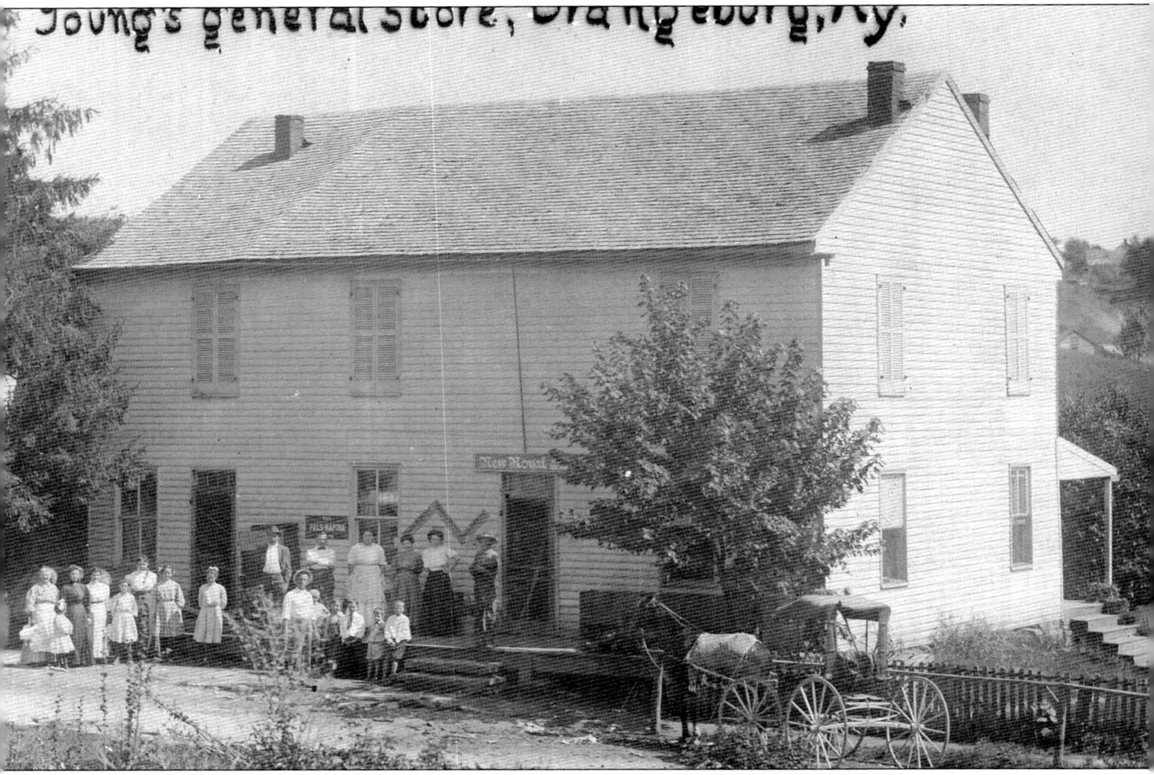

This view of Young's General Store of Orangeburg, Kentucky, was mailed on May 22, 1910, and sent to Ada Breeze in Maysville. This building became known as Red Man Hall, a lodge that catered to Native American culture, then it was turned into housing rentals and later a pool hall. Today, it is still located on the corner of Dixon Pike and Highway 1234 in town.

Three

Bracken County, Kentucky

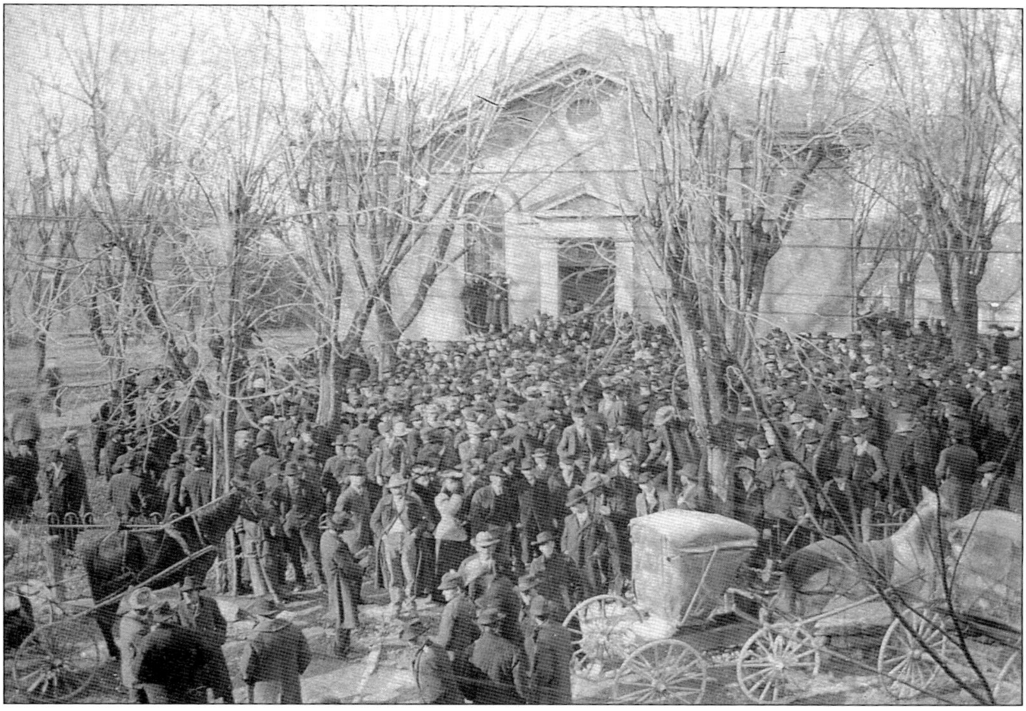

A large crowd gathered at the courthouse in Brooksville, Kentucky, on what is probably Court Day. This photograph is dated 1907, before this courthouse was demolished in order to build the present courthouse that was completed in 1915. Court Day continues to draw many people from the surrounding rural communities.

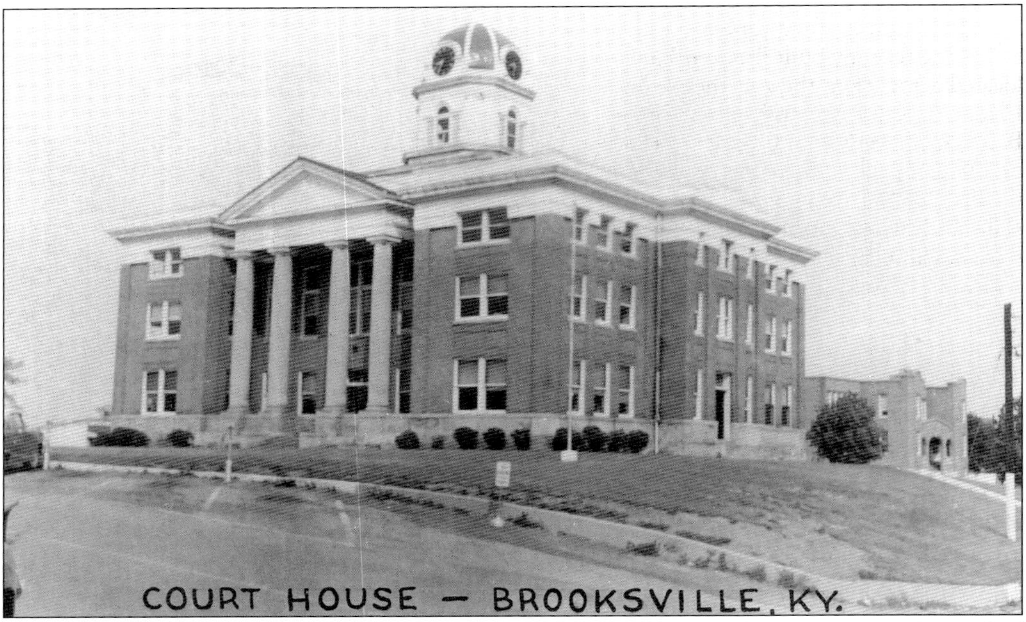

The new Bracken County Courthouse was dedicated on June 14, 1915, to an estimated crowd of 3,000 spectators. Located on the town square in Brooksville, Kentucky, the courthouse still stands today, and the new judicial center has since been built next to it.

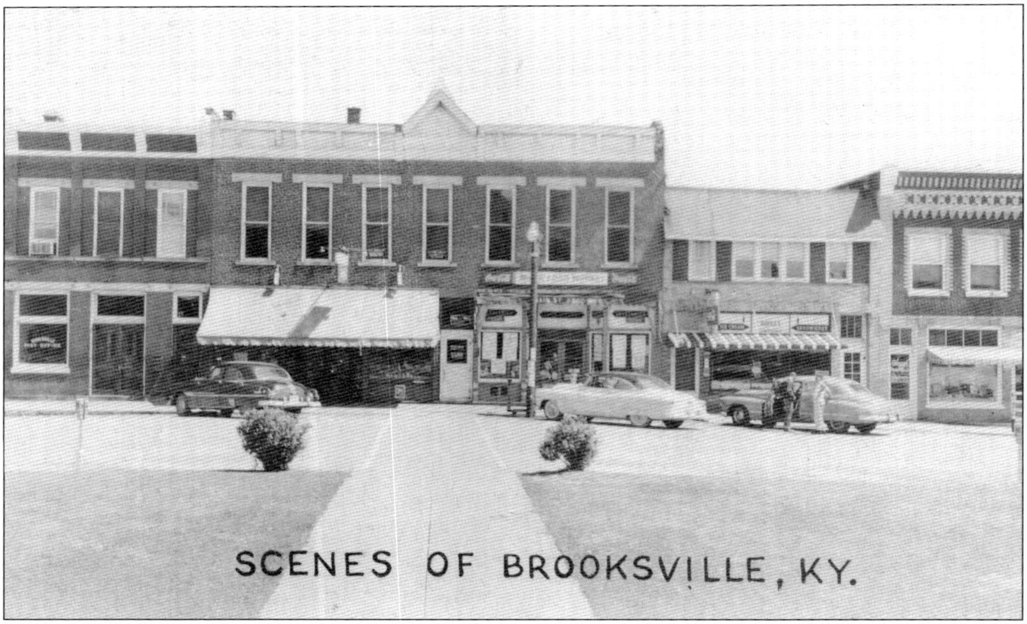

This shows a typical 1940s street scene on Locust Street in the heart of Brooksville. Located on the courthouse square are, from left to right, the post office, which was previously the Brooksville Bank; Bertram's Drug Store; Main Street Food Market; and Burke's Ice Cream and Sandwich Shop. Residents could find just about everything they needed in this day and time.

This photograph, dated June 24, 1907, shows the recently built Bracken Bank, located across from the courthouse on Locust Street in the business section of Brooksville, Kentucky. Carved in stone on the parapet are the name "Bank" and the date "1899." This early bank structure still stands today, but the parapet has been removed and the facade has been changed.

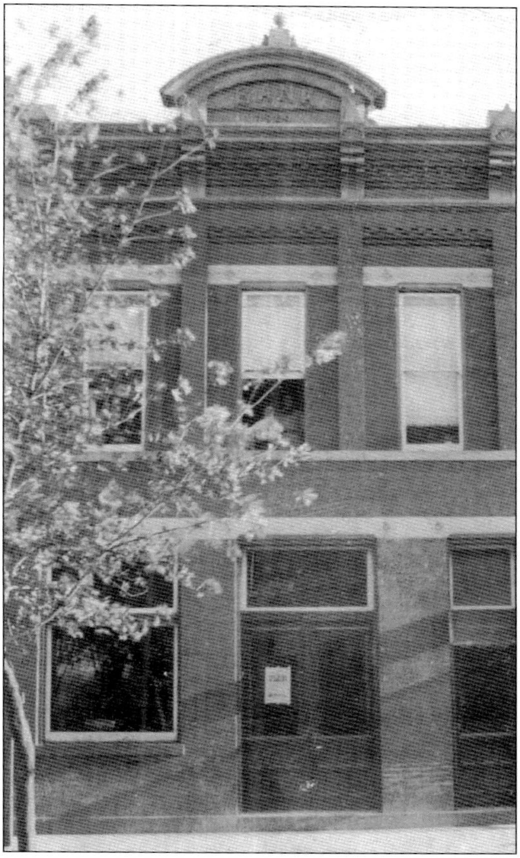

Augusta, Kentucky, was well known for its role in education dating back to the first Methodist college in the world established there in 1825. The first public school, shown below, was built in Augusta and opened in 1887. Like the Methodist college burning in 1852, the public school burned in 1906. The school was rebuilt with additions through the years, and the Augusta Independent School remains active today.

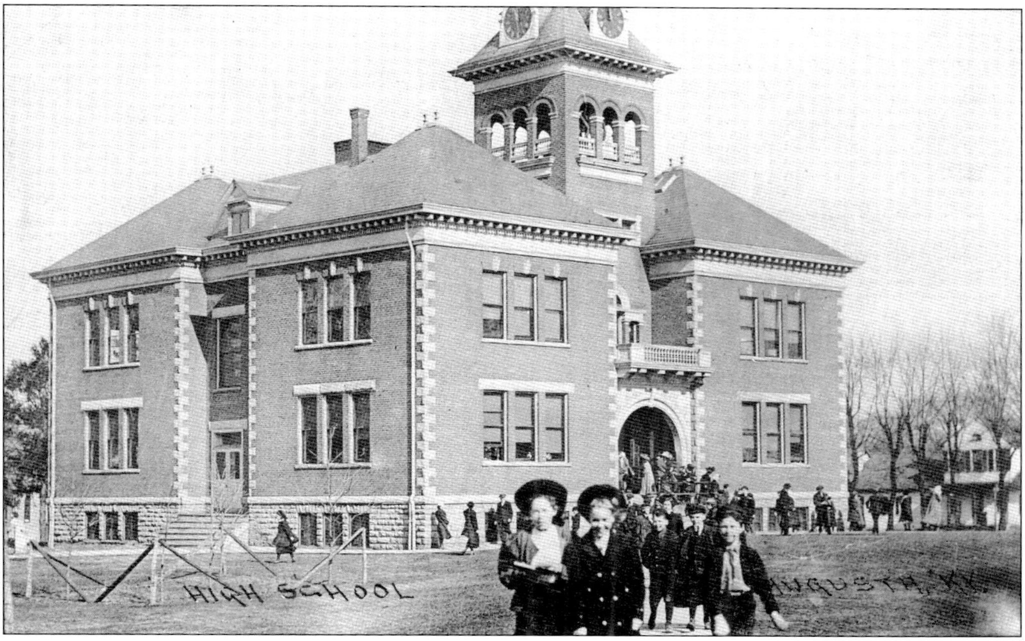

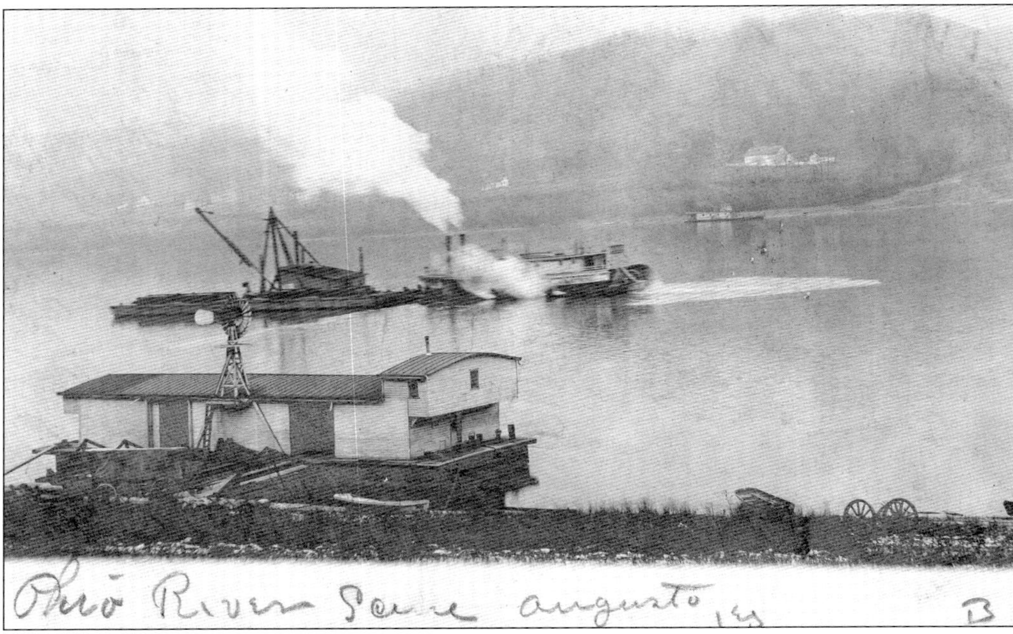

Wharf boats provided a transfer platform to board and depart from the steamers that traveled on the Ohio River, as in this scene at Augusta, Kentucky. A working steamboat pushes two barges, one with a crane attached, while the local ferry is on the Ohio side. Across the river is a community named Boudesferry, Ohio, along Route 52, where the Sunny South Hotel was located.

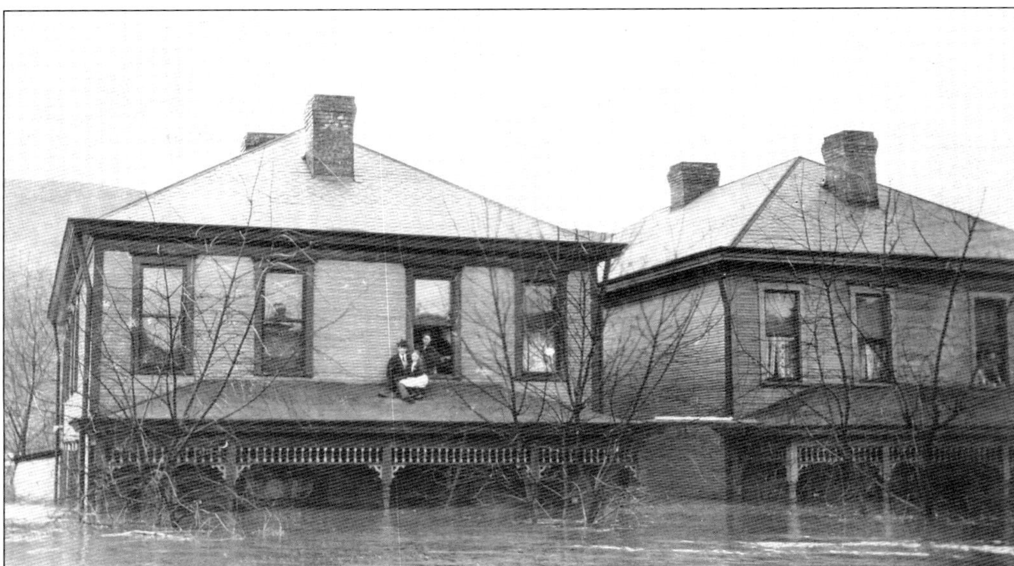

Most of the time there is peace and beauty along the mighty Ohio River here in Augusta, Kentucky, but there was a price to pay when the floodwaters rose and dangerous debris floated along with the current, as seen in this 1907 photograph. Residents had to move their home's contents to higher ground, or if they were fortunate enough, like these people, move them upstairs until the water receded.

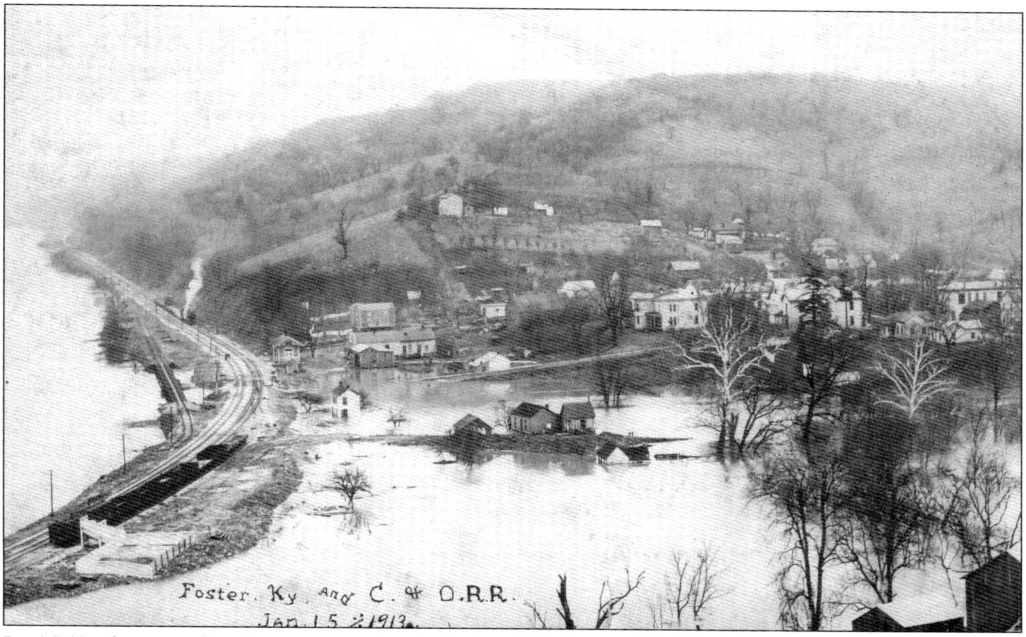

In 1850, this town's name would finally go on the record as Foster, Kentucky, after at least two previous names. The Foster name came from Israel Foster, an early pioneer, who settled in this area along the Ohio River. This flood scene, dated January 15, 1913, was one of the worst to hit this small community until the flood of 1937 occurred. This photograph was mailed from Edna Grimes to Charles Follmer.

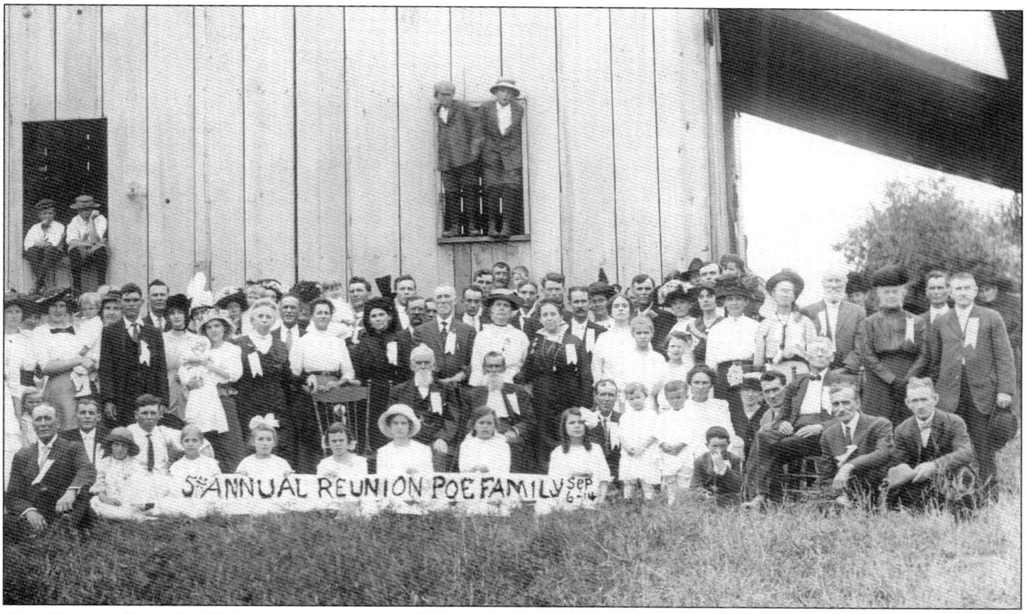

On September 6, 1914, generations of Poes gathered for their fifth family reunion. Poe was a common surname then in Bracken and Mason Counties and remains so today. On the back of this photograph, the location is said to be Wellsburg, Kentucky, a small unincorporated community downriver from Maysville in Bracken County.

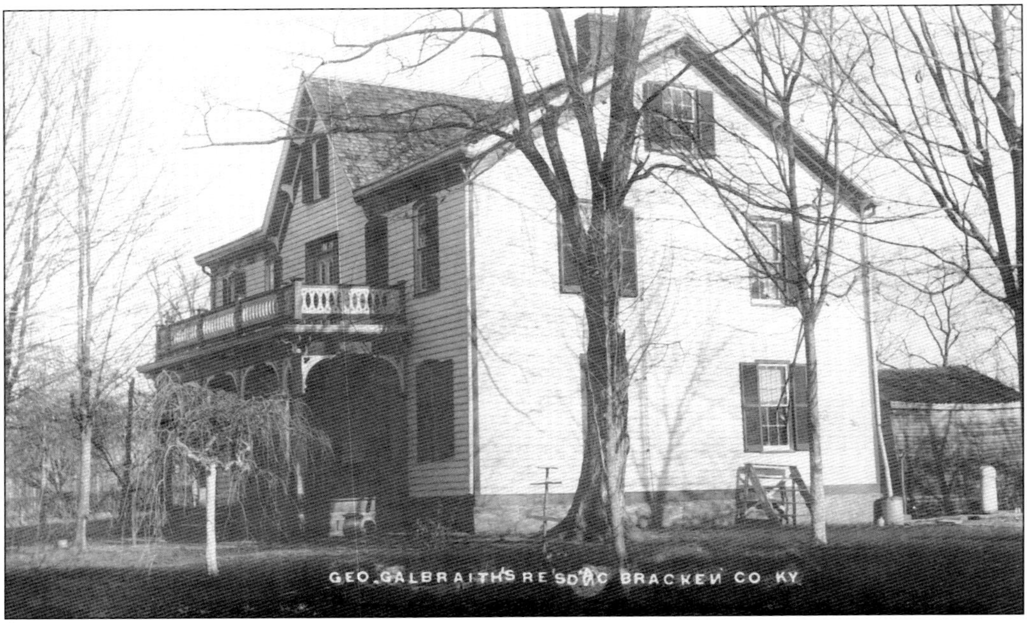

The farmhouse of George Galbraith, a prominent businessman who lived at Bridgetown near Germantown, Kentucky, is still standing today. Galbraith was born on the family farm in Bracken County on December 19, 1853, and died on March 6, 1943, at the age of 89. He is buried in nearby Maple Grove Cemetery. Galbraith and his wife, Elizabeth, had six children, and many of their descendants live in the area today.

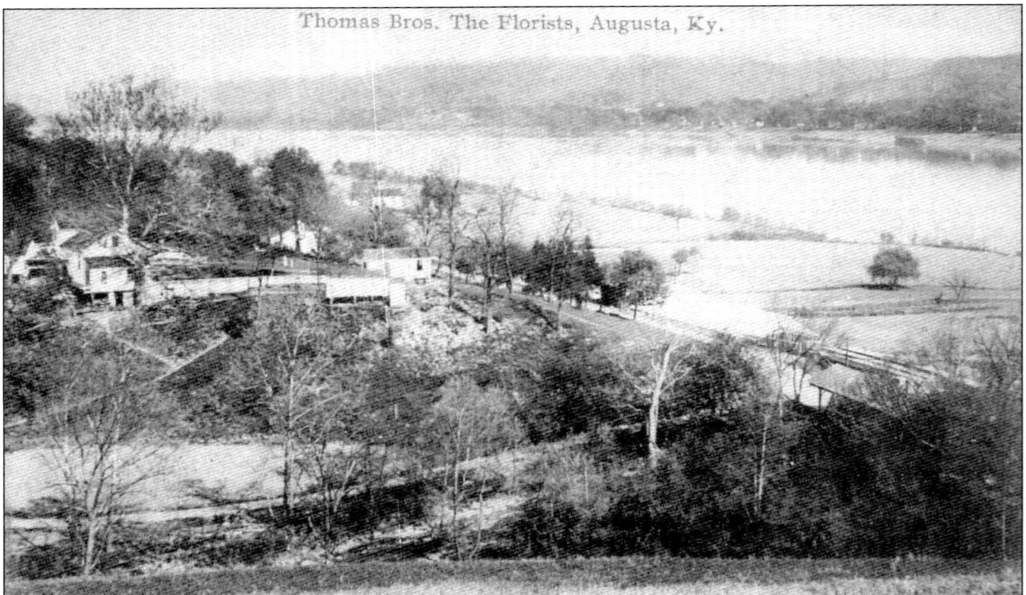

This photograph dated August 26, 1914, shows the greenhouse of Thomas Brothers Florists, located just south of the C&O train tracks in Augusta, Kentucky, near the Ohio River. Charles Thomas Brothers was born in Lewis County on August 8, 1885, and later moved to Augusta, where he died on October 12, 1926, at the age of 41 and was buried in the Highland Cemetery.

Four

Fleming County, Kentucky

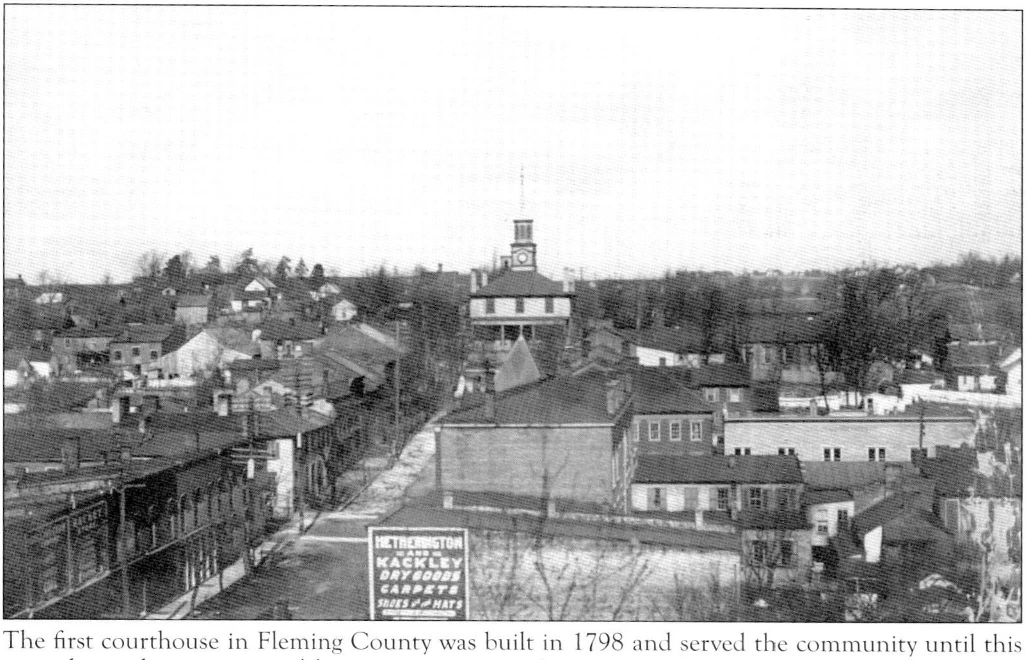

The first courthouse in Fleming County was built in 1798 and served the community until this second courthouse, pictured here, was constructed in 1830 and served until 1952. The second courthouse was torn down, and a third courthouse was built on the same site where it served until 2012 and is now the clerk's office. In 2012, the Fleming County Judicial Center was dedicated on the corner of West Water and North Main Cross Street and serves this community today.

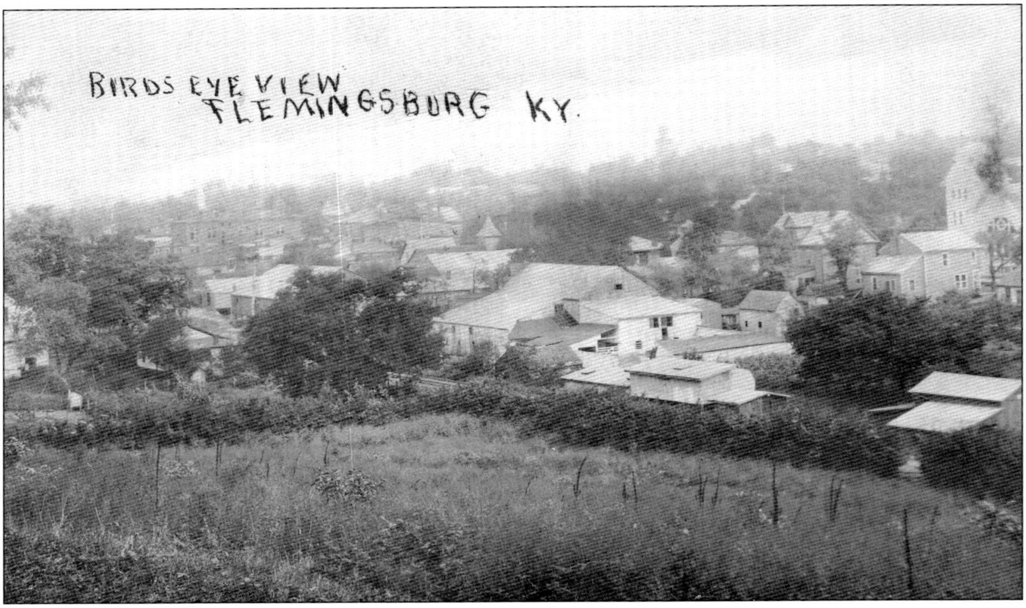

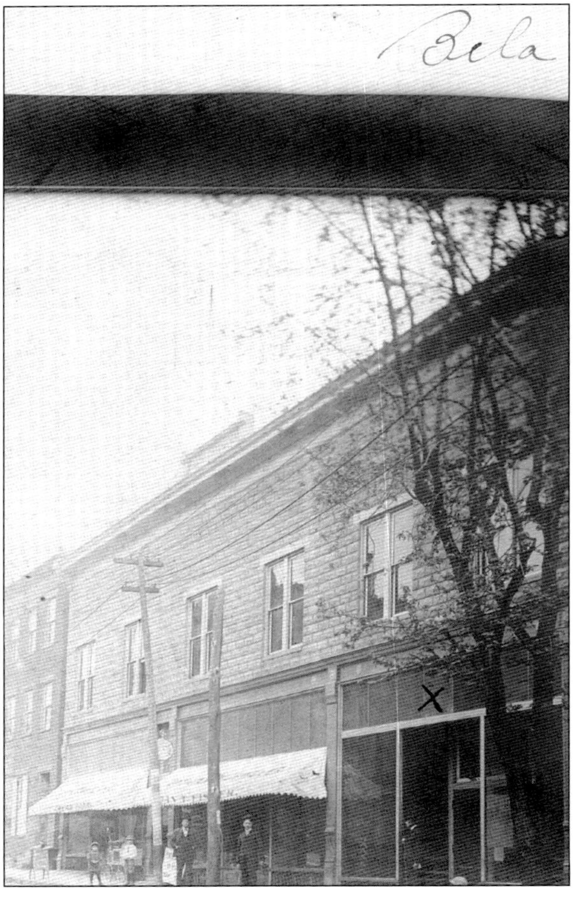

Pictured here is a bird's-eye view of Flemingsburg, Kentucky, just east of downtown, with the courthouse visible on the top of the hill above North Main Cross Street. This view is dated March 14, 1922, and shows how rural the town was at the time, with a cattle barn just a few blocks from the courthouse. The L&N train tracks run right through the middle of town.

Many Fleming County photographs and postcards during the early 1900s were sold by Dan T. Fischer, a jeweler and optician in Flemingsburg, Kentucky, at this location. The post office and ice cream parlor in this July 10, 1907, view were also located in this building owned by Fischer. To his credit, many early views of Fleming County were preserved by Fischer, who also wrote the book *Condensed History of Fleming County*.

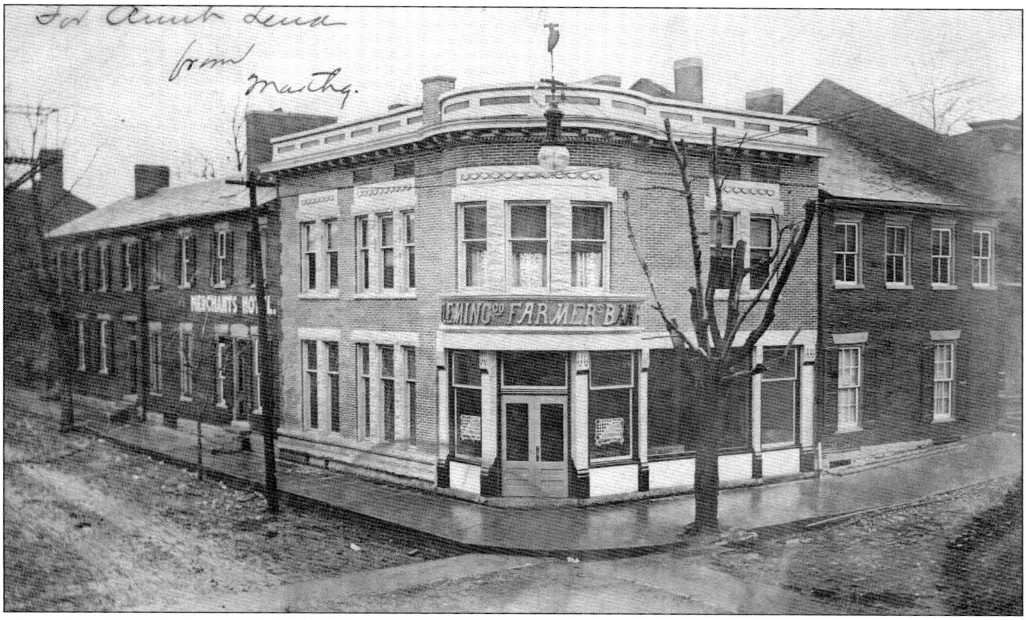

The new Farmer's Bank in Flemingsburg, Kentucky, was on the corner of West Water Street and North Main Cross Street. Christman, "the Photo Man" from Flemingsburg, preserved this image of structures that stood where the new judicial center building sits today. Although these structures were torn down, Flemingsburg has saved many historic buildings.

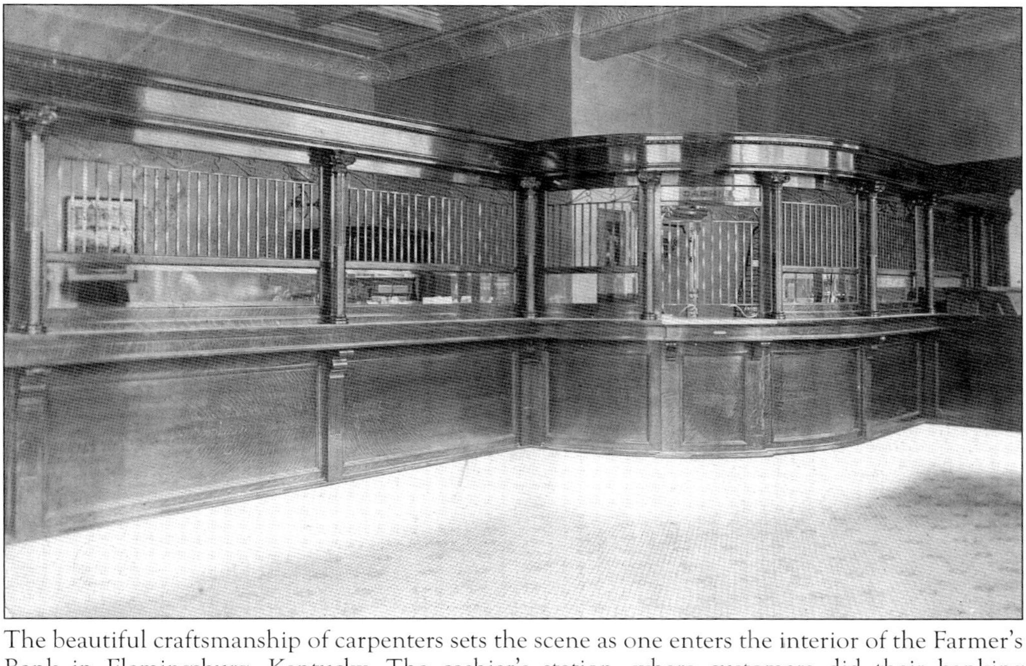

The beautiful craftsmanship of carpenters sets the scene as one enters the interior of the Farmer's Bank in Flemingsburg, Kentucky. The cashier's station, where customers did their banking business in the early 1900s, was located in the curved area of the tiger oak grain woodwork. The craftsmanship continues to the coffered ceilings and large, decorative crown moldings.

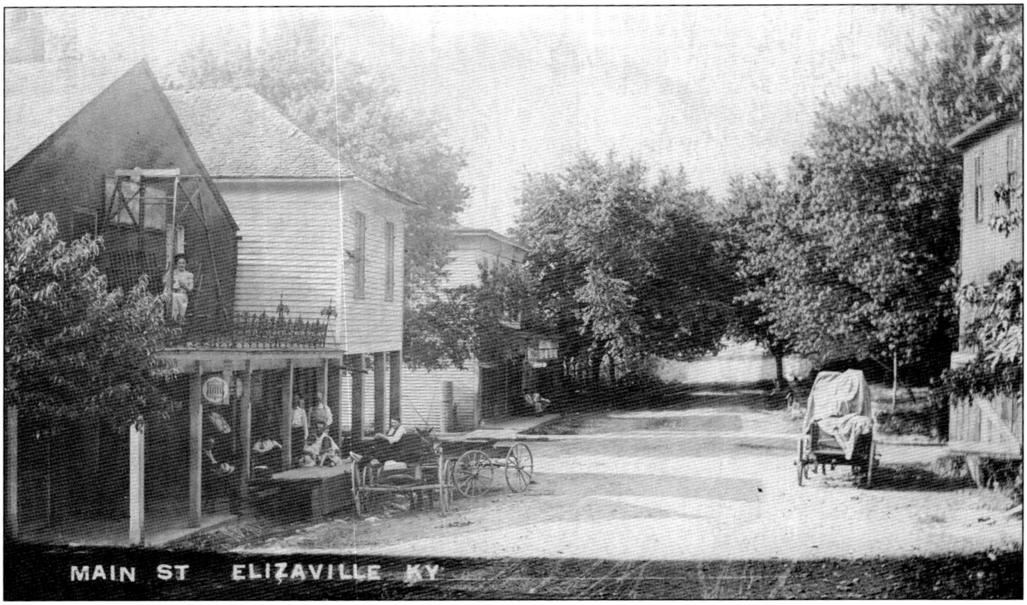

Elizaville, Kentucky, located in Fleming County and seen here around 1907, maintained dirt streets, as did most small towns during this time. On Main Street, a lady swings on the roof above a telegraph office and store surrounded by a short, wrought iron decorative rail. Horses and buggies were the primary means of transportation in this era. Dwight Baldwin took this town as his residence in 1840 before moving to Cincinnati and founding the Baldwin Piano Company.

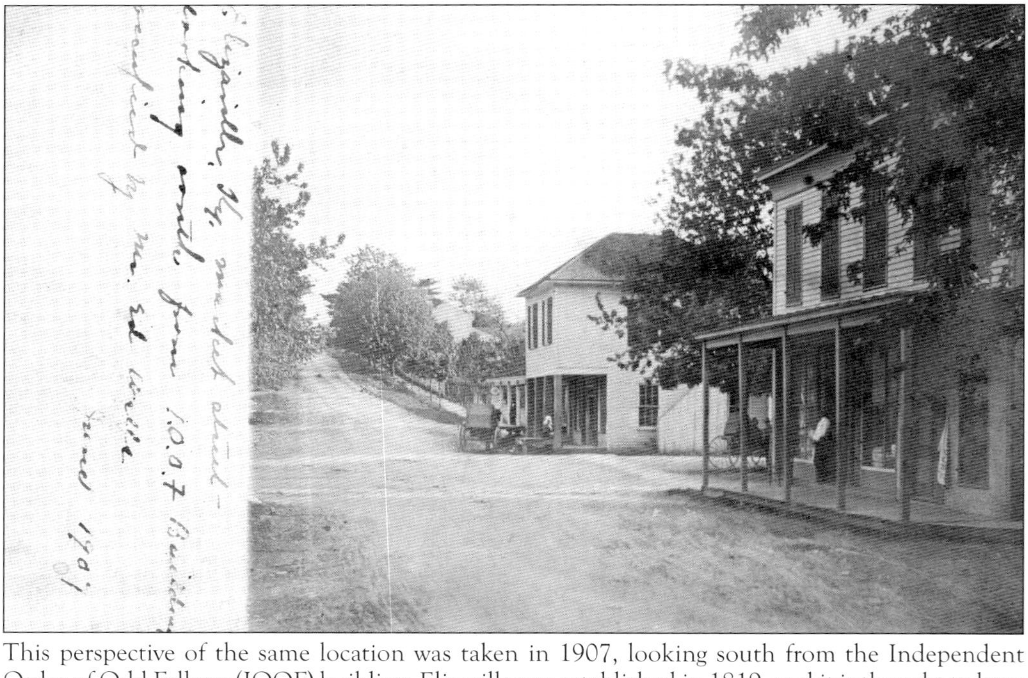
This perspective of the same location was taken in 1907, looking south from the Independent Order of Odd Fellows (IOOF) building. Elizaville was established in 1819, and it is thought to have gotten its name from Eliza Cochran, whose father, John, built the first cabin in this community. The sender locates this as Market Street.

This 1907 view shows the Christian Church in Elizaville, Kentucky, where the Reverend Donald McCalleum from Australia was the pastor at the time. Franklin Sousley, a native son of Elizaville, was born on September 19, 1925, in Fleming County and lived there. Sousley helped raise the flag at Iwo Jima in 1945 during World War II. Tragically, he was killed about a month later and is buried at the cemetery in Elizaville, Kentucky.

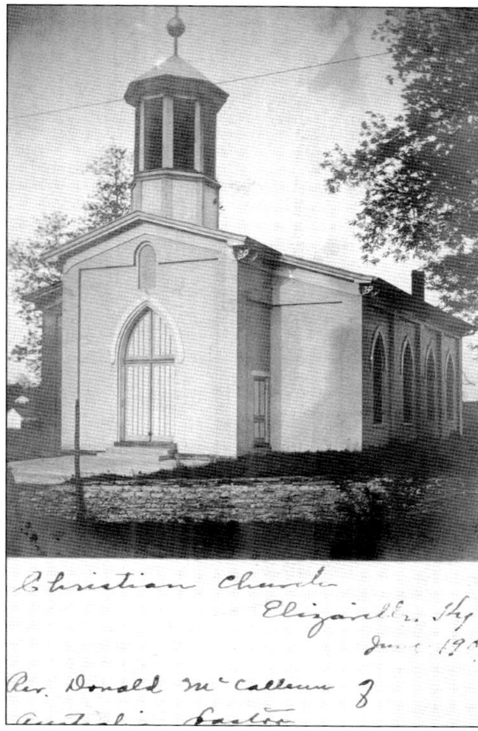

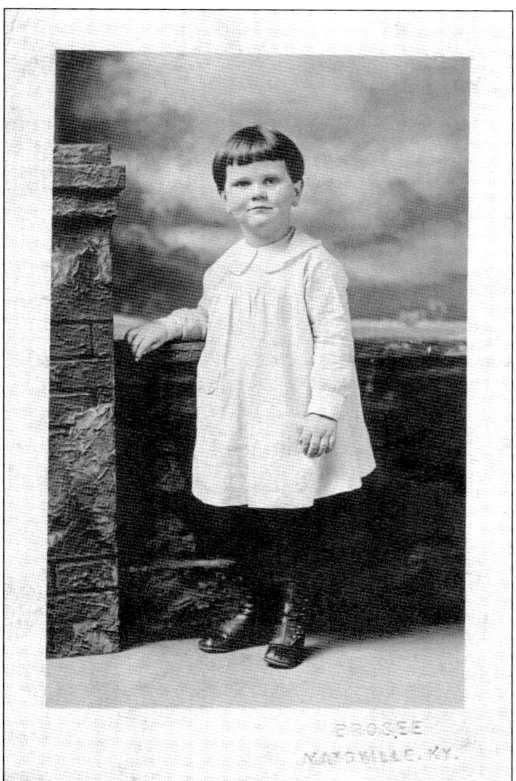

The child pictured here is Virginia R. Workman, a lifelong resident of Elizaville, Kentucky, where her parents, Rueben and Mary Abney Roberson, also lived. Workman was a world traveler and, in her later years, became blind. The old red-and-white family home was the site of one of the first private schools in Elizaville. At one time, there was a small pioneer cemetery behind the home.

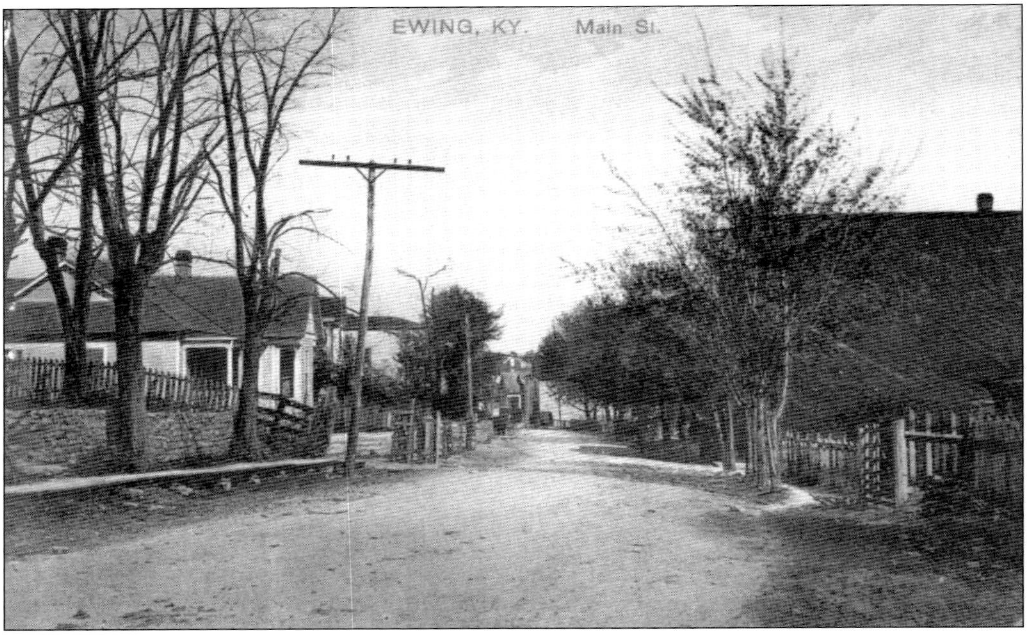

In 1873, the first post office in Ewing, Kentucky, was established, and the town was named after Robert Ewing, who had donated land for a train route to serve this area. This is a Main Street view of a residential area and its dirt streets through this small town. Woody Fryman, a pitcher for 18 seasons in major-league baseball, lived in this community and farmed here after his retirement.

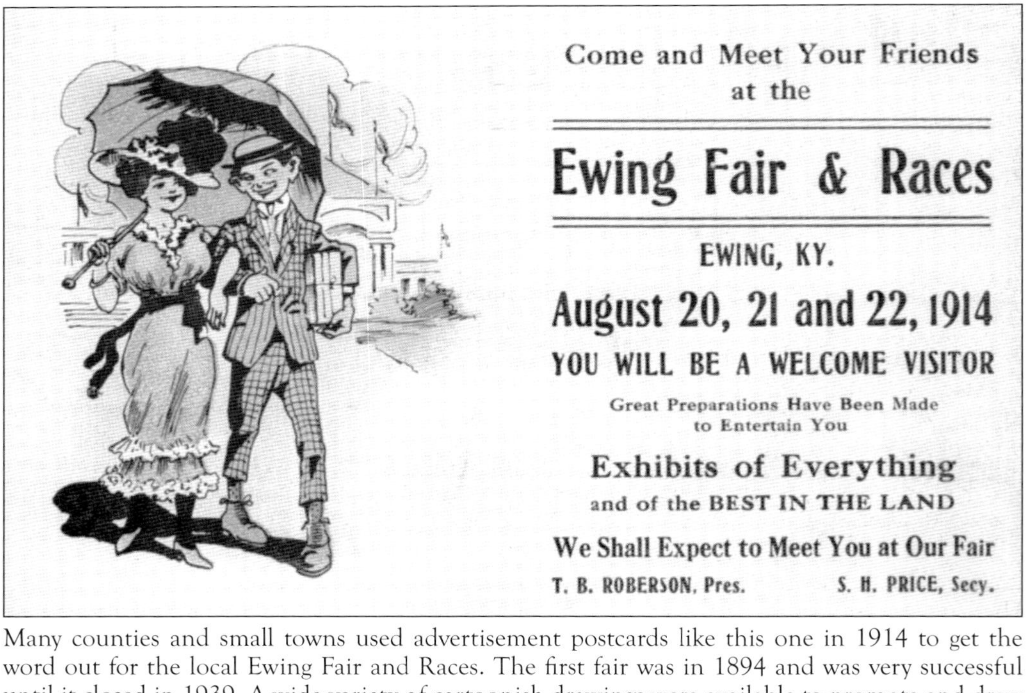

Many counties and small towns used advertisement postcards like this one in 1914 to get the word out for the local Ewing Fair and Races. The first fair was in 1894 and was very successful until it closed in 1939. A wide variety of cartoonish drawings were available to promote and draw spectators from all around the area.

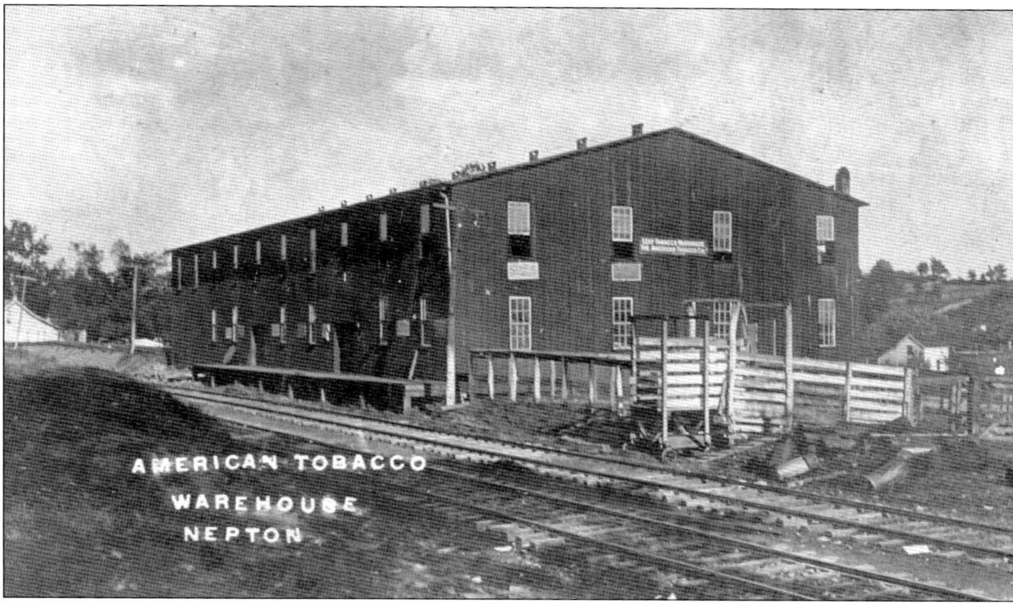

On December 17, 1907, this American Tobacco warehouse in little downtown Nepton, Kentucky, was threatened by the Night Riders, terrorists who burned down tobacco warehouses during the tobacco wars. The Fleming County sheriff and his deputies stayed on guard in Nepton throughout the night. Nepton had no fire service, so residents were in fear for their town all night long. This photograph is dated March 31, 1908.

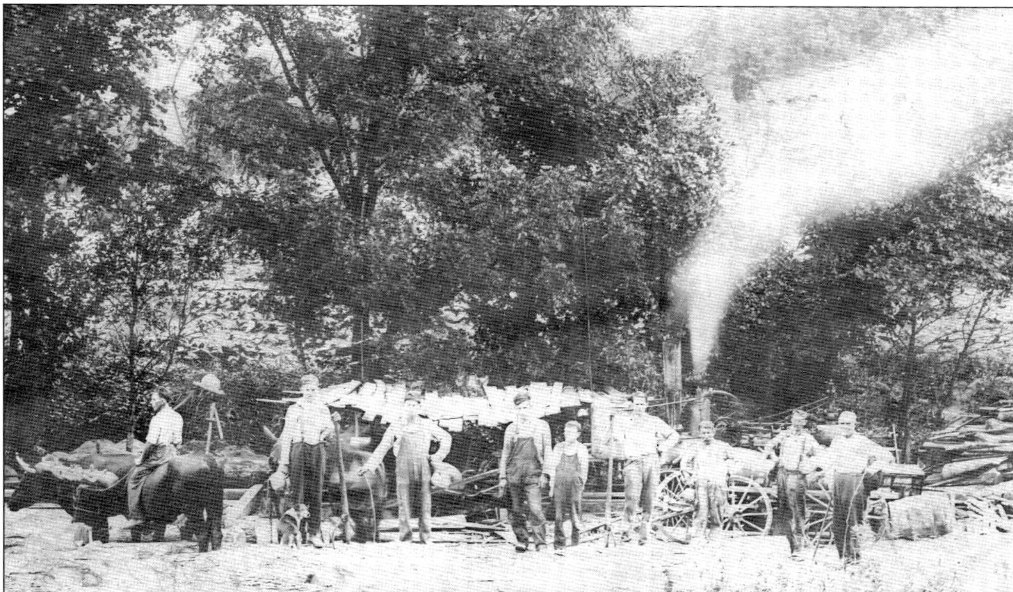

The hardworking men in this photograph from Nepton, Kentucky, traveled from site to site to build new homes using local timber. The heavy green wood was cut to nominal size back in the day when a two-by-four was actually two inches by four inches. The enormous saw blades were powered by a steam engine through a system of pulleys and belts. The photograph is dated September 25, 1914.

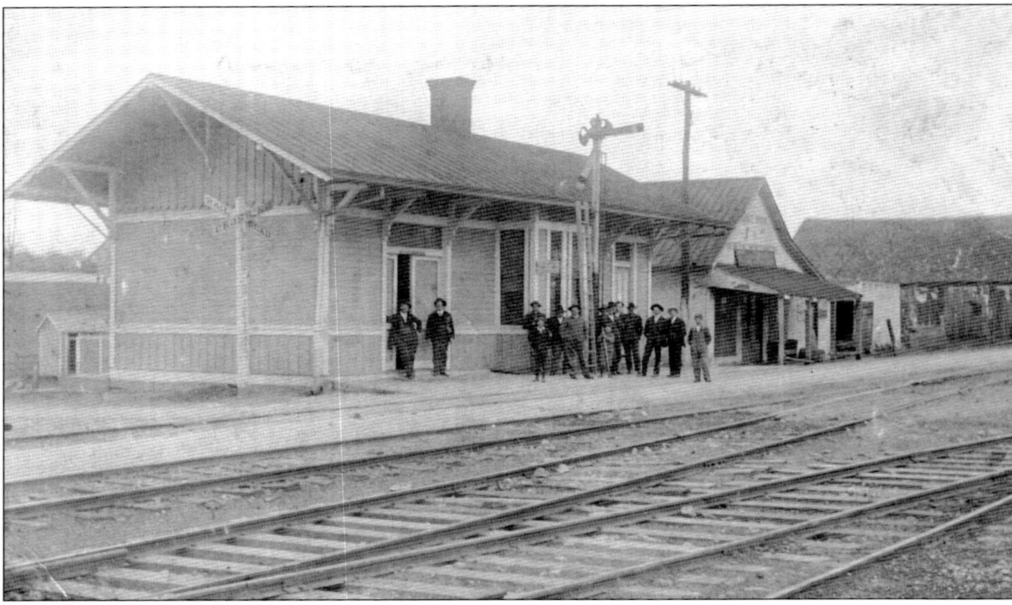

Robert Ewing sold land to the Maysville-Lexington Railroad Company in 1871 to build a depot at Johnson Junction, Kentucky. The depot also served as the local post office. Next to the depot in this photograph is Cole Brothers General Merchandise, which provided needed supplies to locals in this small community. This photograph, dated June 28, 1908, was sent to Mary Riley in Flemingsburg and published by Dan T. Fischer, Jeweler & Optician, in Flemingsburg, Kentucky.

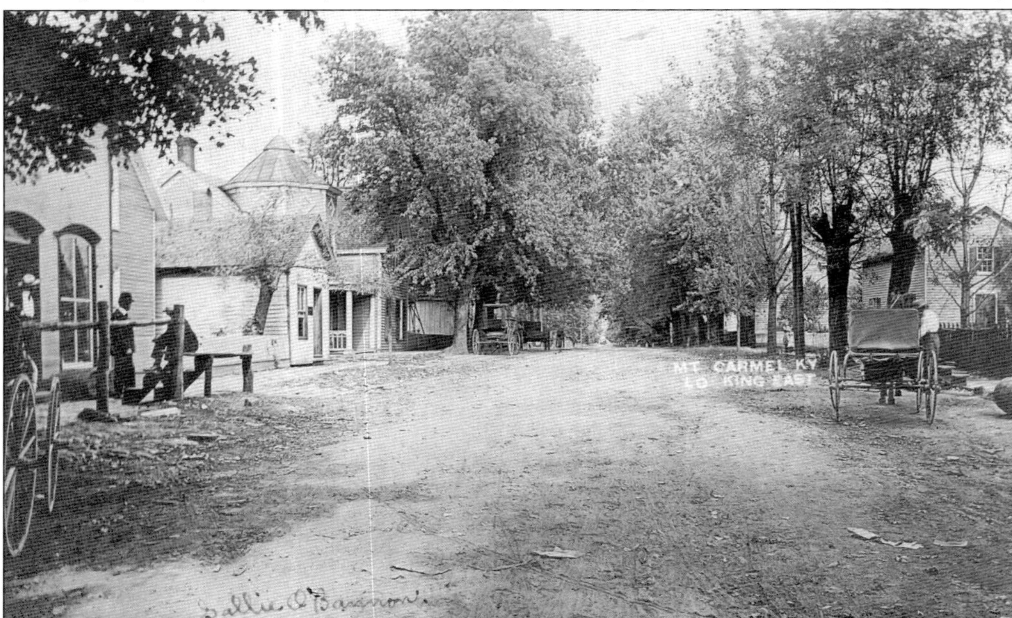

The slow pace of life is apparent as folks go about their lives on this residential street in Mount Carmel, Kentucky. "Steps to nowhere," which were used to unload wagons on Main Street, provided a spot for locals to sit and loaf. The photograph is dated January 2, 1908, with a note from Sallie O'Bannon and published by Dan T. Fischer, Jeweler & Optician, Flemingsburg, Kentucky.

Shekell & Co. General Store was located at Mount Carmel, Kentucky. Stores like this one sold a wide range of merchandise and served as a lifeline to farmers and townsfolk alike. Dated October 7, 1909, the photograph has a message on the back to E.P. Smoot in Mayslick, Kentucky.

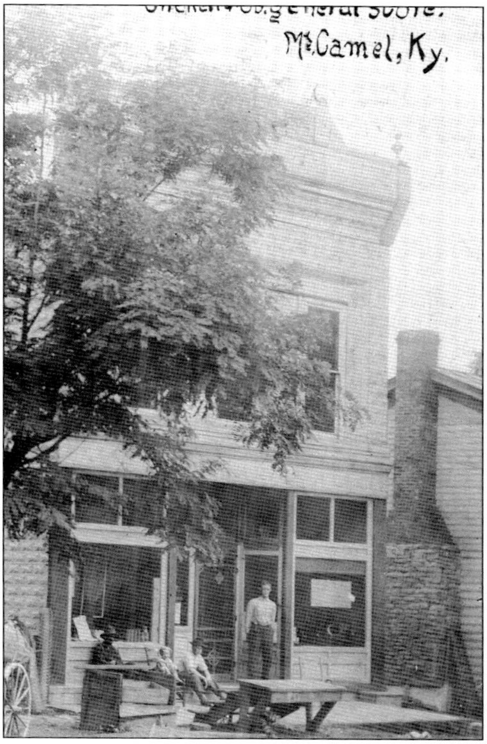

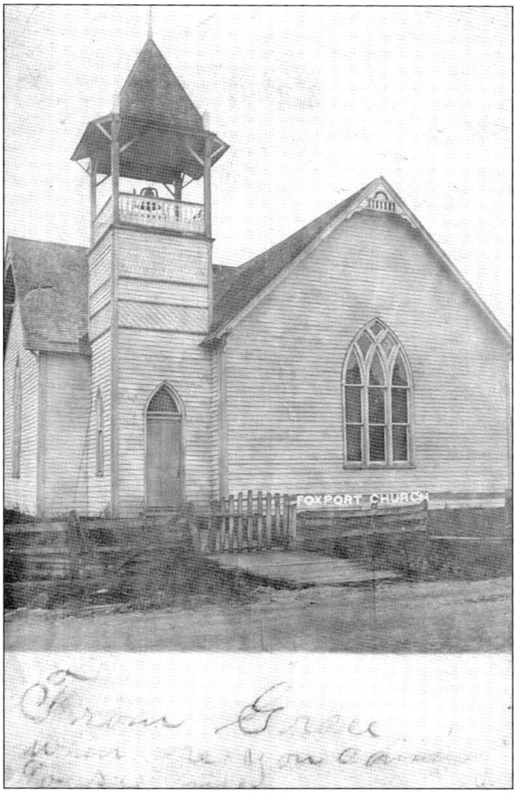

Foxport, Kentucky, is located on Kentucky Highway 344 in a very rural community northeast of Flemingsburg, Kentucky. Even the smallest towns supported at least one church, like the early Baptist church shown here. Published by Dan T. Fischer, Jeweler & Optician, Flemingsburg, Kentucky, this photograph dates to March 16, 1911. There is a newer brick Baptist church in the Foxport community today.

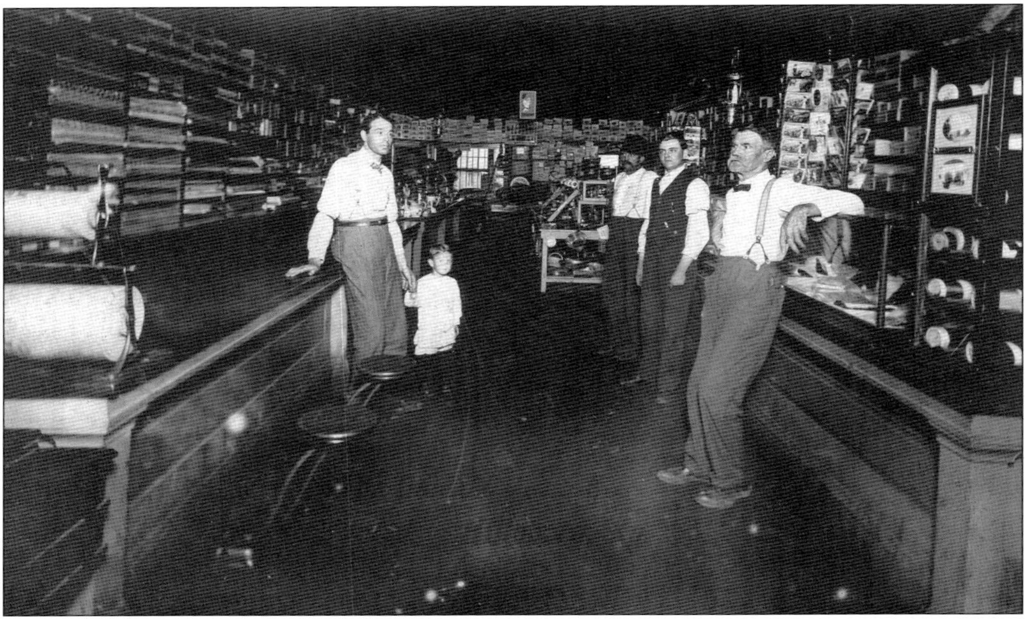

Oliver Denton once owned the Merchant Store in Hillsboro, Kentucky, but at the time of this photograph, his son Minor Denton was the storekeeper. Lorena Alexander grew up in Hillsboro and remembers how local farmers could charge goods here for one year until they sold their tobacco crops. If Denton did not have what they needed, he would order it, and Lorena's dad, Ollie McEntire Riddle, often drove to Cincinnati to pick up supplies for the store.

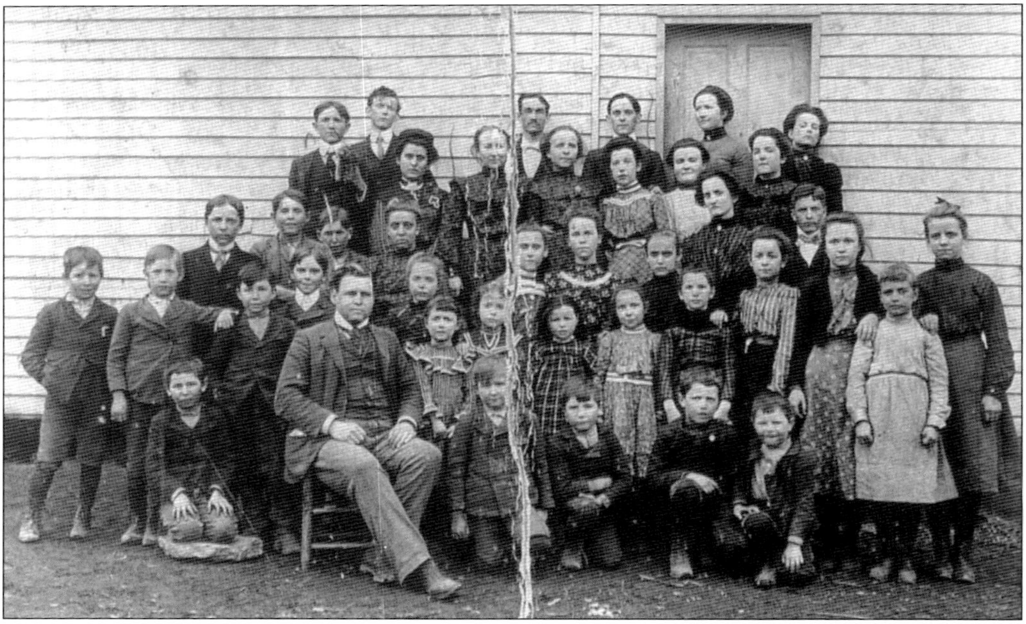

Like many schools of the late 1800s and early 1900s, the local children and their teacher attended a one-room schoolhouse with all ages of students together in the one room. This photograph, although damaged through the years, is of a Hillsboro, Kentucky, school and dates to 1900.

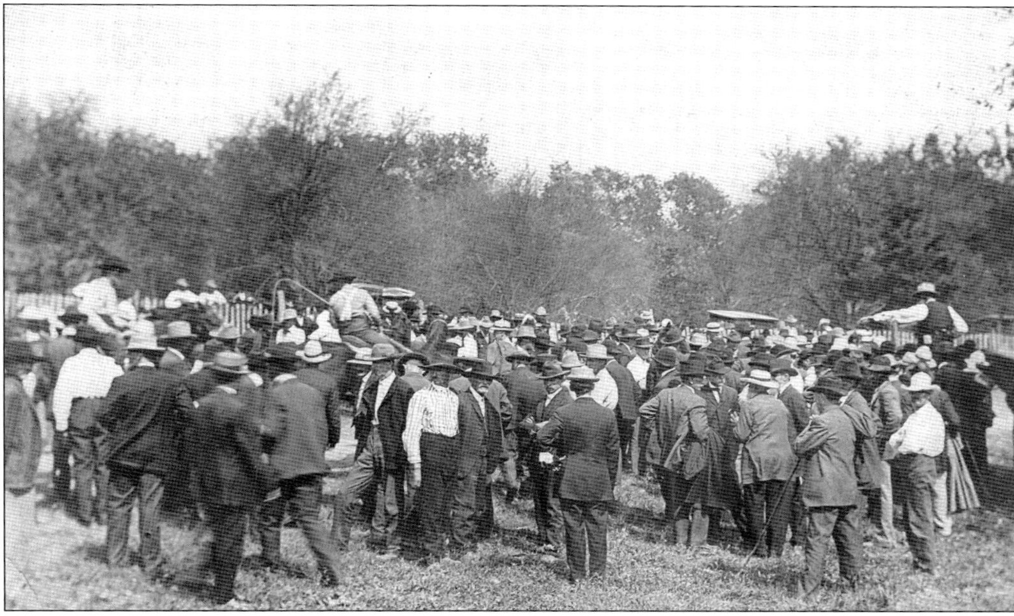

A typical horse auction is shown here in Fleming County, Kentucky, on April 2, 1908. The auctioneer, elevated on the right, directs the bidding of the horses as they parade among the crowd. This card was mailed from a grandmother to her grandson, J.P. Taylor Jr., in Winston-Salem, North Carolina, and identifies the man riding on the front horse as "Charles." This photograph was published by Dan T. Fischer, Jeweler & Optician, Flemingsburg, Kentucky.

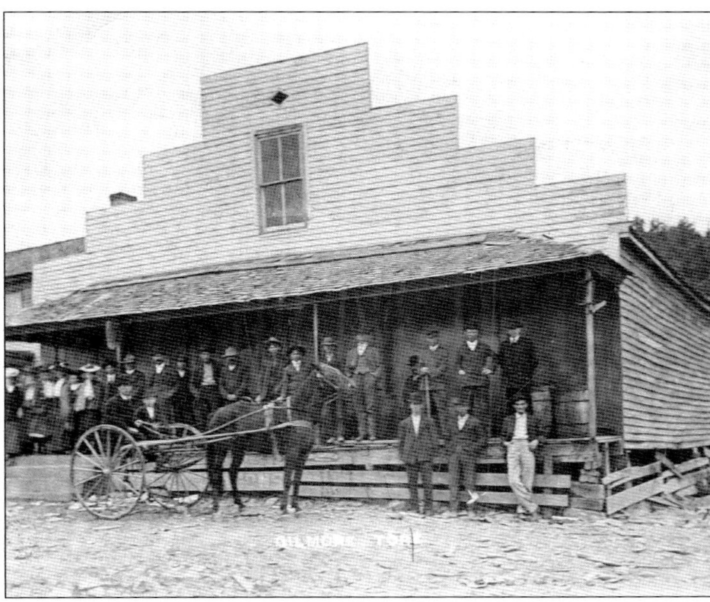

The Gilmore Store was located at Ringo's Mill, Kentucky, and owned by John W. Gilmore. He sold dry goods, notions, groceries, boots, hats, lumber, shingles, and more. The town was named after Joseph P. Ringo. This photograph was postmarked from Ringo's Mill on October 25, 1907, and published by Dan T. Fischer, Jeweler & Optician, Flemingsburg, Kentucky.

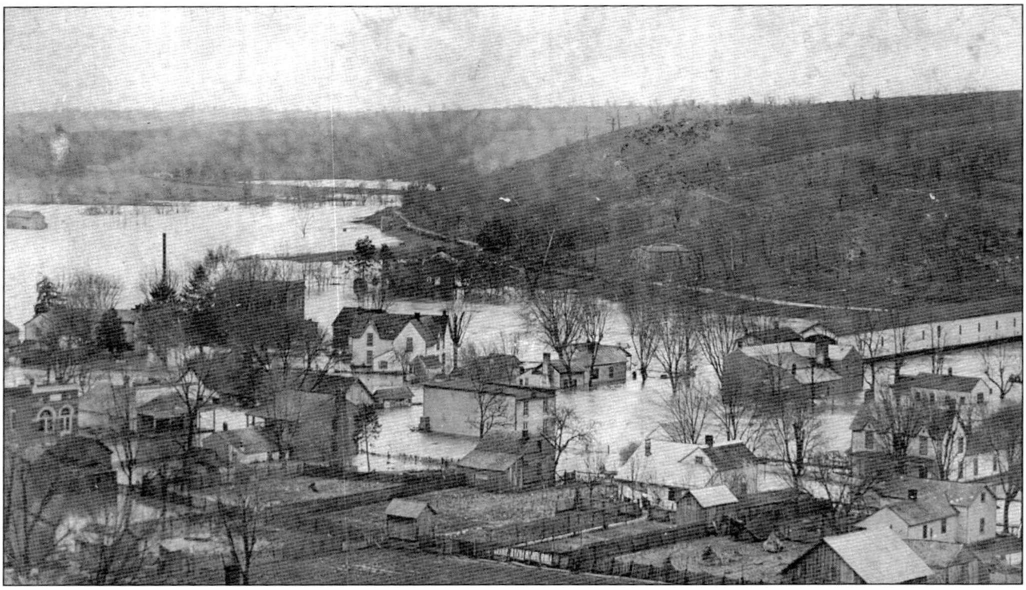

Sherburne, Kentucky, was a special spot on the Licking River due in part to the 253-foot covered bridge, on which construction began in 1867. The historic bridge was destroyed by fire in 1981. It was originally built as a toll bridge and separates Fleming and Bath Counties. This 1907 flood scene of the community was taken by Dan T. Fischer, Jeweler & Optician, Flemingsburg, Kentucky, and sent to Joseph Hawkins in Sherburne.

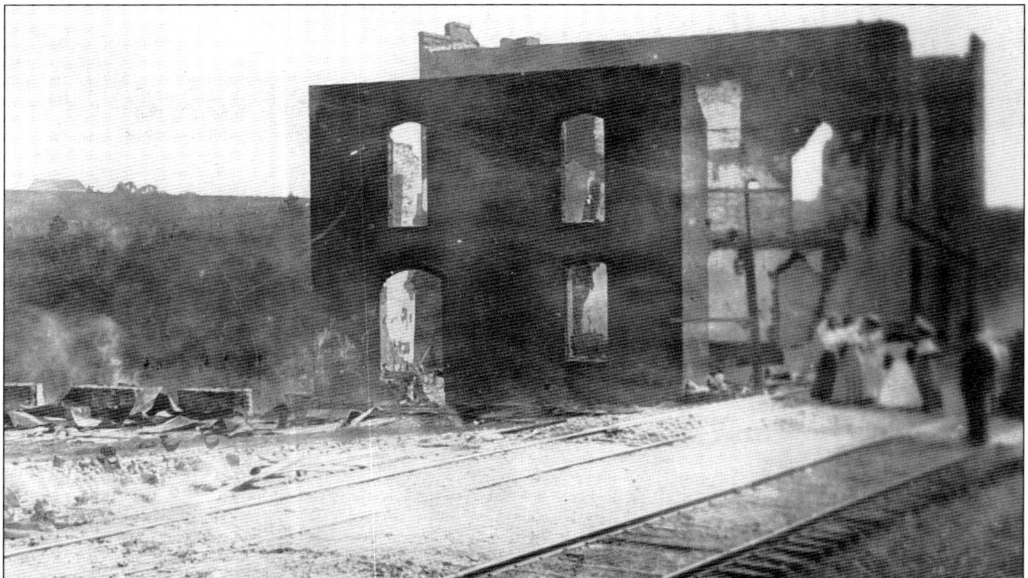

The worst fire to happen in Flemingsburg, Kentucky, occurred on September 1, 1905, and destroyed nine businesses, including two newspaper offices. No cause for the fire was ever determined, but it was thought to have started near the Covington, Flemingsburg & Ashland depot, which was consumed. Some businesses had homes above, and many other buildings were damaged. The estimated damage amount was about $75,000, and very few of the structures were insured.

Five

Lewis County, Kentucky

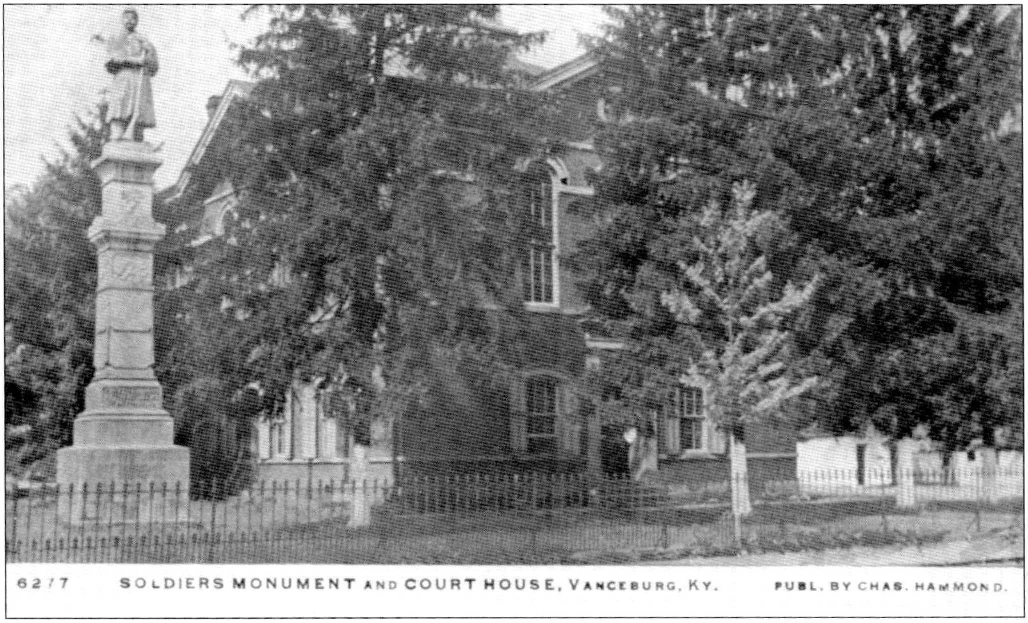

The first county seat in Lewis County was in Clarksburg, Kentucky, but in 1864, the county seat moved to Vanceburg. The monument shown here is the only Union monument south of the Mason-Dixon Line. This postcard, dated 1908, was published by Amelia Art Company, Amelia, Ohio, and sent to Addie Lucas in Wallingford, Kentucky.

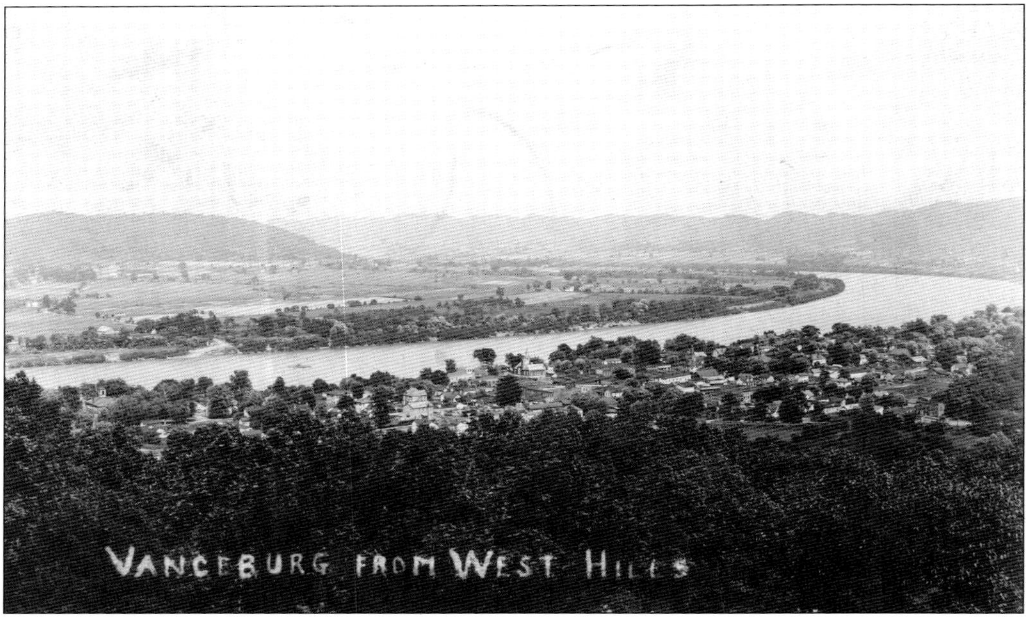

From the western hills overlooking Vanceburg, Kentucky, a six-mile view of the Ohio River horseshoe bend reveals a ferry crossing over from the Ohio side. In this small rural town, this was the local residents' main means of connecting with the population on the other side.

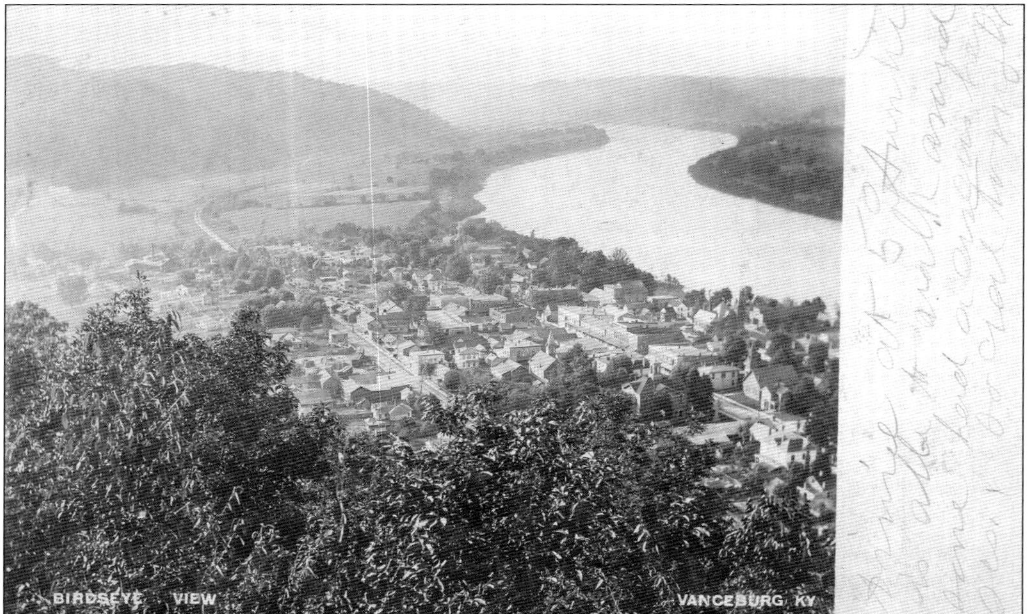

This is a 1907 view from the eastern hills looking downriver toward Vanceburg, Kentucky, and the mighty Ohio River. In the lower right section of this photograph, the courthouse and soldier's monument show the location in relation to the rest of the town. The C&O train tracks run right through the middle of town.

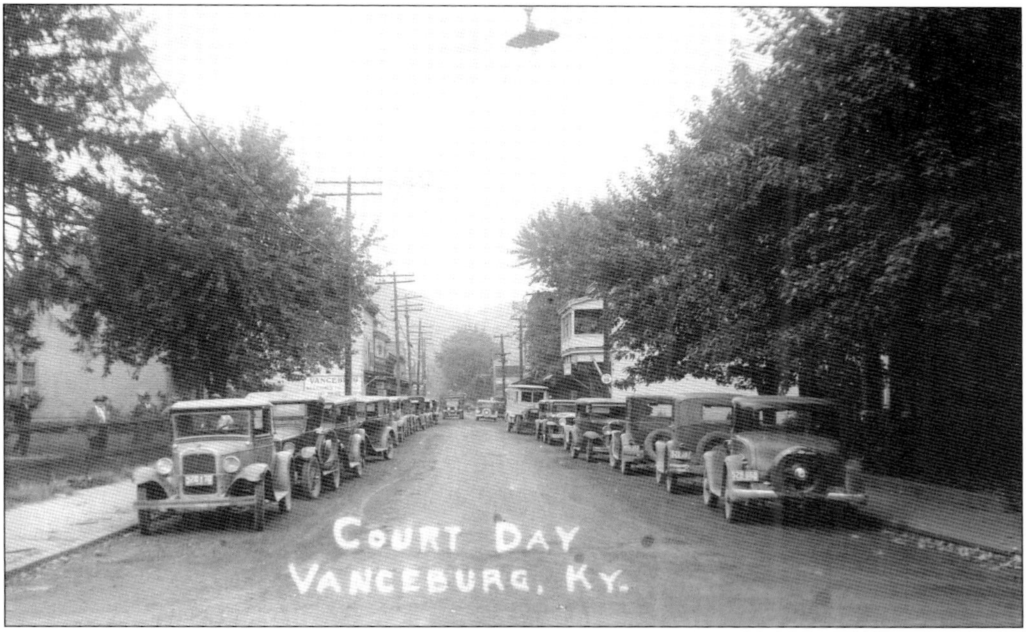

In the 19th century, the Kentucky General Assembly decided that one day a month each county should hold court; thus, it was called Court Day. Townsfolk quickly chose a day in October to hold court and have a big festival where people would gather to buy, sell, or trade their goods, crafts, and animals. This is a photograph of vehicles lining the streets on this special day in Vanceburg, Kentucky, where even schools are closed.

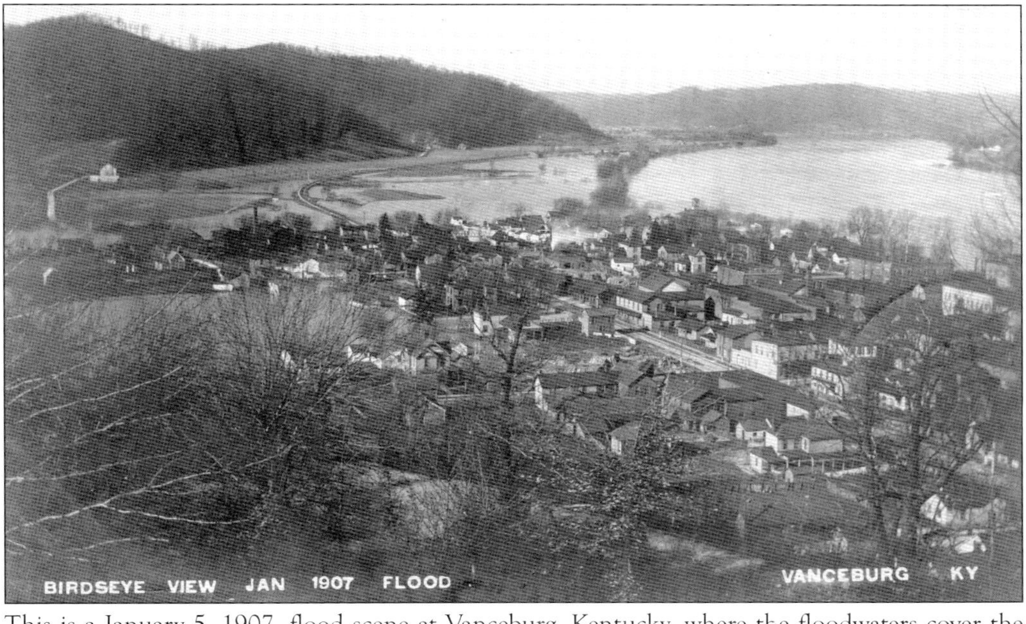

This is a January 5, 1907, flood scene at Vanceburg, Kentucky, where the floodwaters cover the fertile flatland at the west end of town. That year's flood, along with the 1913 and 1937 floods, extended to most of the structures in this river town. When the waters receded, the townspeople had a silty, muddy mess to clean up in their homes and businesses.

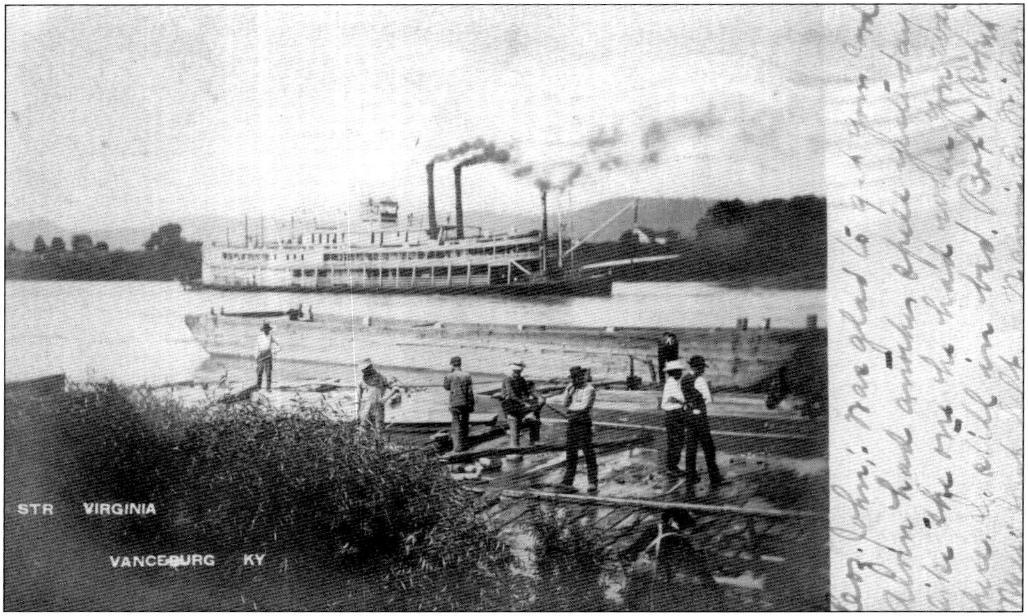

In this photograph sent from Trinity, Kentucky, on October 7, 1907, the steamer *Virginia* is passing Vanceburg, Kentucky, while workers are doing repairs on the barges along the shoreline. This steamboat ran aground in a cornfield on March 6, 1910, near Willow Grove, West Virginia, during a flood on the Ohio River, and it was an enormous task to get it back in the water.

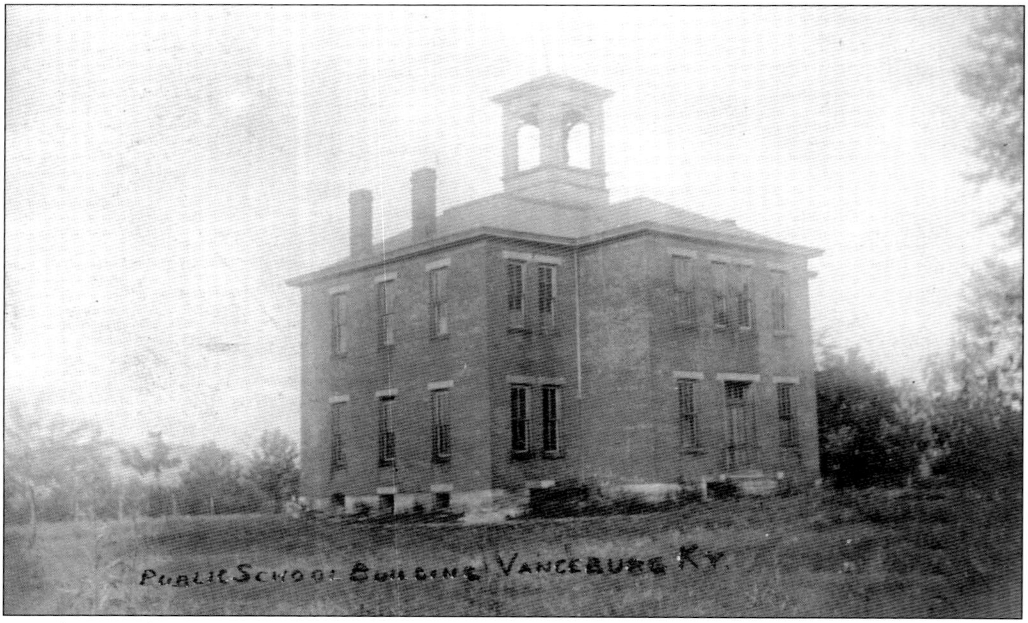

Dated September 1911, this photograph is of the "Public School Building" in Vanceburg, Kentucky. The town also built the Riverside Seminary, and both educational facilities were a testament to the people who lived in this area and the desire they had to educate their children. A new county high school was also built for all who were living outside the city school district.

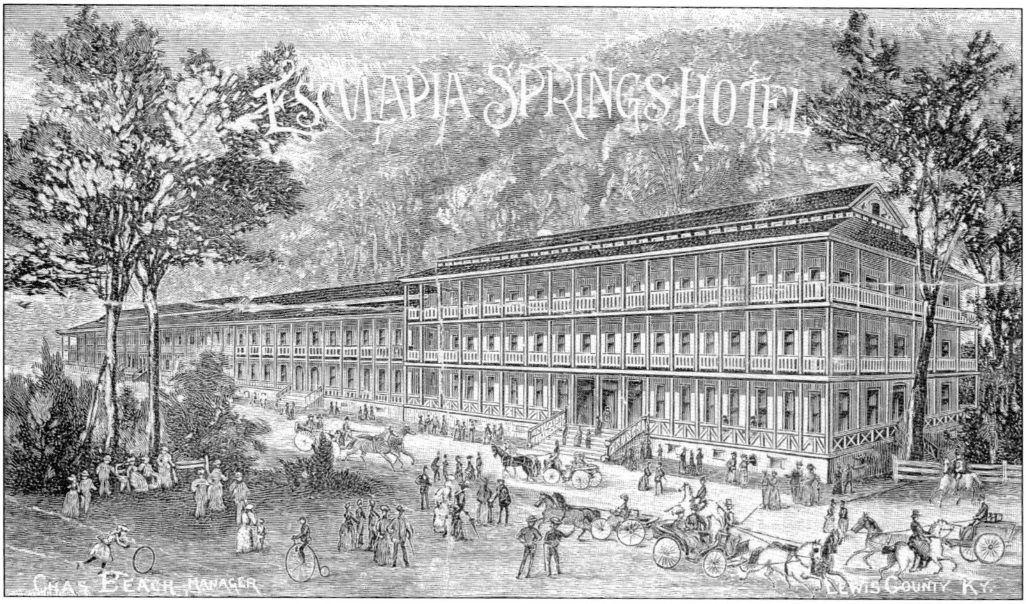

Early steamboats cruising the Ohio River gave people easy access to the original Esculapia Springs Resort a short distance away, but fire destroyed the resort in 1860. In 1892, the Esculapia Springs Company erected this new building, which opened in 1893 and competed with Glenn Springs, also in Lewis County. Below, on the back of the previous picture is this advertisement for the 1891 season for the Esculapia Springs Resort. The manager for the new Esculapia Springs Hotel that season was Charles Beach. It boasts a half mile of porches and room for 300 guests. People came to natural springs like this one located throughout Kentucky to vacation and to soak in the white sulfur water for remedies and recreation.

ESCULAPIA SPRINGS HOTEL,

—SEASON 1891.—

Opens June 15.—Only three hours ride on C. & O. from Cincinnati. Round Trip $5.50, including carriage ride. Excursion every Friday during the season, $4.40 round trip. Hotel 400 foot long, half mile of porches, capacity, 300 guests; many rooms ensuite. The table will be a leading feature. A select orchestra has been engaged for the season. Hops and entertainments every evening for the enjoyment of the guests. Rates, $2.00 per day, $10.00 to $12.00 per week. Resident physician. Electric bells, telephone connection with W. U. telegraph office. Hot and cold Mineral baths. Out-door sports of every description.

Analysis of White Sulphur Water, A Specific Remedy for all Kidney and Bladder Diseases,

BY DR. R. PETER.

ONE PINT CONTAINS--SOLIDS.

Carbonate Iron,	0.046 grains.	Carbonate Lime,	0.421 grains.
Chloride Potassium,	0.062 "	Chloride Sodium,	9.960 "
Chloride Magnesium,	3.641 "	Sulphate Soda,	0.434 "
Sulphate Lime,	7.515 "	Hyposulphite of Soda,	0.536 "
Phosphate of Soda,	0.135 "	Bromide of Magnesium,	0.083 "
Sulphuret of Sodium,	0.156 "	Silicate of Soda and Organic Comp.	1.167 "
		Total,	24.56 Cubic Inches.
GAS—Sulphuratted Hydrogen,			0.683

Cincinnati Beference, R. H. LANGDALE, Attorney, N. E. Cor. 4th and Walnut.
W. H. BALDRIDGE, Nevada Building, 5th and Sycamore.

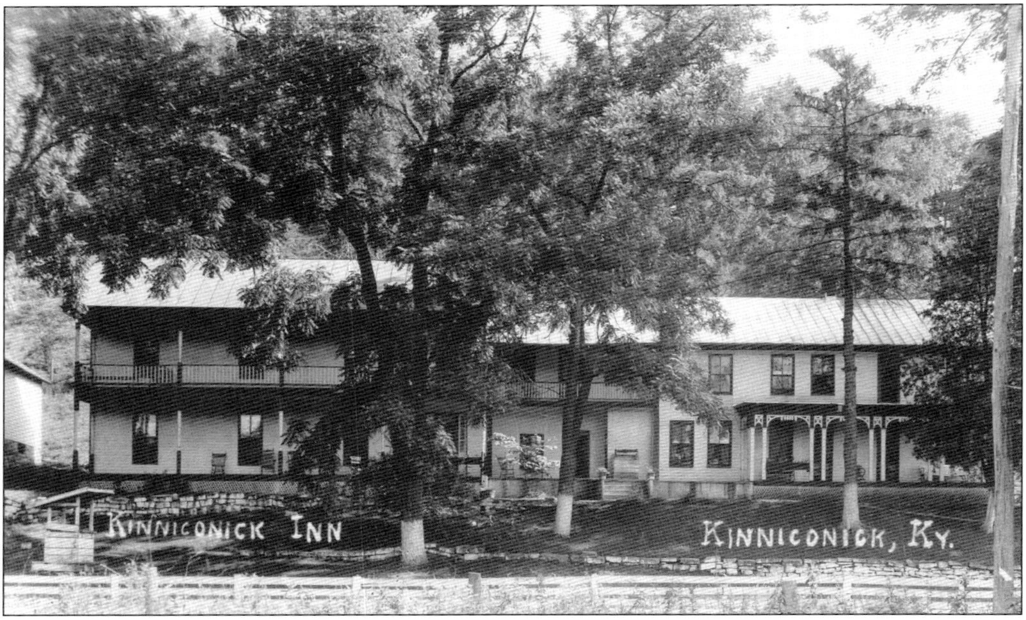

This area, called Kinniconick, Kentucky, located on Kinniconick Creek, was once a small community with a school and post office, among other services, for the people who lived in this area. Many fishermen came to this area to fish for bass and muskellunge from two creeks, both named Kinny many years ago. While here, many visitors stayed at the Kinniconick Inn.

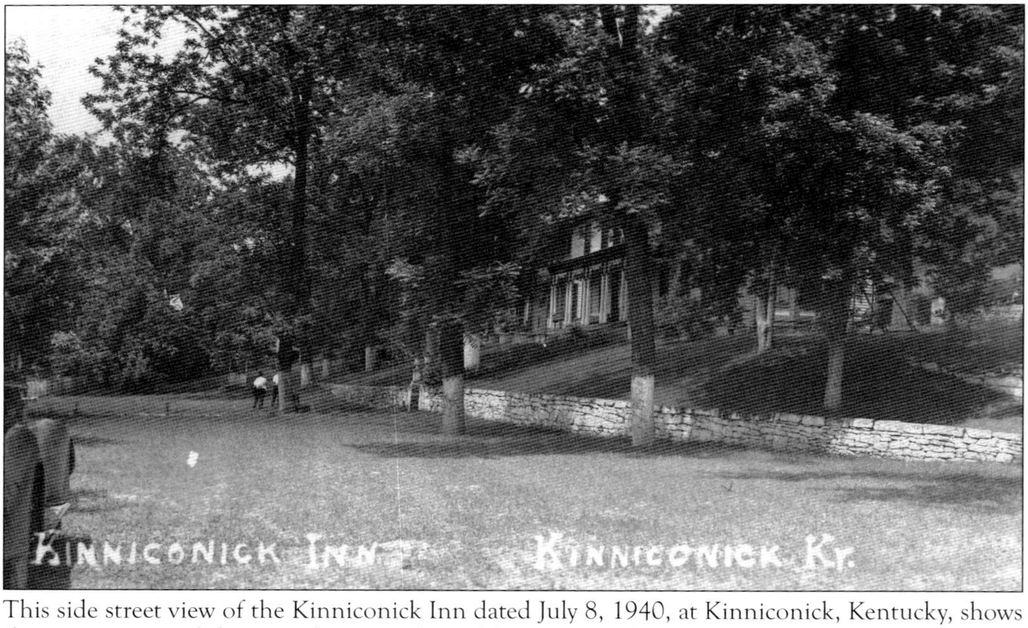

This side street view of the Kinniconick Inn dated July 8, 1940, at Kinniconick, Kentucky, shows the scenery around this inn where people could get away and vacation. Years ago, there were seven mills in this area along the local creeks. A Kentucky historical marker nearby says the father of Ulysses S. Grant was associated with three tanyards in this area.

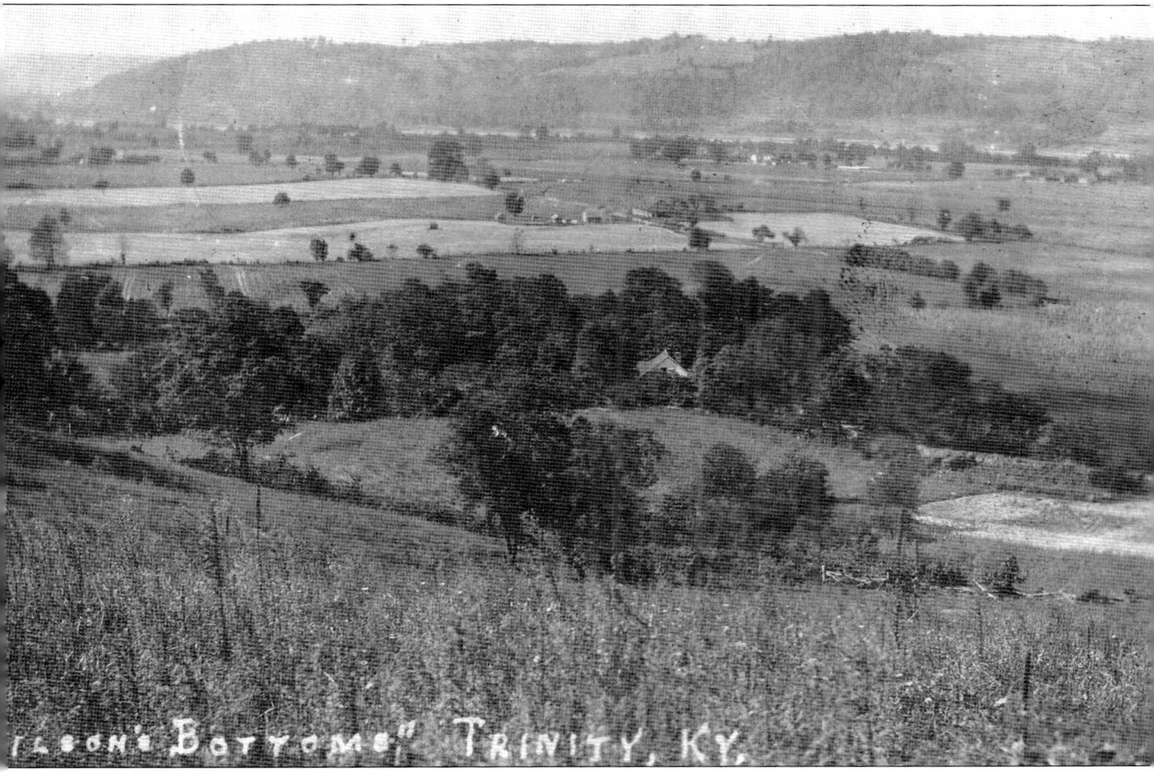

Wilson's Bottom, a community established in 1785 near Trinity, Kentucky, is named for John Wilson, one of the first settlers. Because this area has very sandy soil, the first post office here was named Sand Hill. This photograph of the area is dated April 22, 1908, and postmarked from Manchester, Ohio. The Ohio River can be seen in the distance beyond the flat bottoms.

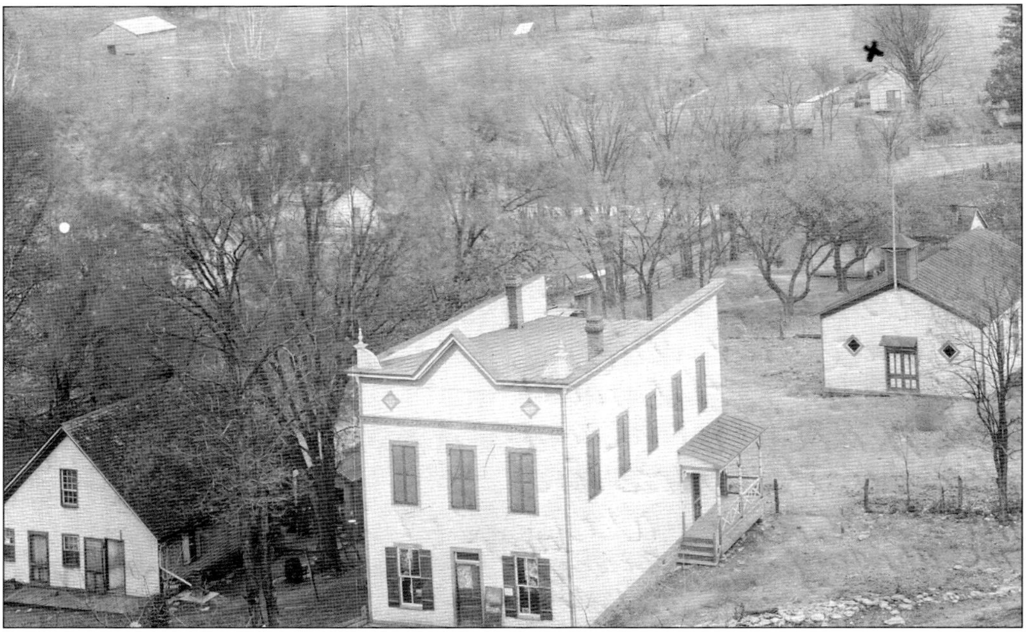

Sent to Grace Shelton in New Richmond, Ohio, and dated May 2, 1910, this overhead view of Trinity, Kentucky, reveals an impressively designed store towering over its humble surroundings with the Sand Hill School to the far right. Notice the cistern on the old house with the downspout used to gather rainwater. The sender, Alvin, says the "X" in the photograph is his home.

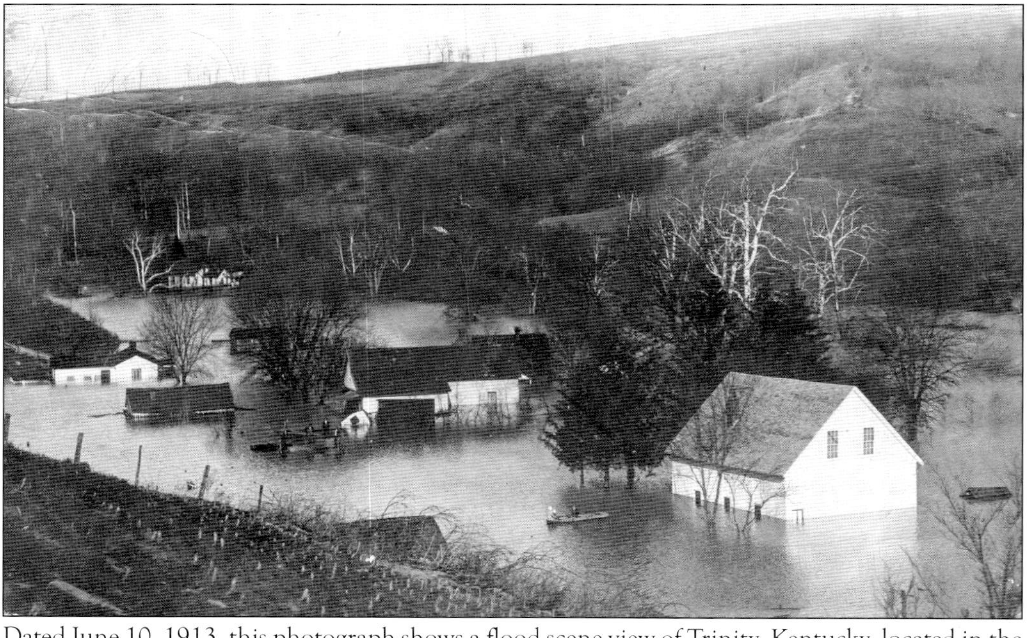

Dated June 10, 1913, this photograph shows a flood scene view of Trinity, Kentucky, located in the northwestern part of Lewis County. Situated near a large bend in the Ohio River on the western edge of Manchester, Ohio, this community relied on farming as the main source of income.

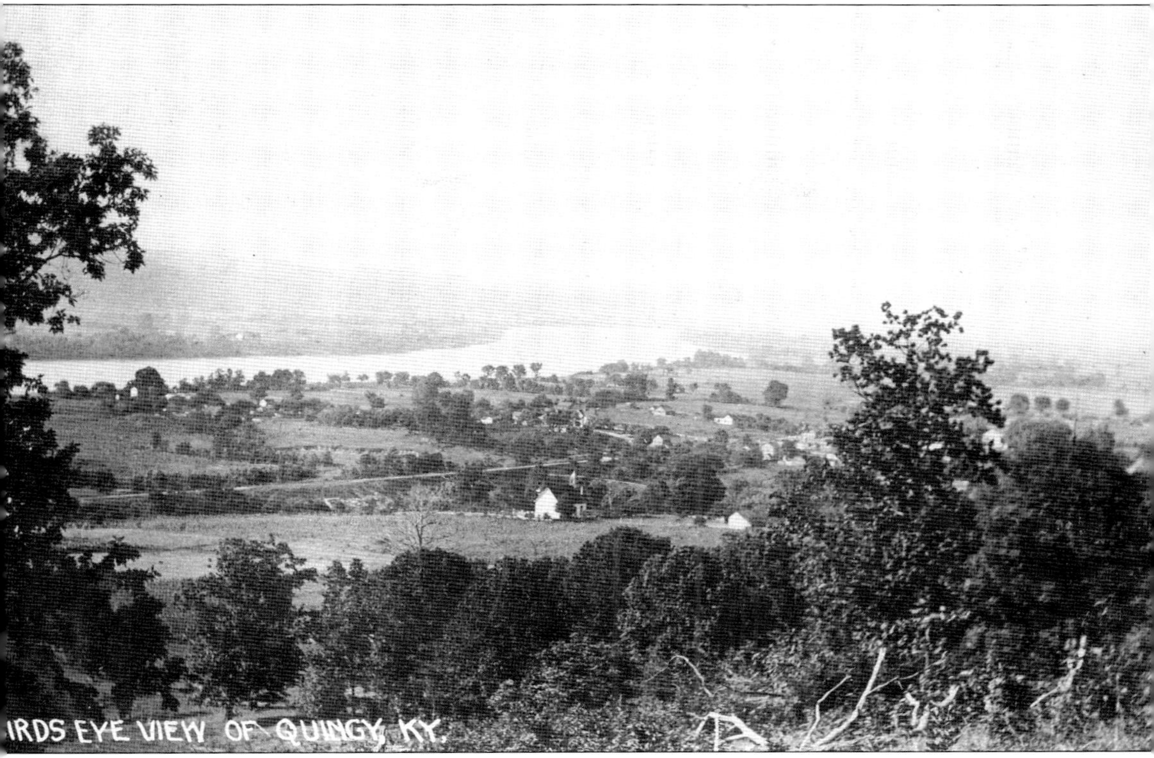

Located on Route 8 along the Ohio River about 10 miles east of Vanceburg is the small town of Quincy, Kentucky, founded in 1819 by John Wood. This small valley town photograph is dated July 1, 1910. In 1825, both Quincy, Kentucky, and Adams County, Ohio, were named after John Quincy Adams, the nation's sixth president.

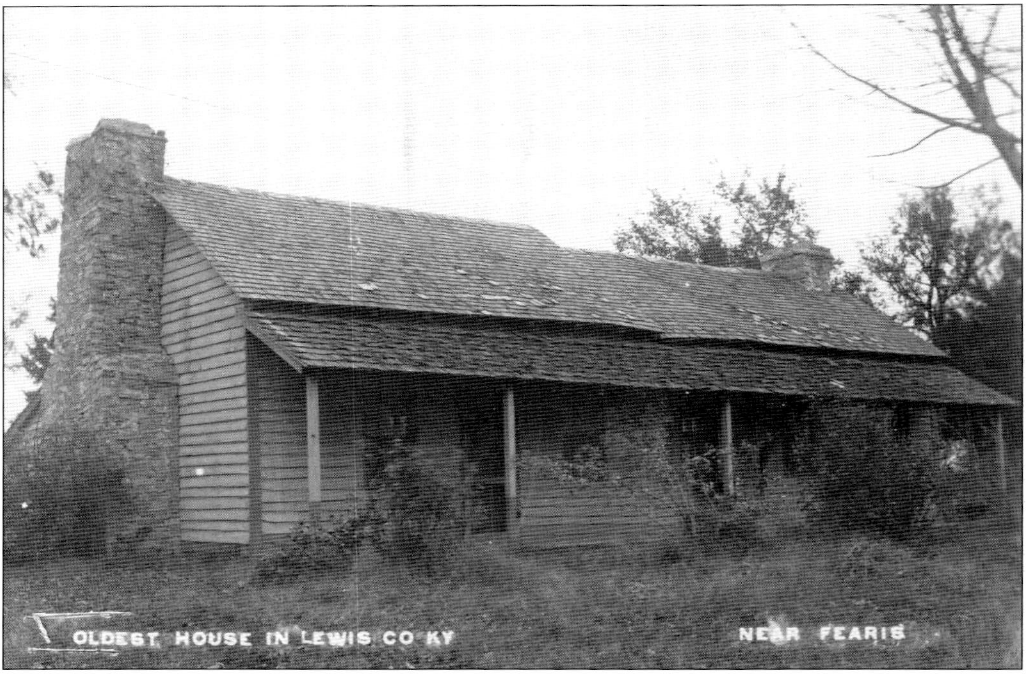

This photograph was published by Dan T. Fischer, Jeweler & Optician, Flemingsburg, Kentucky, and shows the oldest home in Lewis County, near Fearis, Kentucky. This community is now called Fearisville and is located at the intersection of East Cabin Creek Road and Trinity Station Fearisville Road. This photograph dates between 1907 and 1910.

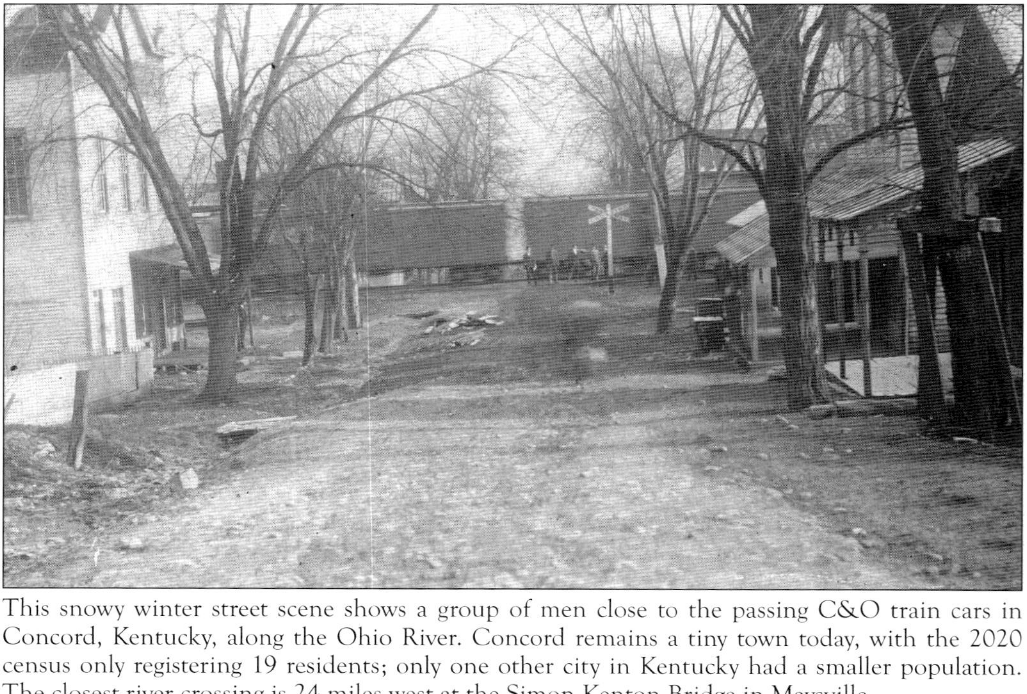

This snowy winter street scene shows a group of men close to the passing C&O train cars in Concord, Kentucky, along the Ohio River. Concord remains a tiny town today, with the 2020 census only registering 19 residents; only one other city in Kentucky had a smaller population. The closest river crossing is 24 miles west at the Simon Kenton Bridge in Maysville.

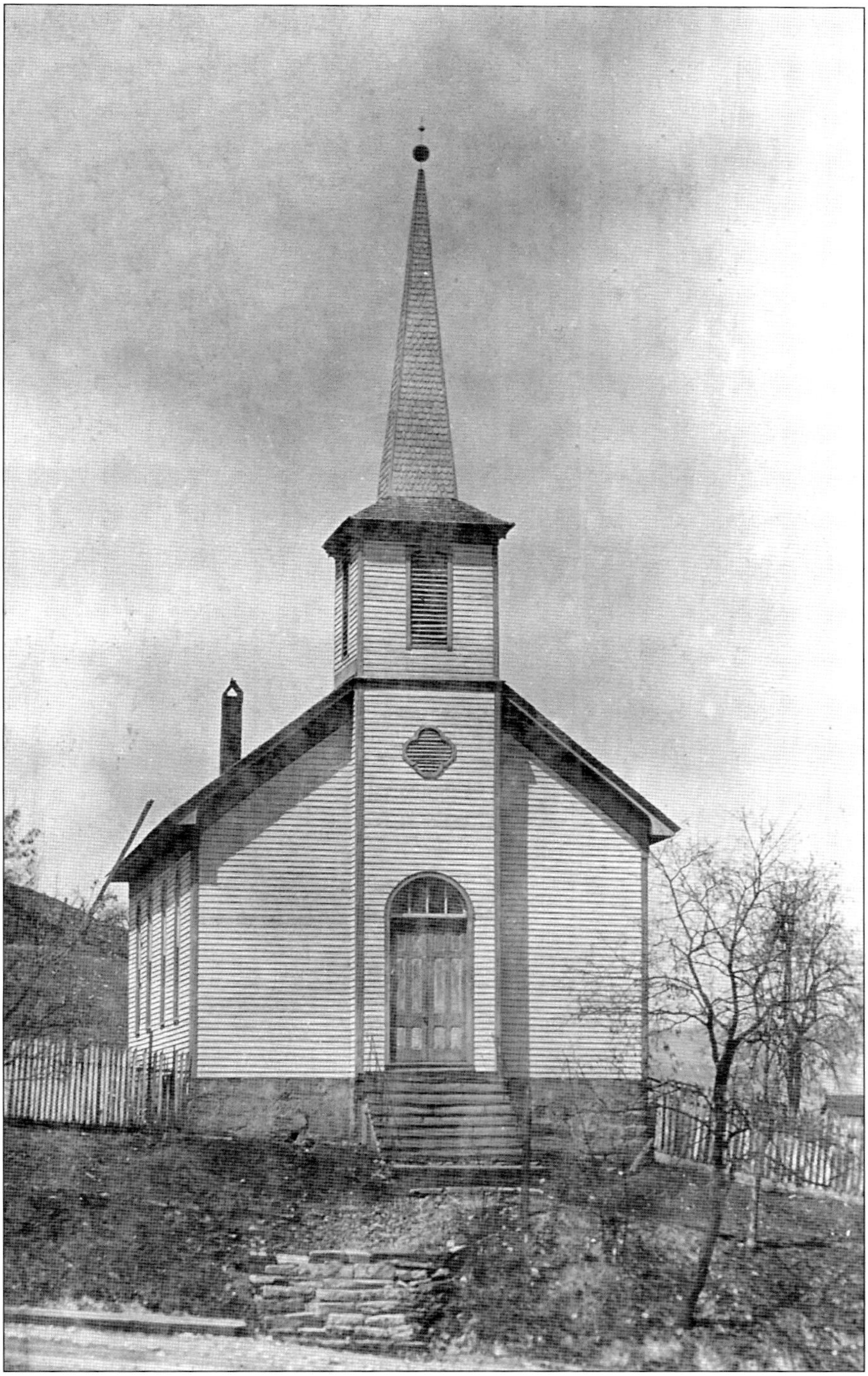

According to Rev. O.G. Ragan's *History of Lewis County*, this Freewill Baptist Church was built in 1888 in Concord, Kentucky. The other two churches in the town, according to Ragan, were the Methodist Episcopal Church, built in 1848, and the Union Church, built in 1830. This photograph is postmarked from Concord.

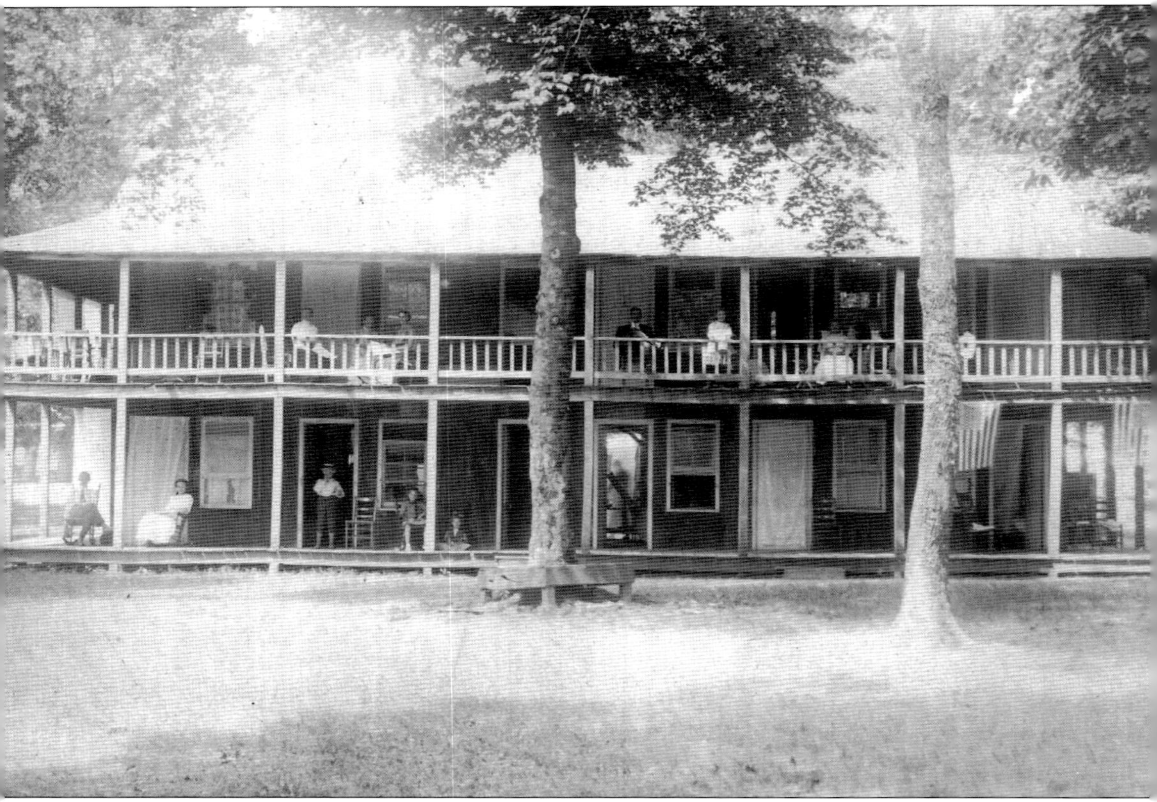

Ruggles Camp was established in 1873 by the United Methodist Church on land once owned by local farmer William Ruggles. Christian revivals attracted the faithful from near and far with large tents and even cabins and housing, built for extended stays and summer youth camps. One of the founding members of the camp, Rev. W.E. Seddon, went on to found Seddon Methodist Church in Maysville. The camp continues to thrive today.

Six

ROBERTSON COUNTY, KENTUCKY

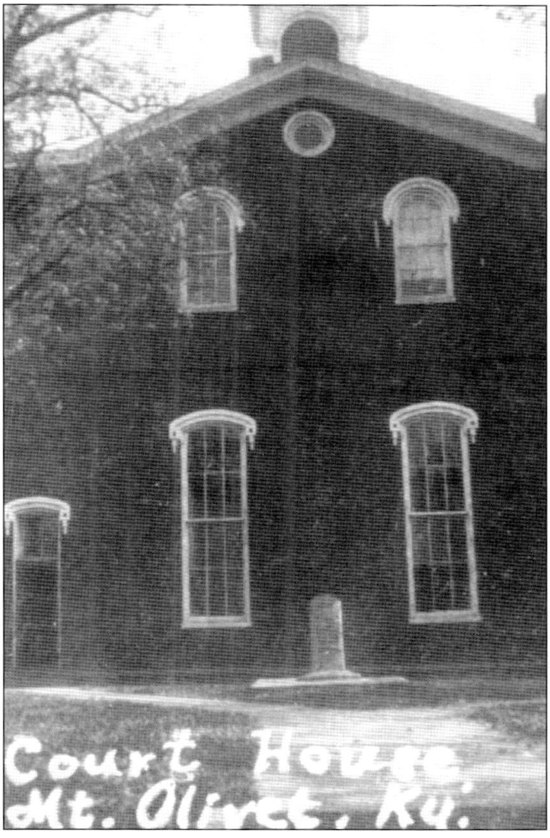

Dated prior to 1907, this photograph is of the Robertson County Courthouse, which was constructed in 1870 by local builder G.M. Williams. The courthouse was located on Court Street in the county seat town of Mount Olivet, Kentucky. Robertson was at one time part of Nicholas, Harrison, Bracken, and Mason Counties and has the lowest population in Kentucky. In 1978, this old courthouse was put in the National Register of Historic Places.

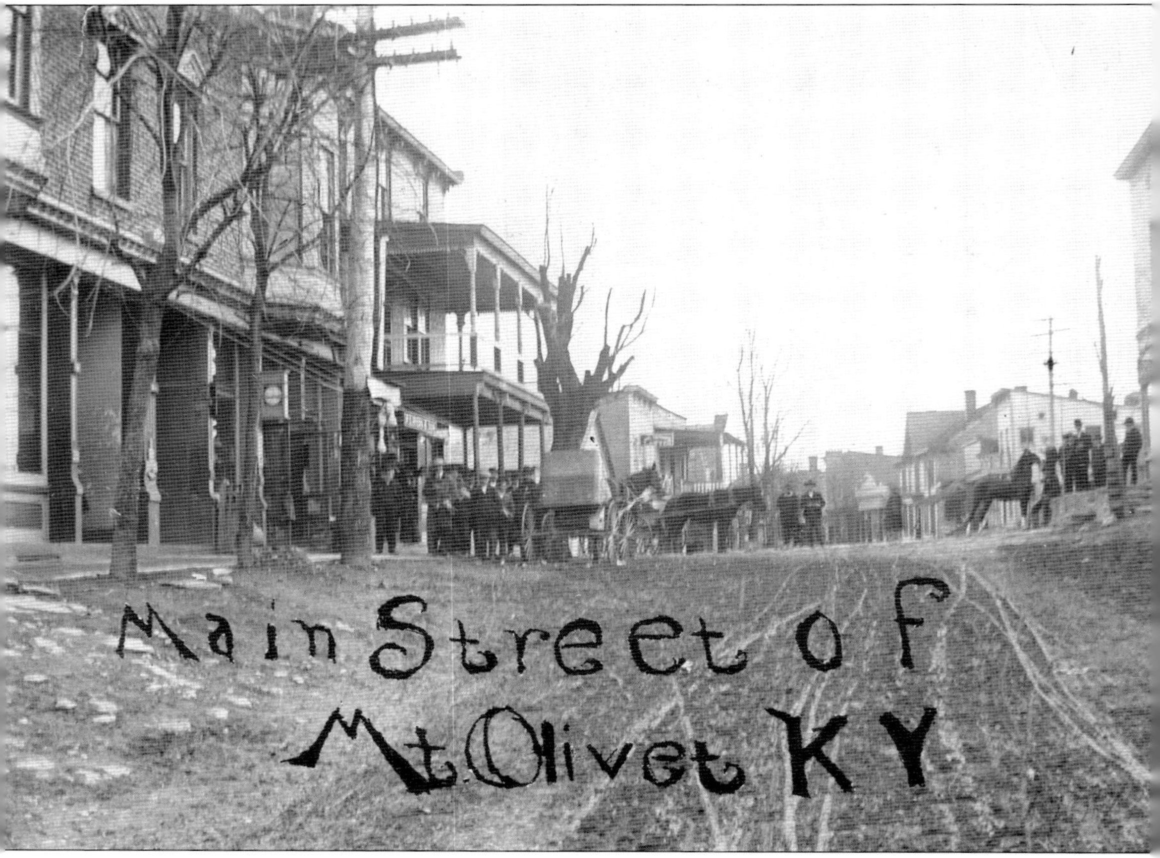

Like many rural, small-town county seats at the turn of the 20th century, Mount Olivet, Kentucky, still had dirt streets. This photograph shows South Main Street just before the intersection of West Walnut Street with North Main Street in the distance. Most of the buildings are gone today, but a few remain to identify this photograph dated January 24, 1908.

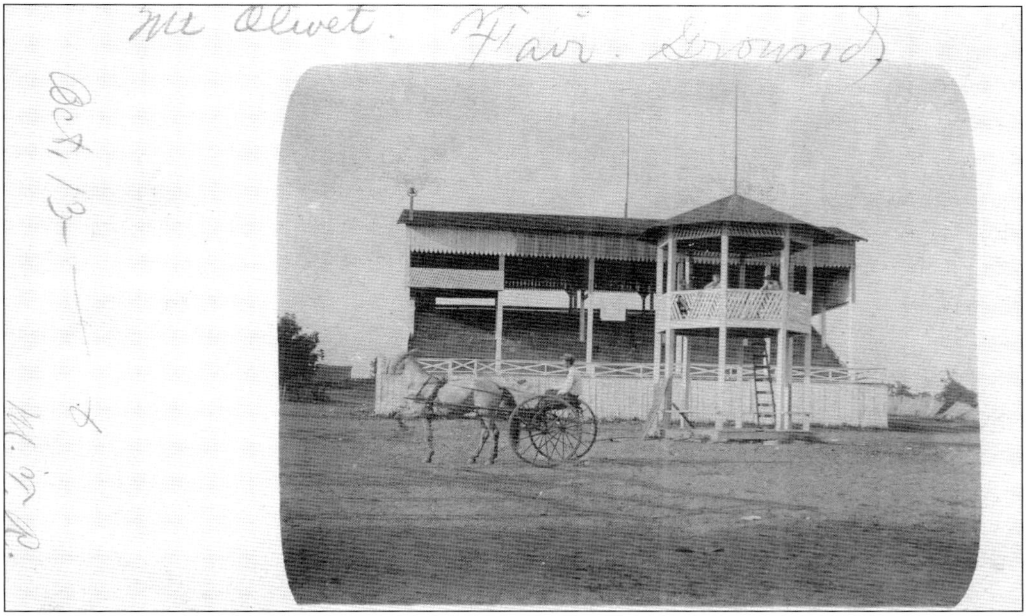

A few children climbed up the ladder to watch a harness racer on his large two-wheel sulky, trying out the track for an upcoming race at the Robertson County Fair. Notice the small grandstand, which illustrates just how rural the community was. This photograph of the Robertson County Fair was taken at the fairground location on Bee Lick Road. The photograph, dated October 13, 1906, was sent to Ada Moneyhon in Augusta, Kentucky.

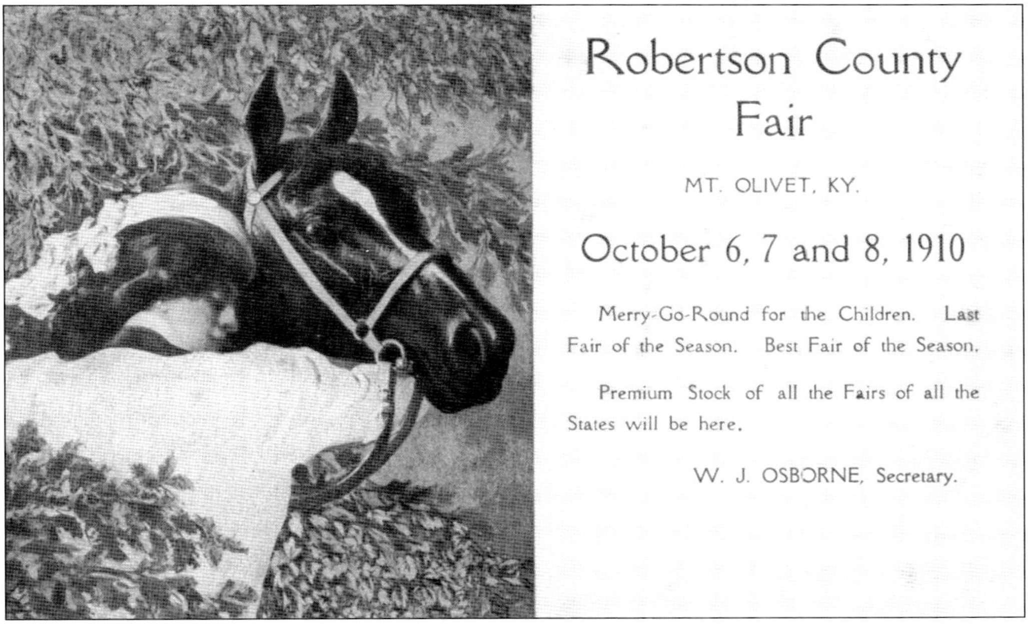

Many rural fairs throughout Kentucky used the Fair Publishing Company in Norwalk, Ohio, to publish advertising cards with the upcoming fair schedule. This card is numbered 3009 and promotes the 1910 fair in Robertson County, Kentucky. These fairs drew spectators for competitions in cattle shows, horticulture, bakery goods, and more, just as fairs do today.

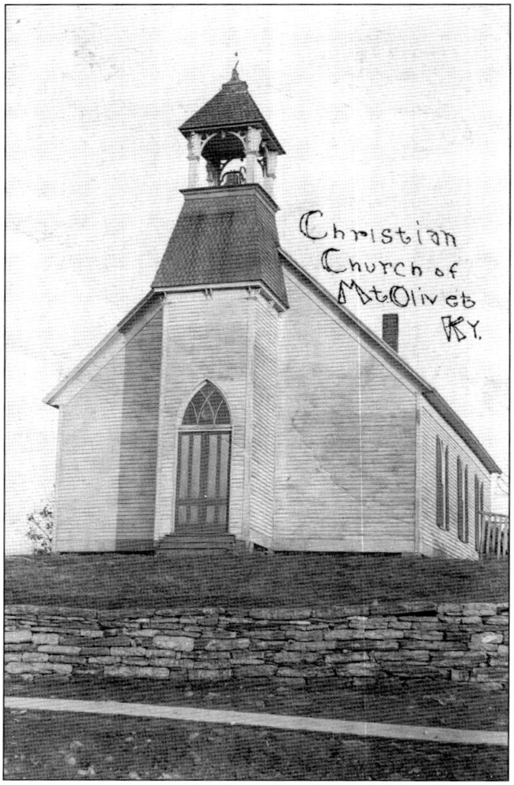

Published by H.B. Rood Photo, Poultry, Vermont, this photograph reveals the elevation of the Christian Church in Mount Olivet, which was remodeled in 1911. Doors were installed on both sides of the front, and a set of double windows was added in the center. This church served the community until 1954, when another Christian Church was built.

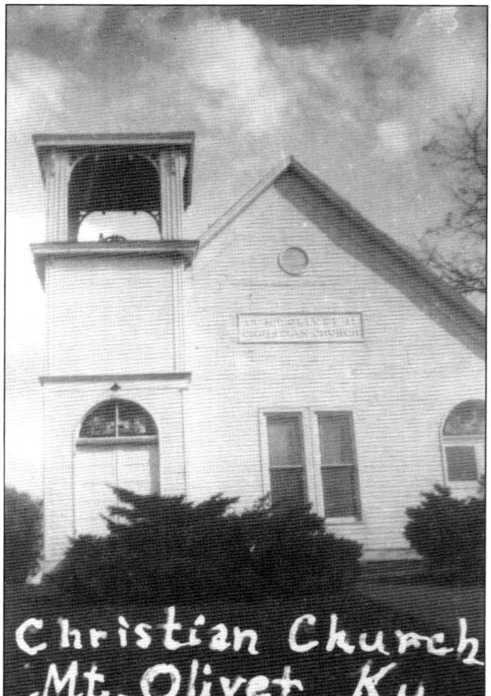

The original Church of Christ in Mount Olivet, Kentucky, was built in 1860. The front elevation here shows a remodeled extended entrance, but the window above the door remained the same. In 1906, some churches changed their name to the Christian Church for the first time. On November 2, 1908, this photograph was sent from Mount Olivet, Kentucky, to Lucy Wood in Augusta, Kentucky. This Christian Church has been rebuilt three times.

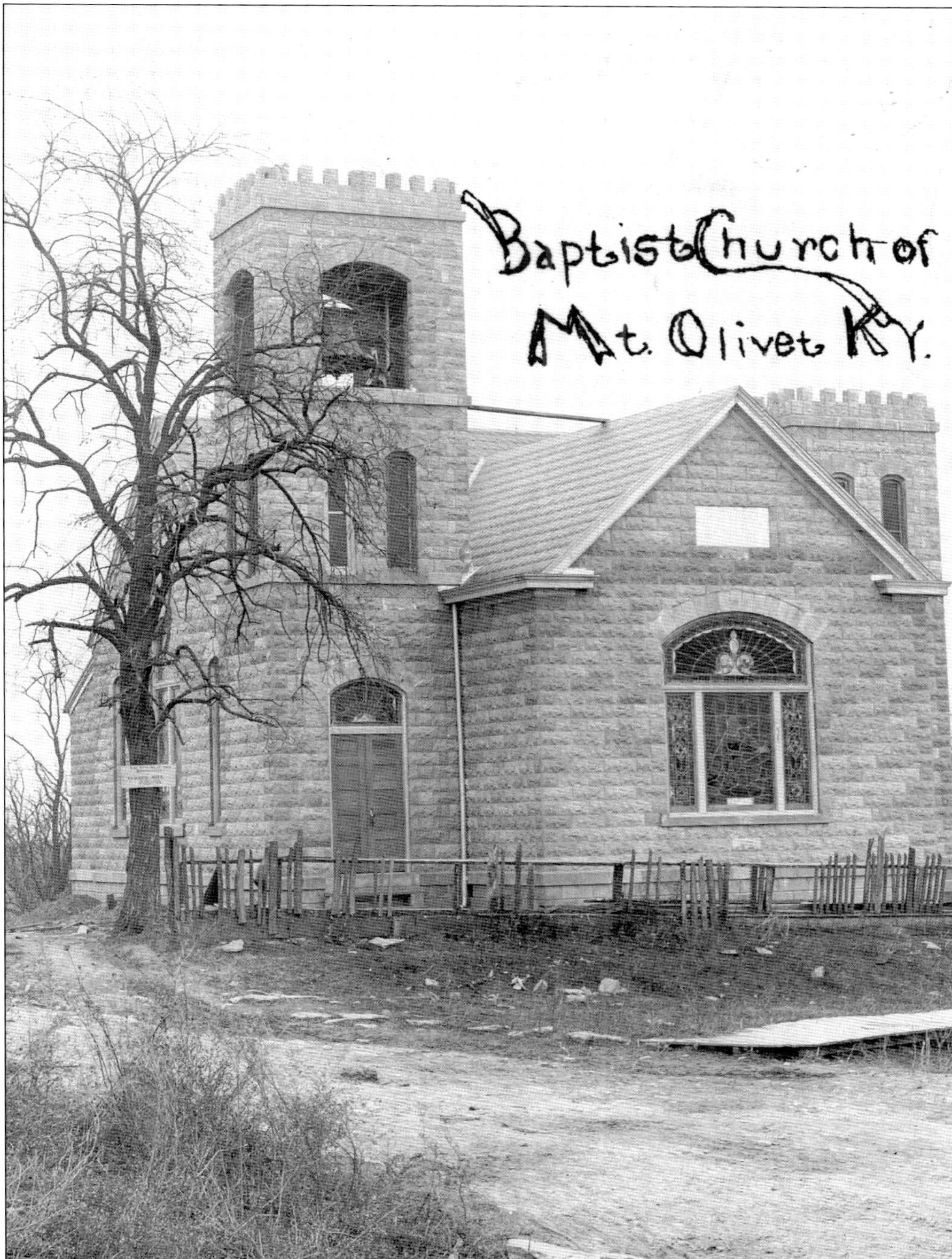

The date carved into the stone above the front window of the newly constructed Baptist church in Mount Olivet, Kentucky, is 1907. Addressed to Ada Moneyhon, Augusta, Kentucky, the photograph is dated February 15, 1908, with an inscription saying, "Compliments of Mrs. C.E. Colyer." The juxtaposition of an imposing bell tower and ornate stained-glass windows with its bleak surroundings surely inspired a faithful following that continues to gather there today.

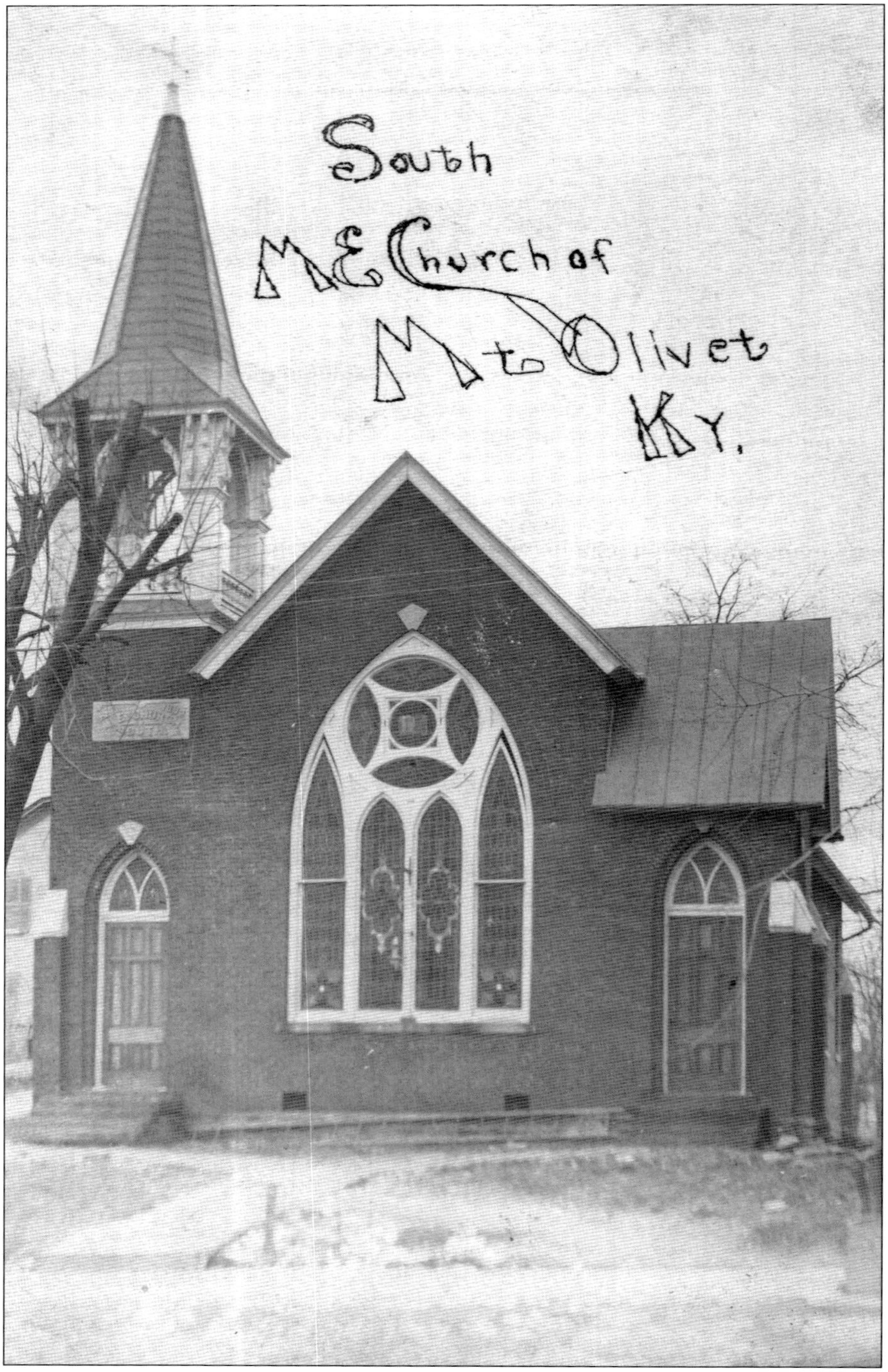

Dated January 14, 1908, this photograph reveals the South ME Church in Mount Olivet, Kentucky, where the sender's father preached. The church was torn down from this original location to make a parking lot for what is now the Peoples Bank. A new church was rebuilt on Highway 165, Oakland Road out of town, but now that church is the Christian Baptist.

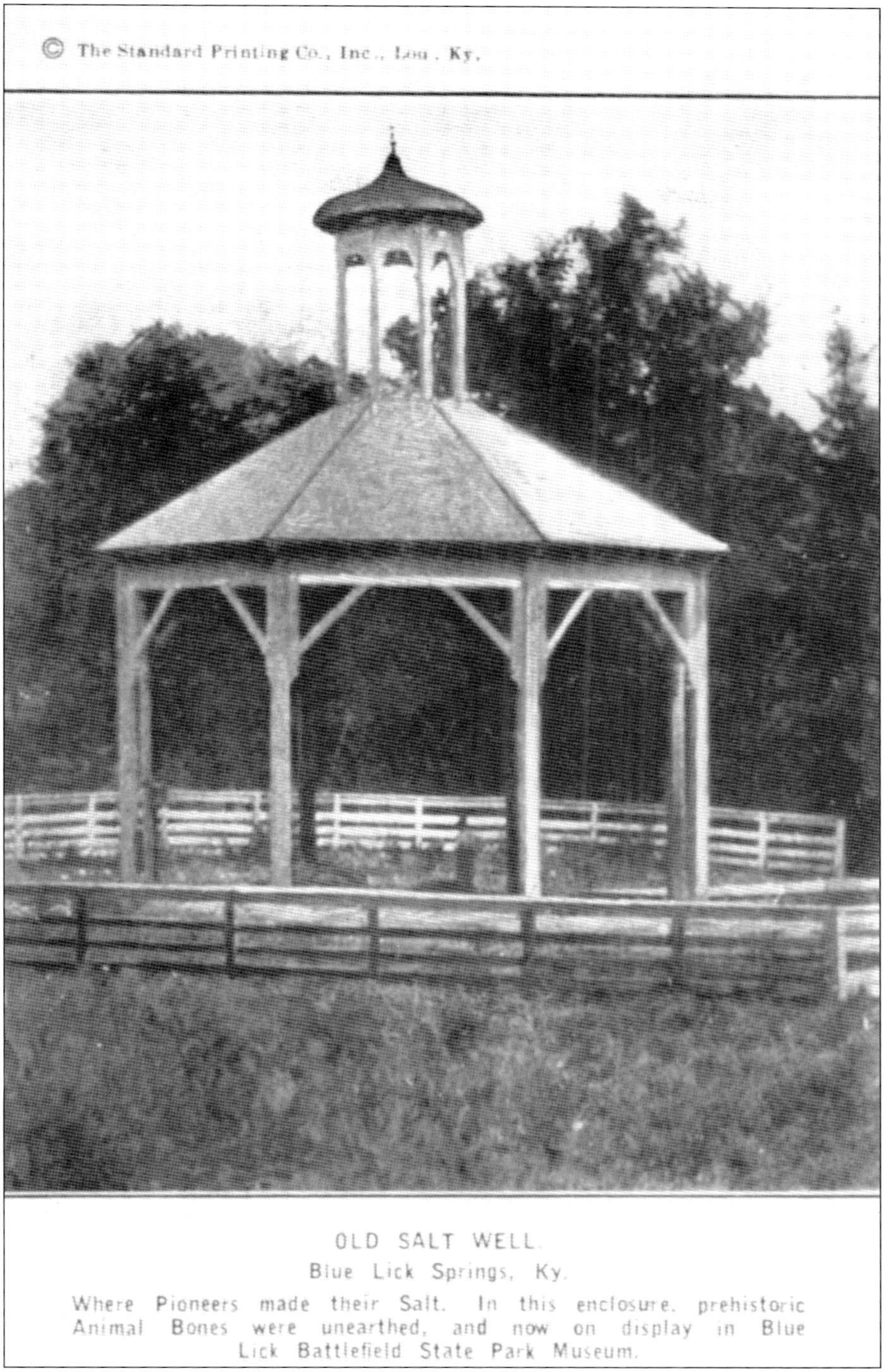

Early pioneers found the upper and lower areas of Blue Licks, Kentucky, to be a great source of salt for gunpowder and the preservation of meats. The Blue Licks area is split by the Nicholas and Robertson County lines, and it is now a state park where the last battle of the American Revolutionary War was fought on August 17, 1782.

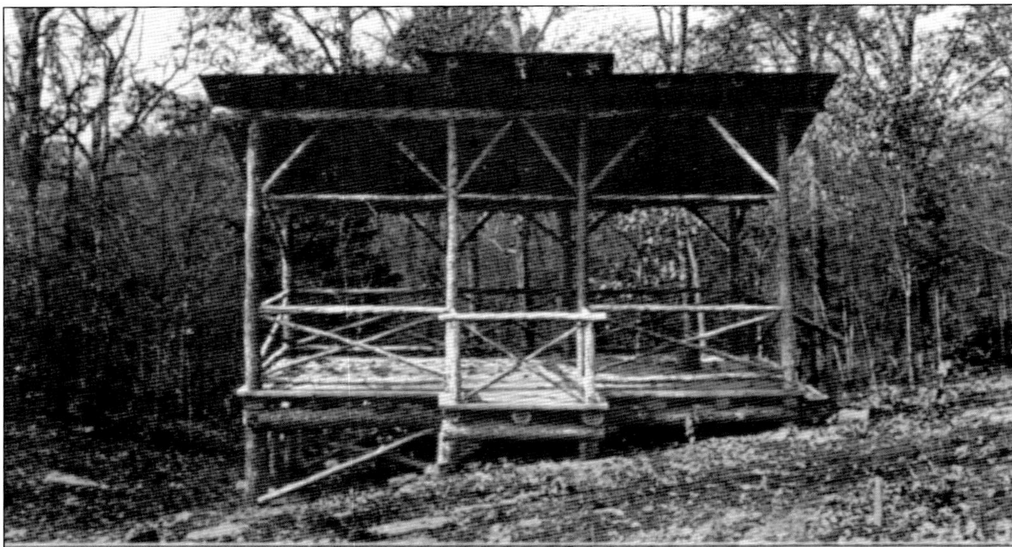

Natural Amphitheatre with Speaker's Stand. Blue Licks Battlefield State Park.

Pictured here is a rustic amphitheater that was used in the early 1900s for the reenactment of the last battle of the Revolutionary War. Pioneers were building homes and settlements in this area as early as 1783, along the Licking River. Reenactments are still performed on this site with authentic guns, knives, and clothing. A campground and museum with walking trails make this a great place to visit.

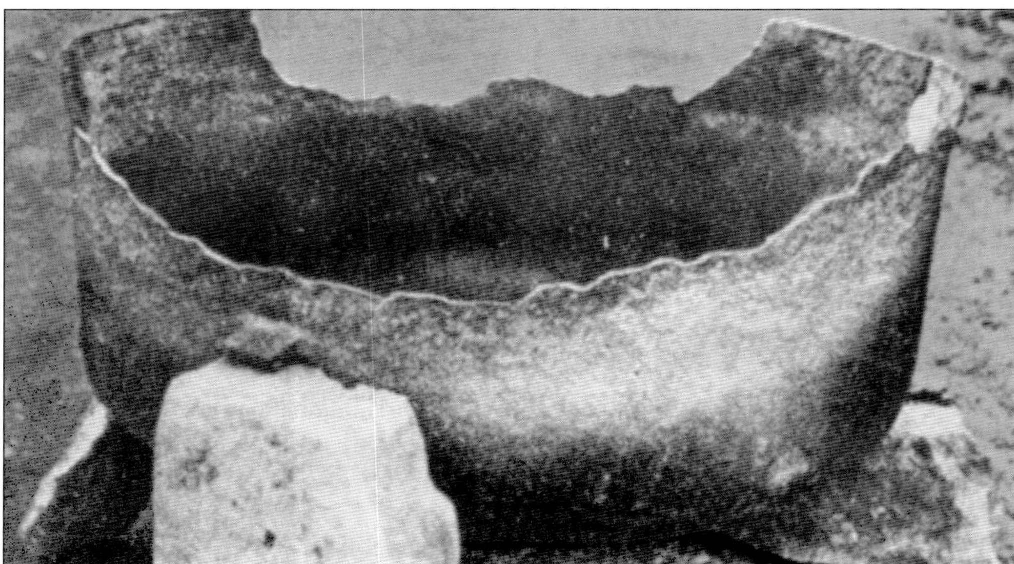

Salt Kettle of Daniel Boone brought to Blue Licks in 1778 (a Gift to Pioneers of Kentucky by the Government of Virginia). Blue Licks Battlefield State Park.

This salt kettle belonging to Daniel Boone provided salt to the early pioneers to preserve the meats from the plentiful wildlife in Kentucky. This photograph was taken at Blue Licks, Kentucky, where a salt spring allowed the workers to get up to 50 pounds of salt from every 1,000 gallons of water boiled. From the looks of the uneven edges of this kettle, it must have produced a large amount of salt.

Seven

Adams County, Ohio

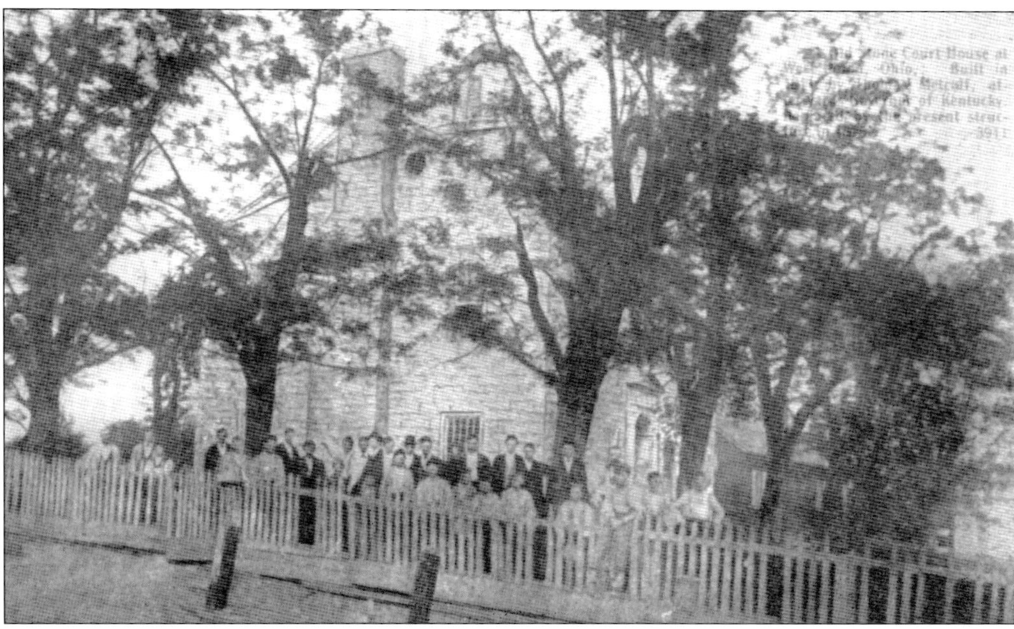

The first county seat in Adams County was in Manchester, Ohio, but there was no courthouse ever built there. The first courthouse to be built was in West Union, Ohio, and was built from logs. In 1811, the courthouse seen here was built in West Union by Thomas Metcalf, who later became the governor of Kentucky. This courthouse burned in 1875, and a third courthouse was built in 1876.

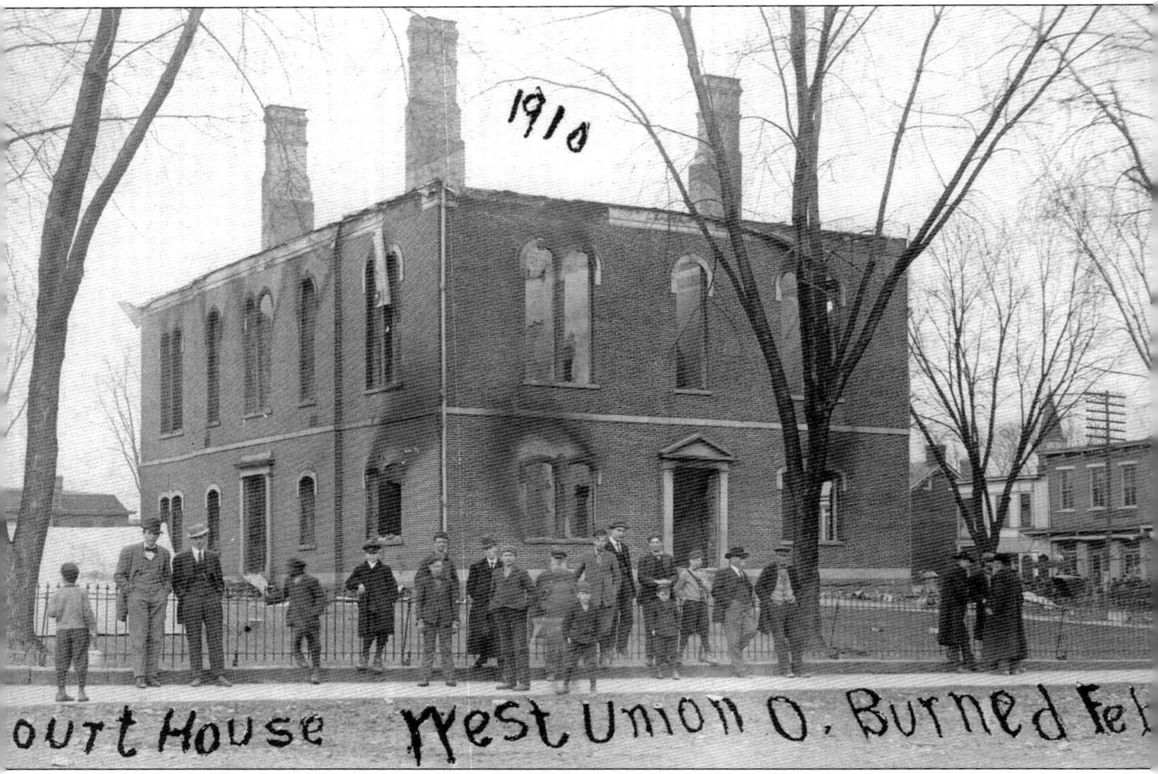

This is the third courthouse for Adams County, Ohio. The Ohio General Assembly officially relocated the county seat from Manchester to West Union and built this courthouse in 1876. A fire burned all records on February 25, 1910, and a new courthouse was built during 1910 and 1911 and is still serving the county today.

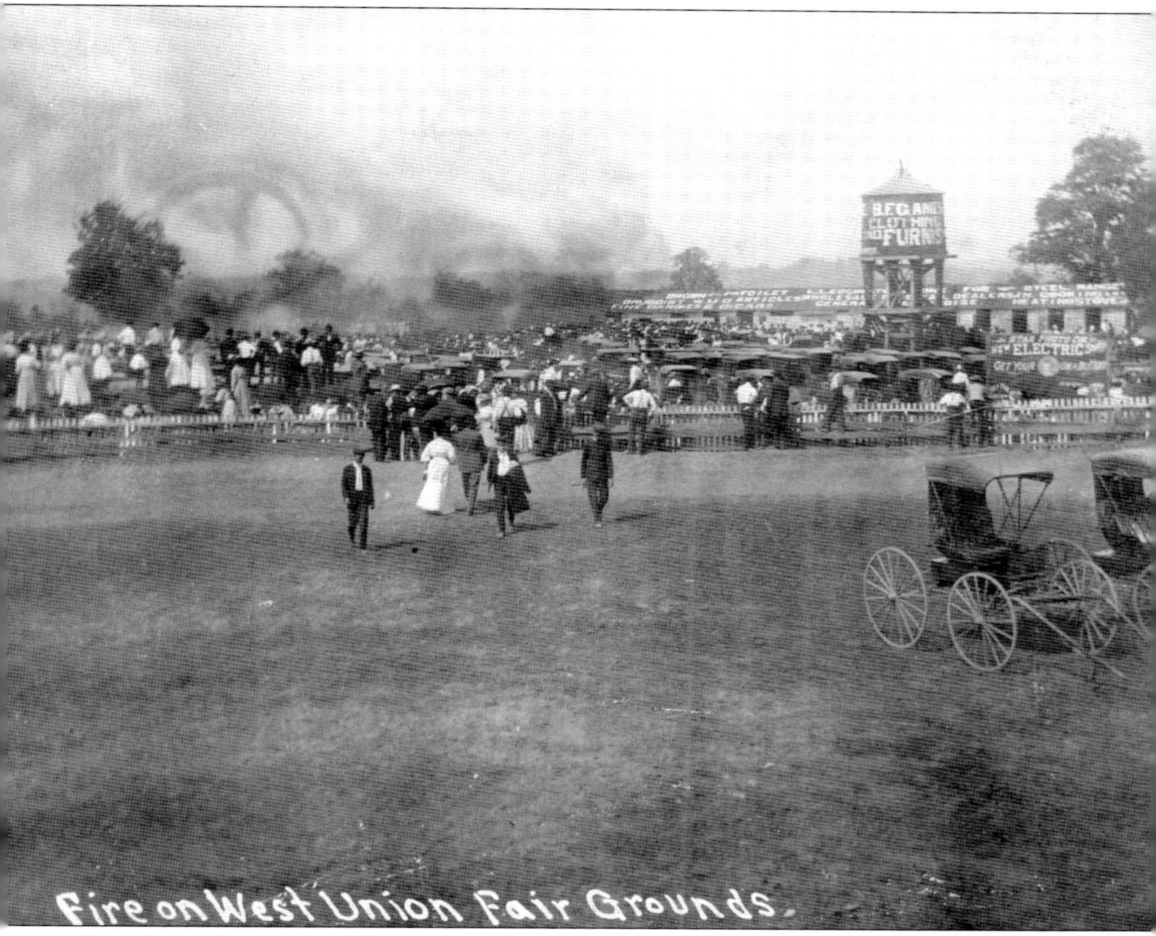

The West Union fair in Ohio, dating back to 1853, was located on land donated by Judge George Collings at the corner of West and South Streets. A fire is burning somewhere on the grounds, scattering the crowd. Some of the advertisements include BFG Ames Clothing and Furnishings; Star Photographs; and New Electric Studio, where one could get a photograph on a button. This photograph dates to around 1910.

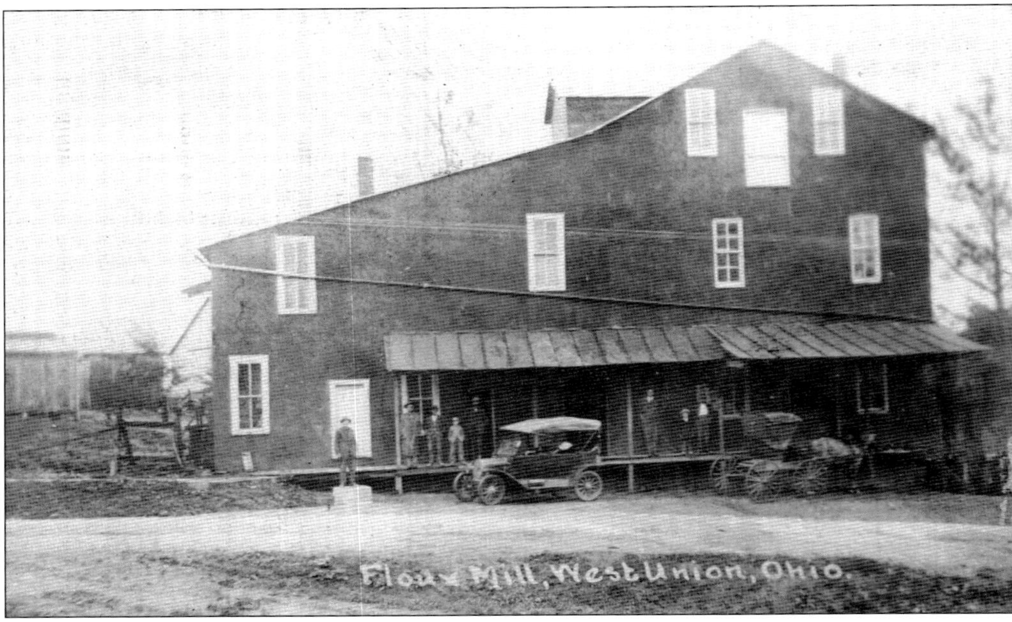

Prior to the mill shown in this photograph was the Stroman Brother's Mill, which shut down in 1908. This image depicts the Paul and Satterfield Flour Mill, which was in business from 1907 through 1915, although this photograph of the mill is dated August 13, 1918. Shortly afterward, the local stores were supplying the big company flour, and most local mills were beginning to shut down.

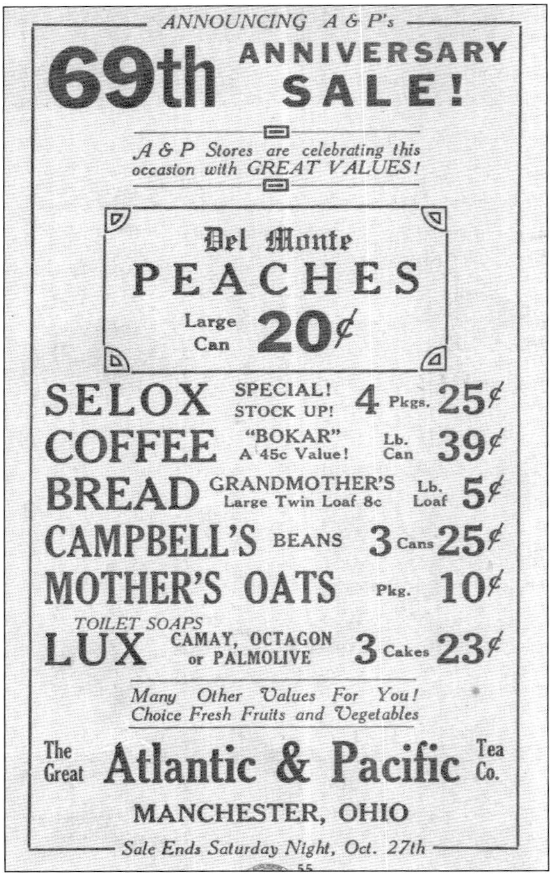

These prices were indeed "Great Values"—if only they held true today. This postcard advertisement for the Great Atlantic Pacific Tea Company (A&P) store located in Manchester, Ohio, was mailed to a resident on Route 3 in Manchester. The date on this card was October 22, 1928, and the sale ended on October 27, 1928.

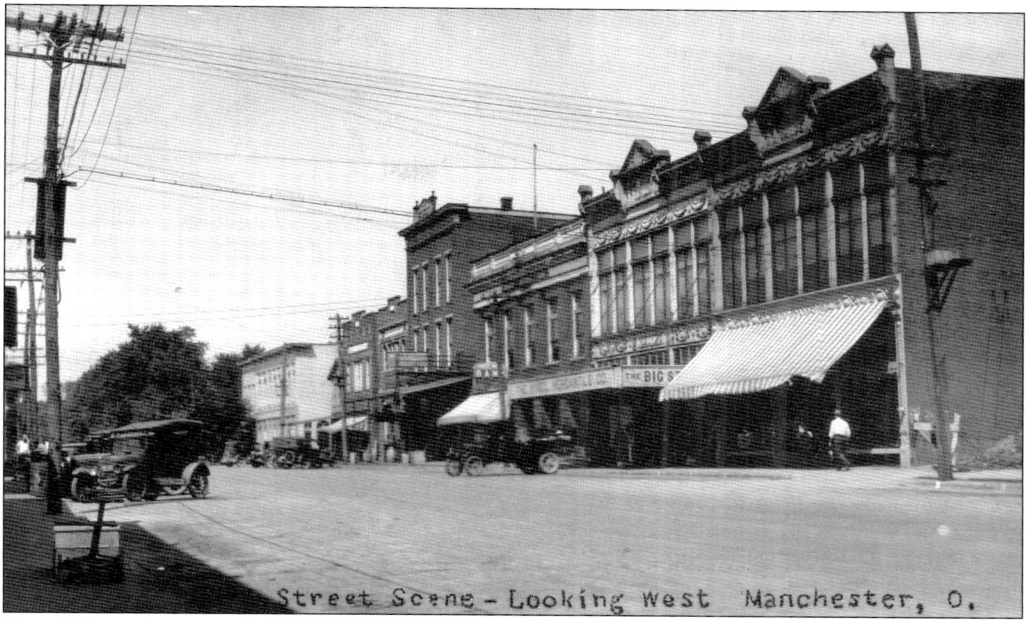

Dated Thursday, October 18, 1928, this photograph was taken looking west on Main Street in Manchester, Ohio, which is the north side of US 52. It appears to be a normal weekday, unlike most Saturdays in this small town, when the streets and shops would have been full of people. The first structure seen here is the Vance Building, dated 1892, and a little farther down is the Bank of Manchester, with a date of 1922.

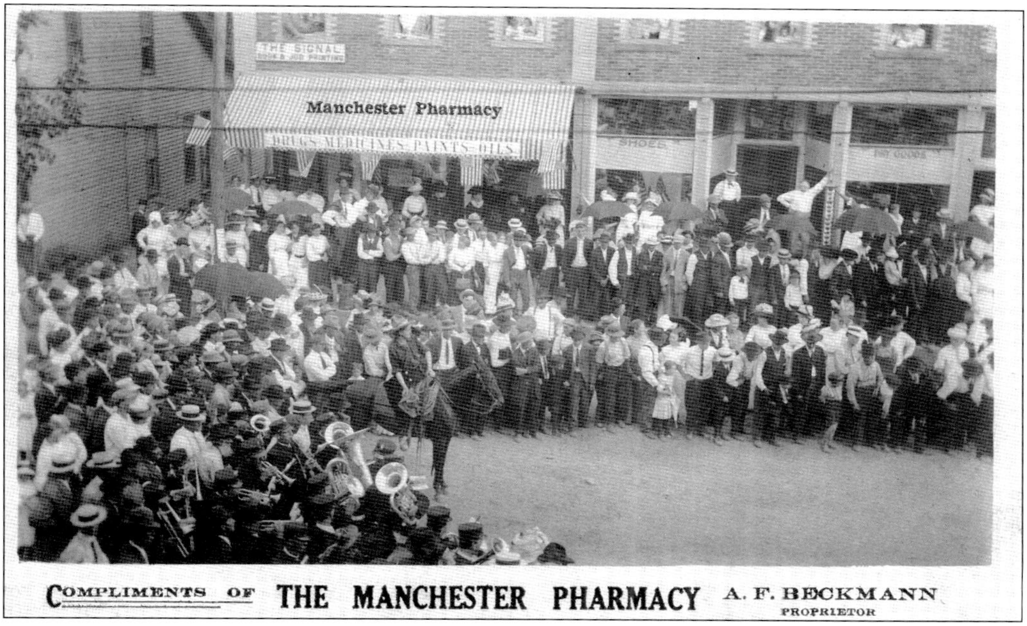

This large crowd is looking down the street toward some unidentified event taking place in front of the Manchester Pharmacy in Manchester, Ohio. The lady on the horse appears poised to toss up a hat as the band plays for musical entertainment. This photograph, taken in front of the pharmacy located on the south side of Main Street, shows the sign above the awning of the *Signal* newspaper.

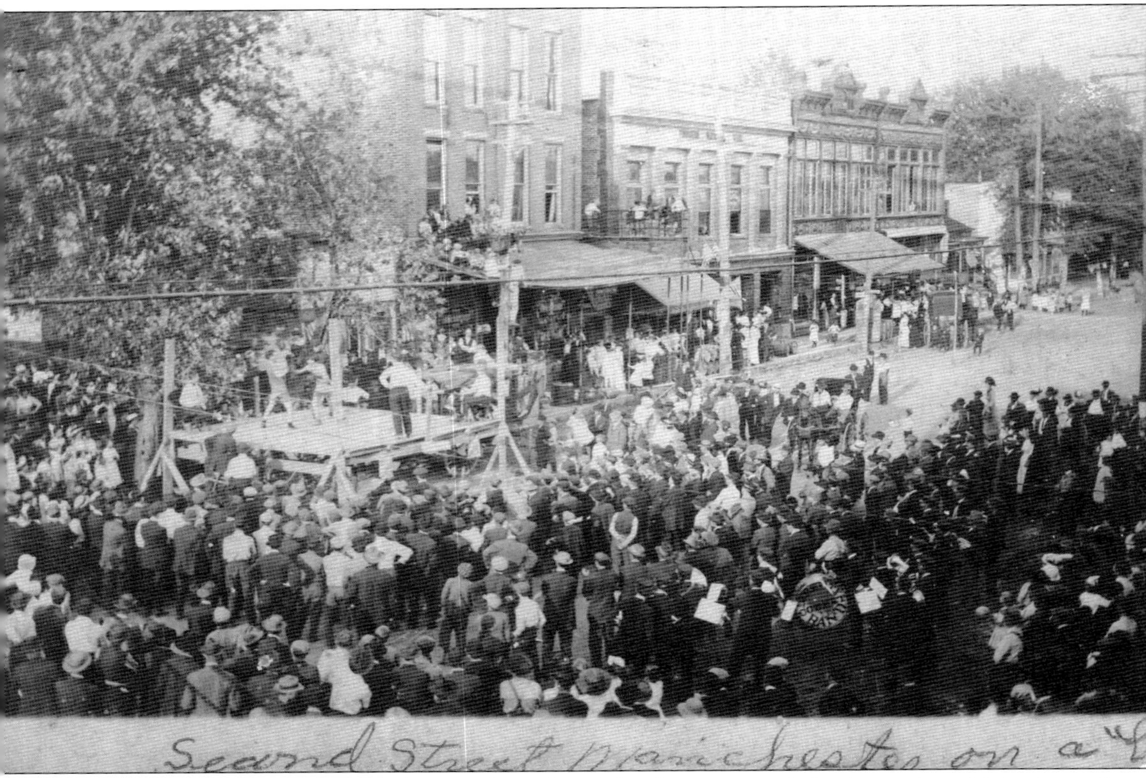

The County Cornet Band plays to the right of this boxing ring fight, located on Main Street in Manchester, Ohio, on what is called a "Big Day." Local resident Elwood Ayers told Tommy Conway that anyone could get in the ring, and he sometimes did. Not only are the streets full, but people are looking out windows and sitting on business roofs watching the action. This photograph once belonged to Lelah Forman.

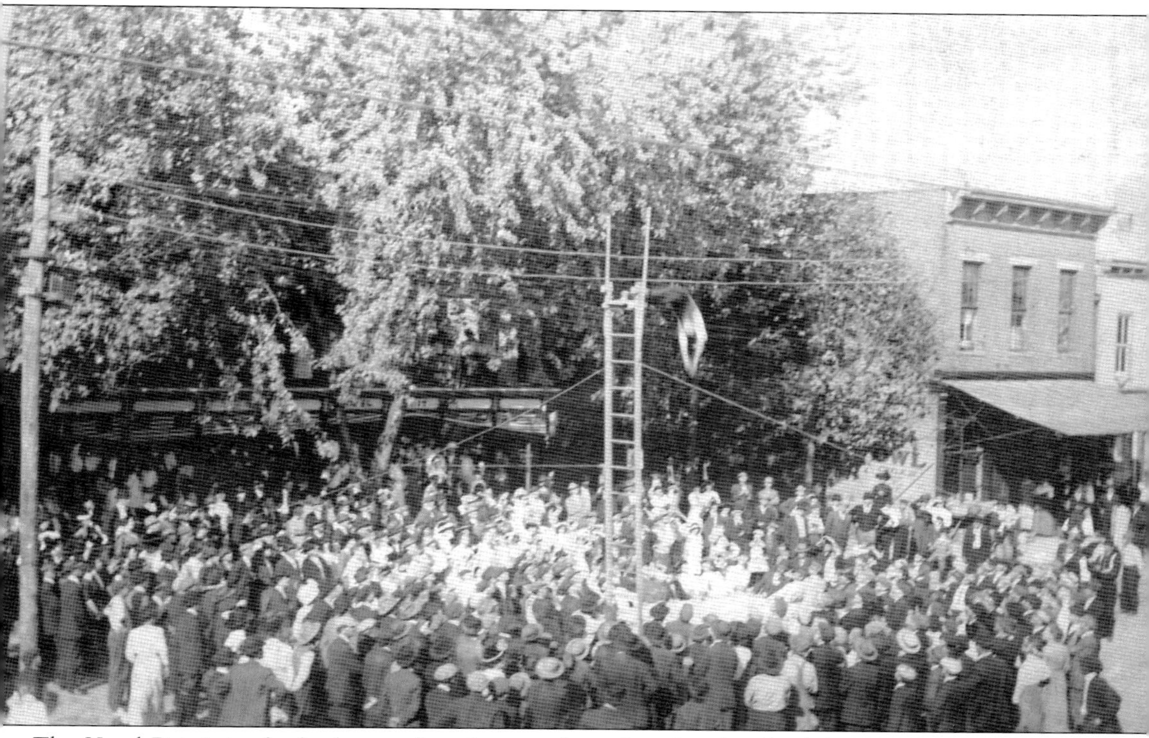

The Hotel Brit is in the background as the crowd watches this daredevil dive off the makeshift platform into a small tank of water on Main Street in Manchester, Ohio. This would have been on the north side of Main Street, just left of the Duffey Building, dated 1883. The boxing match and the diver are probably at the same event as both photographs came from the same lady.

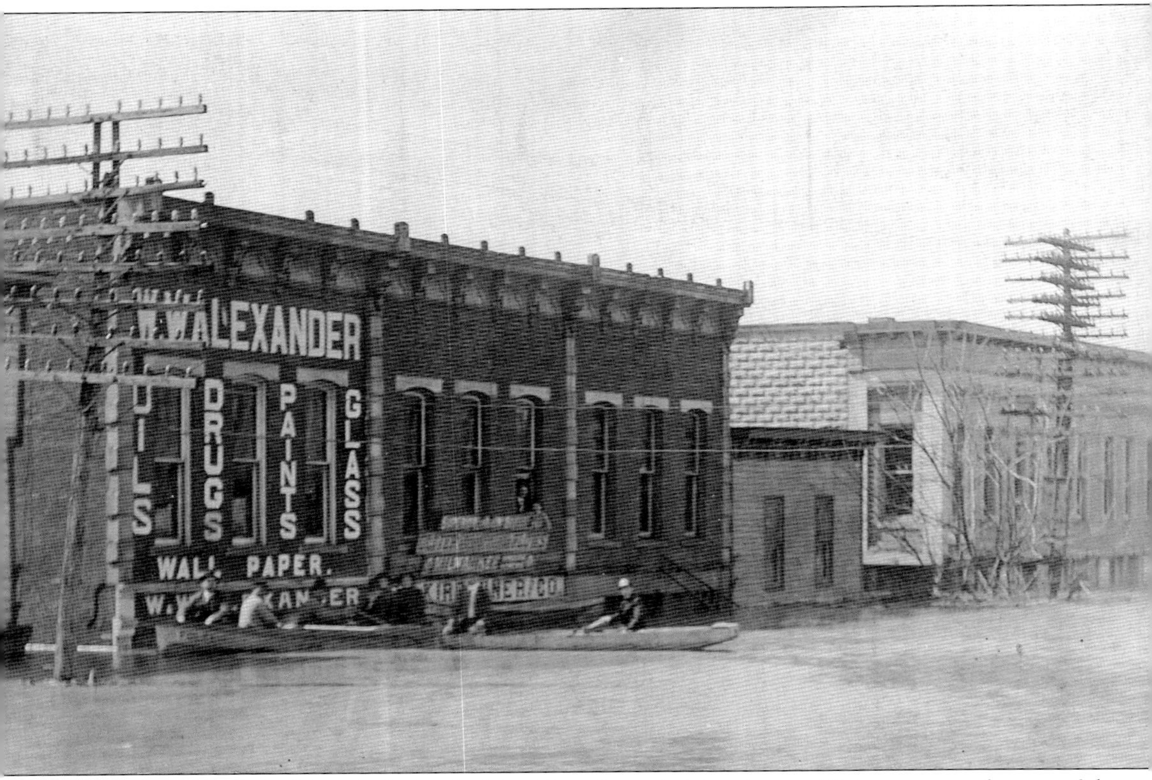

The floodwaters of the 1913 flood of the Ohio River in Manchester, Ohio, are near the top of the first-story buildings along Main Street. Small flatboats were the means of travel above the streets below. Alexander Drugs is on the left, and F.Y. Kirshner Company is to the right of the drugstore. Kirshner sold Oliver plows and farm machinery.

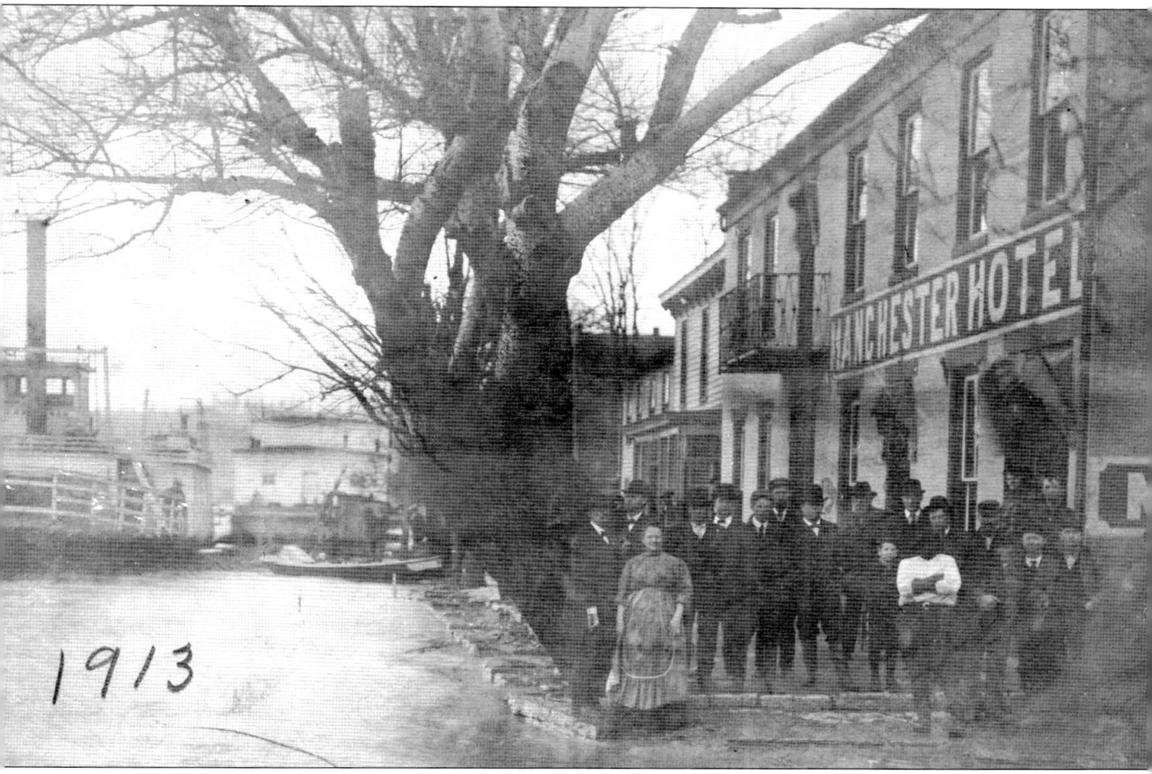

During the flood of 1913 in Manchester, Ohio, the wharf boat and ferry were docked and tied off in front of the Manchester Hotel on Front Street. The hotel was owned and operated by J.W. Lightbody. Lightbody also owned another hotel at another location in Manchester, and it was named the Lightbody Hotel, which was the oldest on the Ohio River. One man, John Dade, lost his life in a 1910 fire at the Lightbody Hotel.

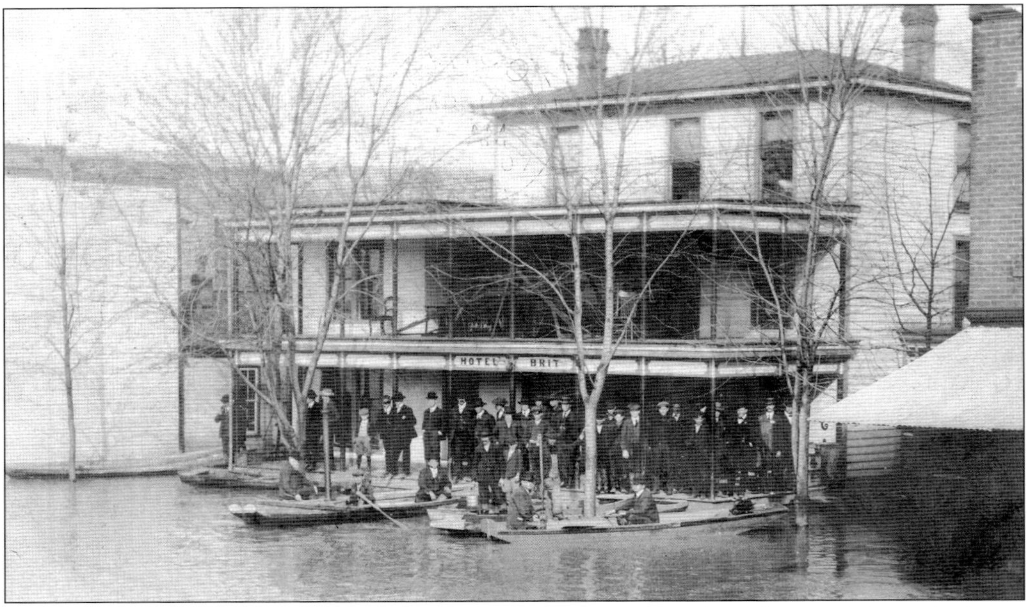

During the flood of 1907, the menfolk gathered on the front porch of the Hotel Brit, which was located on the north side of Main Street in Manchester, Ohio. Five flatboats are on standby to provide transportation. This hotel was later named the Hester Hotel. This photograph was dated April 7, 1907.

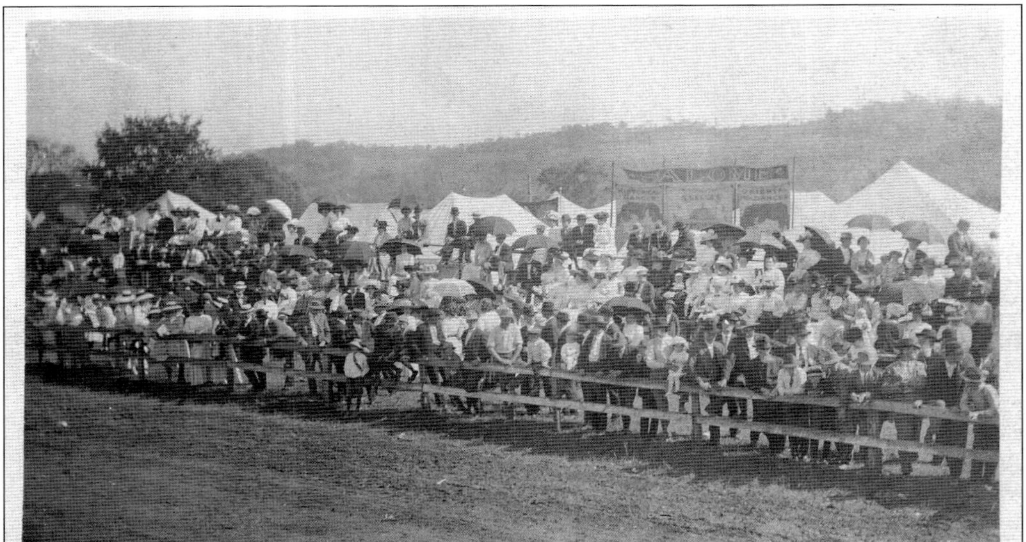

This crowd is gathered at the racetrack of the Manchester Fair, which was held on the west end of town on Route 52. In this photograph, there is no covered grandstand, so many of the men are holding umbrellas over the ladies to shield them from the summer sun. This photograph was taken in the summer of 1910 but not mailed until January 11, 1911.

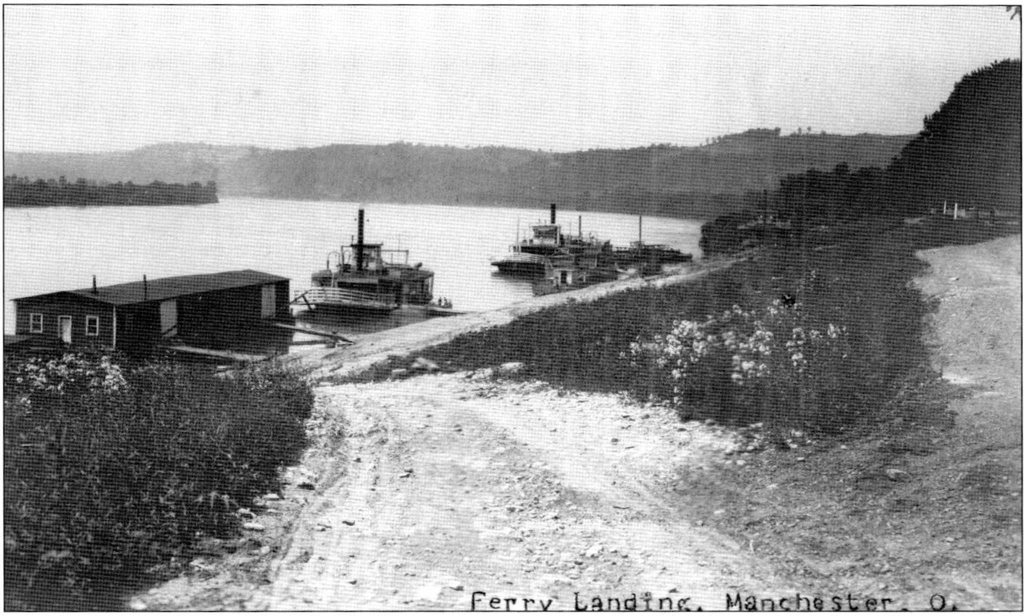

This shows a typical wharf scene in Manchester, Ohio, with a wharf boat and two ferryboats secured to the banks of the Ohio River. Steamboats unloaded cargo or passengers through wharf boats docked at the shoreline, while the ferries would go back and forth across the river. The first ferry in this photograph has the name *W.H. Whiteman* on the bow.

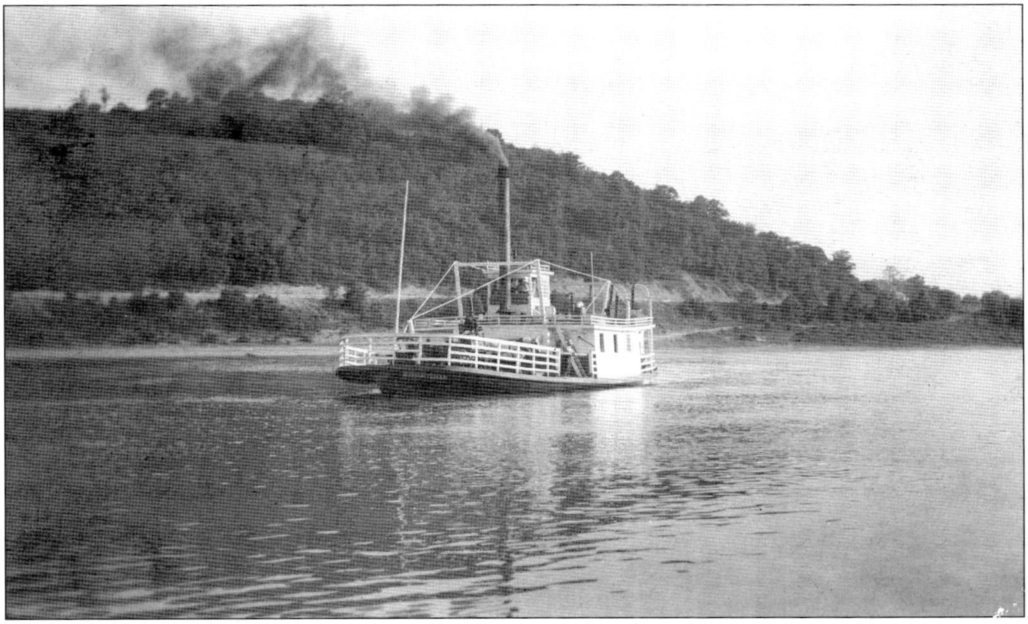

The ferryboat at Manchester, Ohio, crossed the Ohio River just west of the Manchester islands and took people to the community of Trinity, Kentucky, in Lewis County. Many people from this rural Kentucky side would come to Manchester to do their shopping. The name on the bow of the ferry is *W.H. Whiteman*, and his passenger on this trip is a farmer with his horse and wagon.

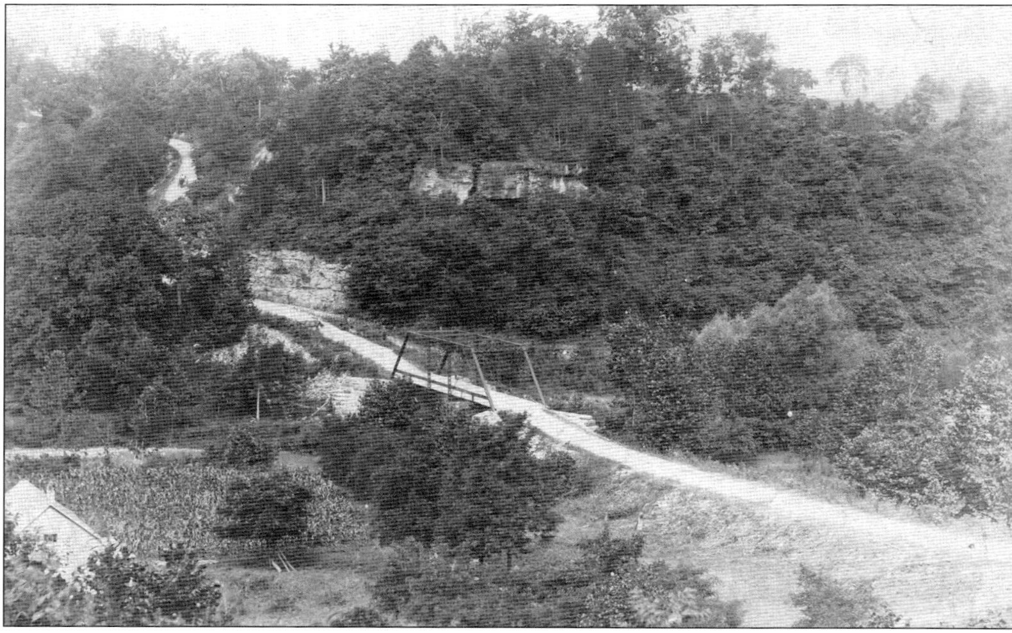

This photograph was taken in Adams County along Brush Creek, located east of West Union, Ohio. Brush Creek Township is one of 15 townships in Adams County and is very rural. Brush Creek itself starts near Belfast in Highland County and runs south to the Ohio River about four miles west of Rome, Ohio, for about 60 miles. It remains today a great river for fishing and kayaking.

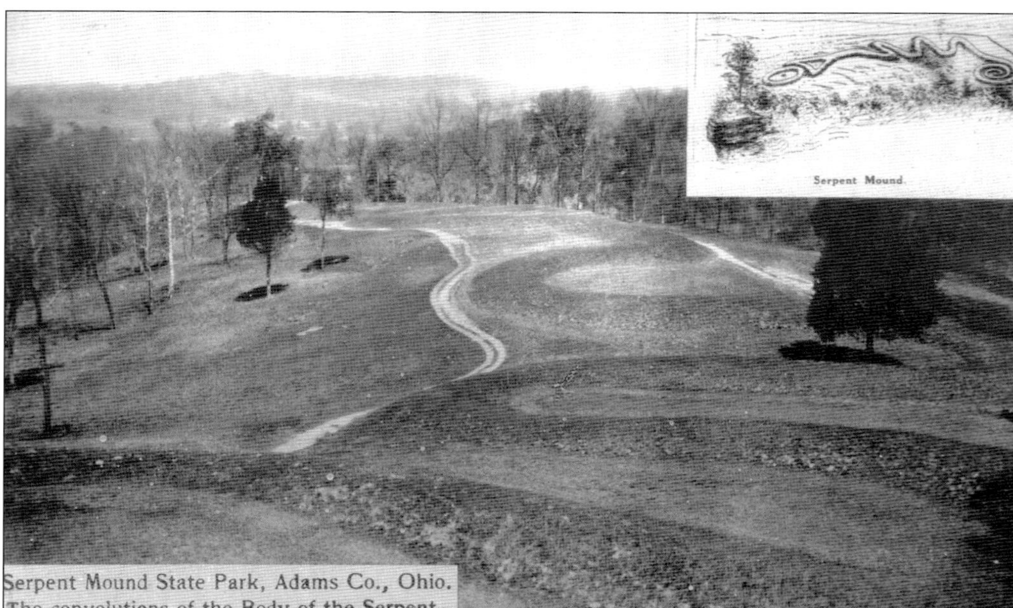

Serpent Mound State Park is located north of Peeples, Ohio, off Highway 73 and near Brush Creek in Adams County. The mound is 1,376 feet long and varies in height from nine inches to three feet. This site was designated as a national historic landmark in 1966, and in 1967, the Serpent Mound Museum was opened near the site where exhibits can be studied.

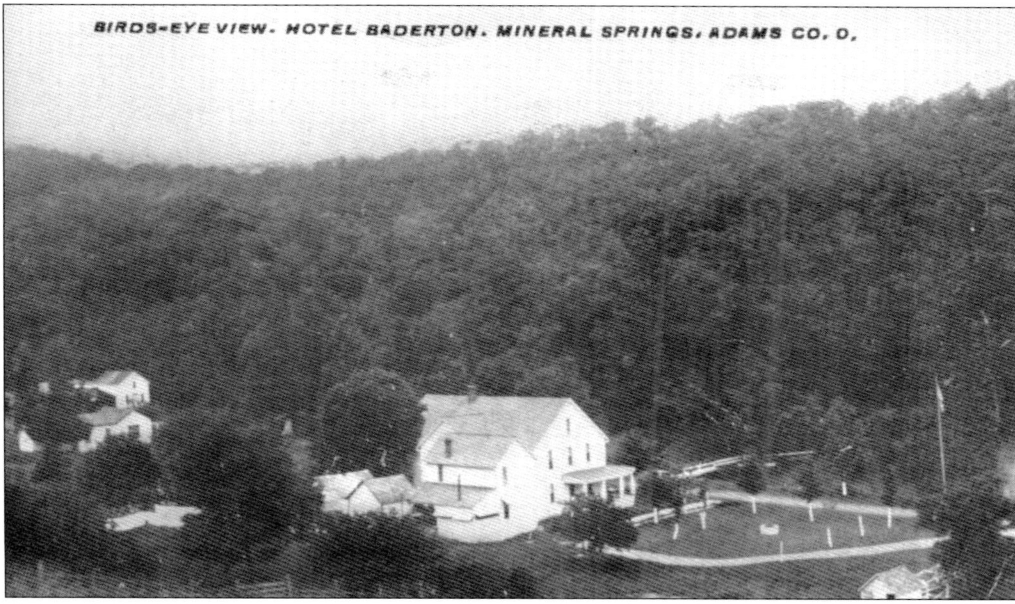

Dated August 26, 1913, this photograph was taken from the hills above the Hotel Baderton at Mineral Springs, Ohio. In 1864, the first hotel was called Sodaville and built where springs flowed from Peach Mountain. The property changed hands many times, but at the time of this photograph, it was owned by the Bader family, who later sold the hotel in 1916. Only a historical marker is left there today.

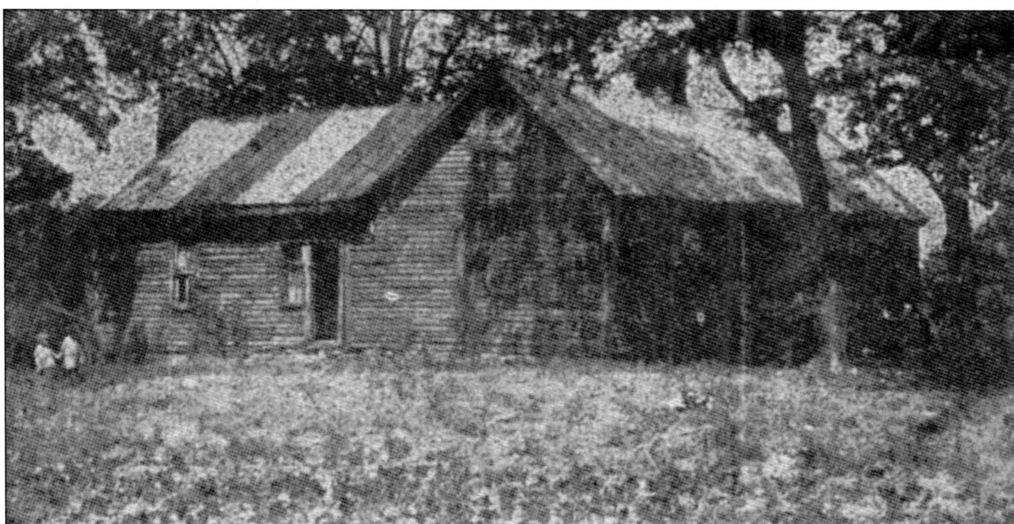

The description on the back of this postcard says, "Buckeye Station was named by General Nathaniel Massie when he built a log cabin at this point in 1791. In the summer of 1797, he erected at this spot a frame house, which still stands today in a fair state of preservation." Buckeye Station is located on a high bluff about four miles east of Manchester on Route 52. The structure is no longer standing.

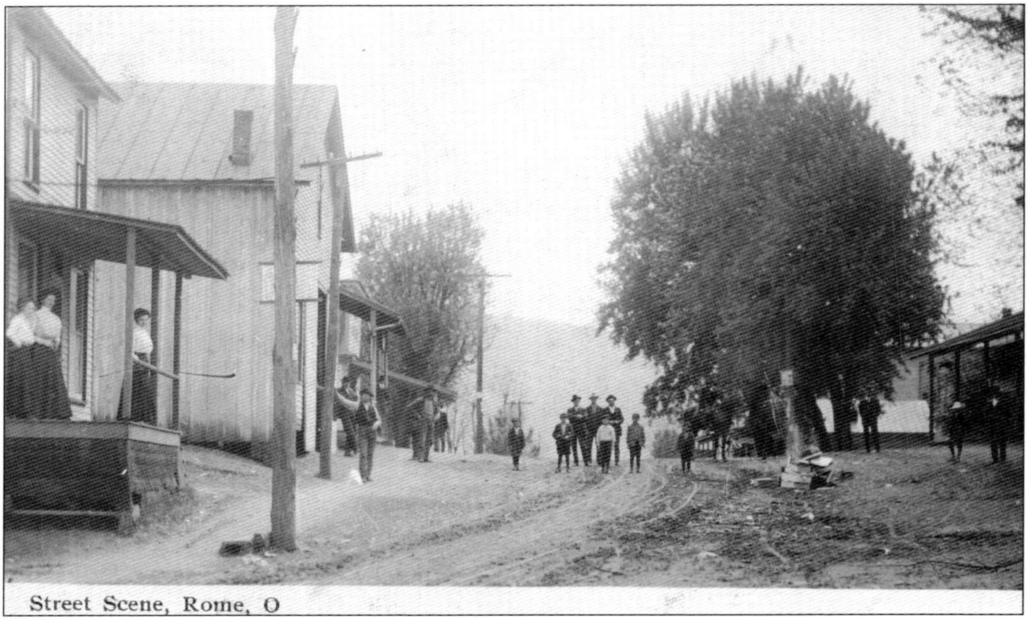

Dated September 20, 1910, this street scene is of Rome, Ohio, in Green Township on the eastern edge of Adams County. The sender of the postcard is Cynthia Montutto, presumably a seamstress, and she says this photograph shows her store on the left, with her and her two trimmers, from the previous year, standing on the porch. The card was sent to Grange City, Kentucky.

Great Transdenominational Revival
With The Donaldson Bros. of Texas
August 16-27 - 7:30 Nightly
Burning Heart Campgrounds, Bentonville, Ohio
– FEATURING –
Recording Stars "MONTANA SLIM" and DONNA LAURENCE
Spectacular Chalk Drawings - Don & David Donaldson
Bible Centered Preaching with Evangelist Bud Donaldson
EVERYONE WELCOME

This postal advertisement card was mailed to people in the community around Bentonville, Ohio, in Adams County. Montana Slim was born Wilfred Arthur Charles Carter in Canada in 1904. He was known as "Wilf" in Canada, but was also known as "the yodeling cowboy." He wrote over 500 songs, and he is in the Nashville Songwriters Hall of Fame, while Donna Laurence and her husband, Gary, were gospel singers.

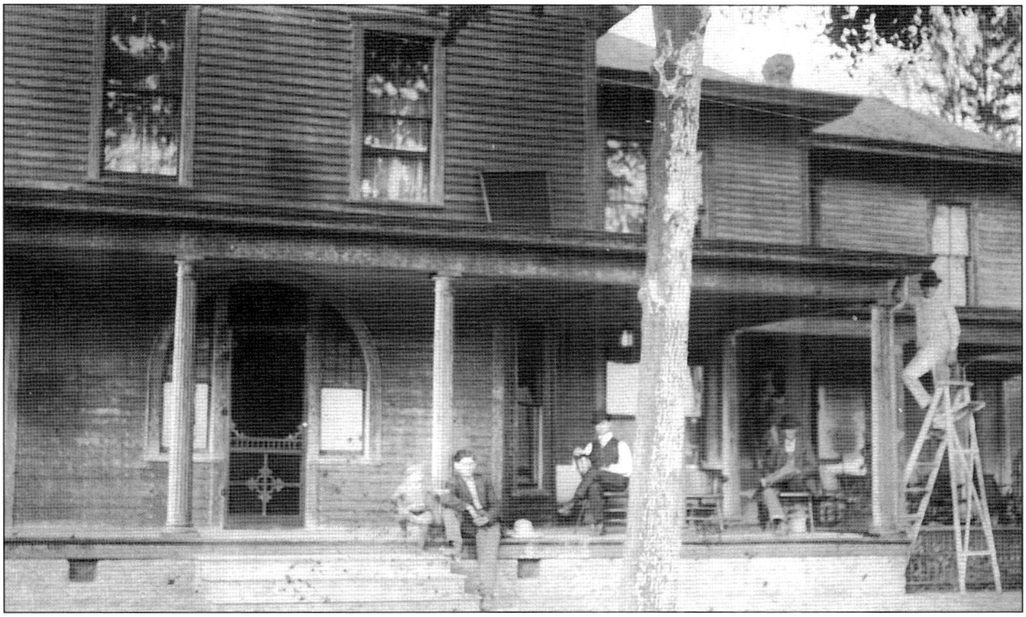

A worker repairs the porch roof while others look on as this photograph was taken of the Spargur House Hotel in Seaman, Ohio, where Frank G. Young was the proprietor. A note on the back says this photograph was taken after the Seaman fire of 1910, and a heading on another advertising card says this hotel is "Good as any, Better'n Some."

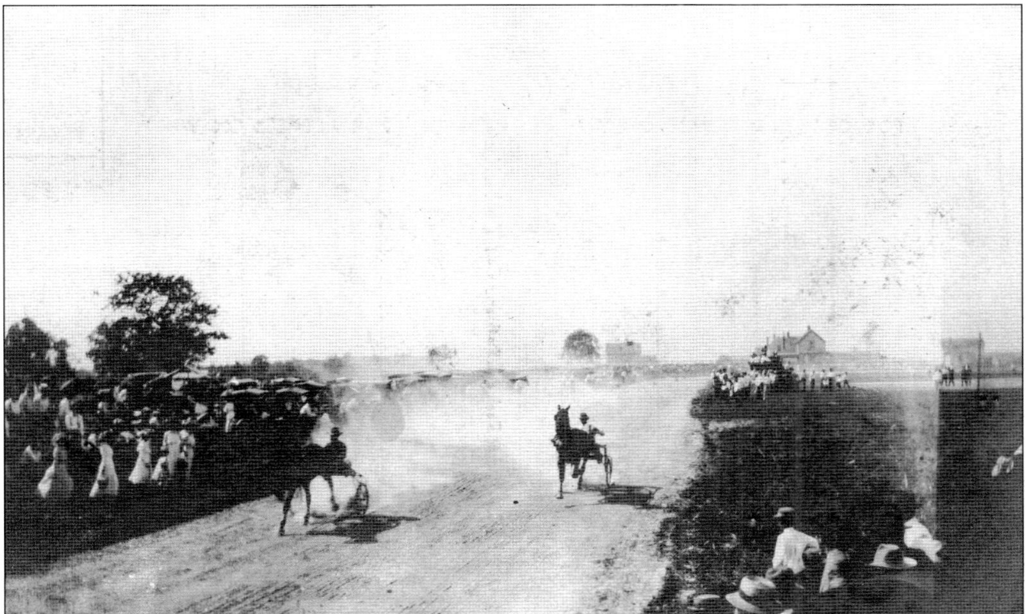

People line both sides of the racetrack to watch Weber Girl and Lady Rags compete in a sulky race at the Seaman Race Track in Seaman, Ohio, located in Scott Township in the northern part of Adams County. The Seaman Fall Festivals have been going on for over 100 years, and the townsfolk are still competing in events that include horses.

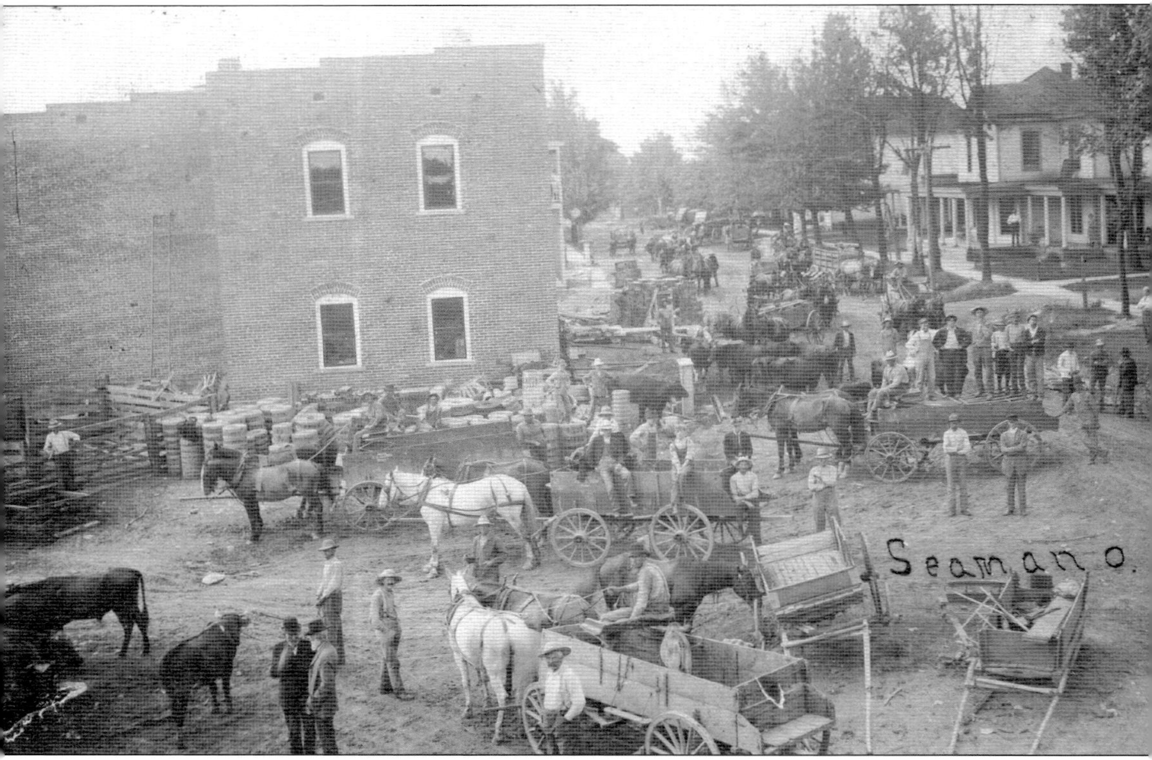

It appears that the people in this photograph in Seaman, Ohio, knew the photographer up above was preparing to take this picture. The note on the back of the card says this is stock sale day. Some of the wagons carry livestock, and a few have wood slats over the wagon beds to keep the small livestock from jumping out.

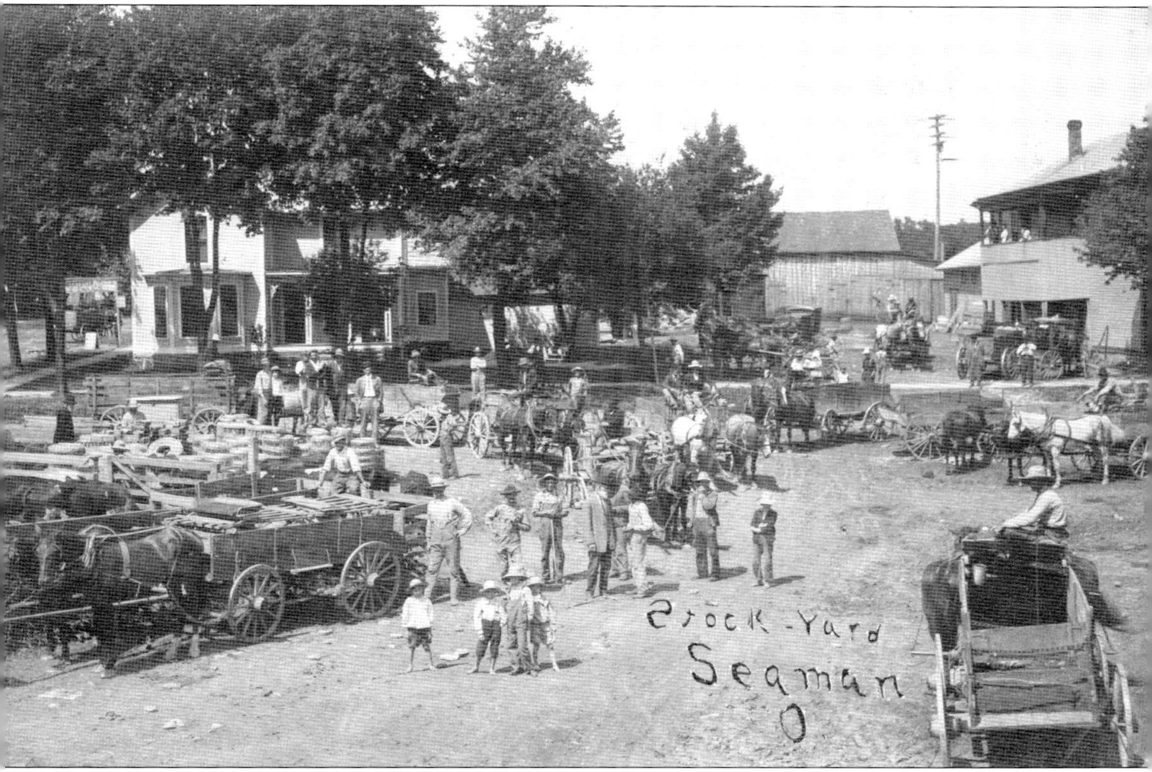

In this photograph, wagons are lined up to get into the stockyards. In both this photograph and the previous one, cubes of concrete block and rolls of fence wire for sale are stacked up near the entrance. This side view of the white house includes a sign on the left showing that it is the entrance to Wickerham Drugs.

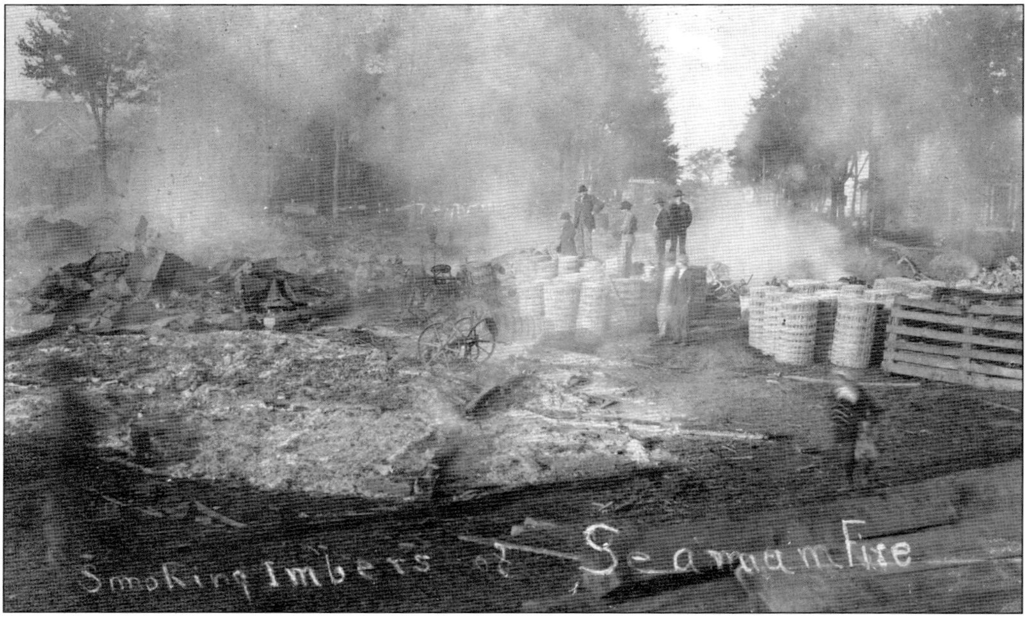

These two photographs were taken after the fire that destroyed many structures in the town of Seaman, Ohio, on October 10, 1910. The fire started at the W.H. McCreight's livery from a discarded cigarette butt and spread quickly to the surrounding framed buildings. In the spring of 1911, people started to rebuild this area using brick building methods and called the area "Merchants Row." Two more notable fires would occur in Seaman: on May 14, 1921, destroying the King Brothers' Lumber Company, and on October 10, 1926, destroying the J.H. Plummer livery barn. Up until 1931, the bucket brigade was the only means to fight fires, but in that same year, the town bought its own REO fire truck; established its own fire department; and had its own fire chief, R.R. Powell, along with other firefighters.

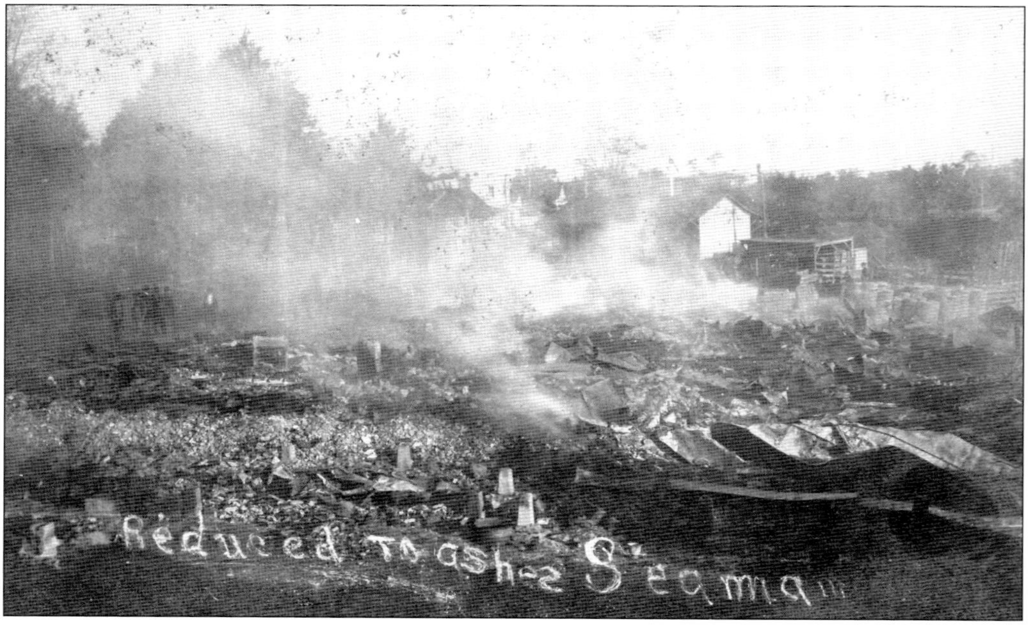

Eight

Brown County, Ohio

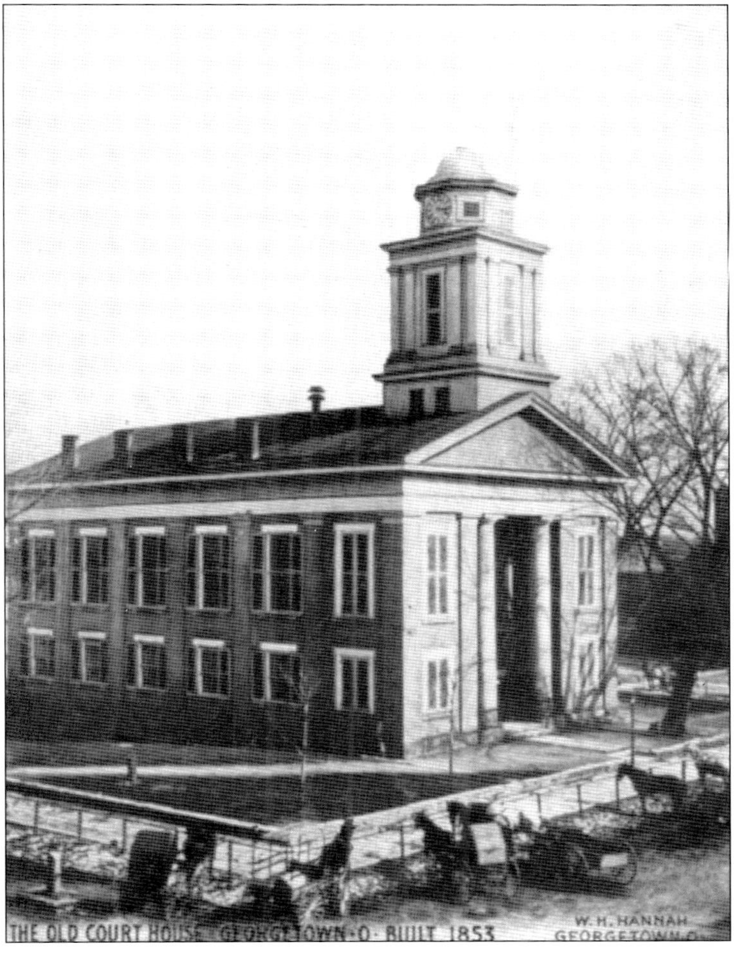

Originally the county seat for Brown County, Ohio was in Ripley, but it was later moved to the town square shown here in Georgetown, Ohio, where construction on the courthouse began in 1849. Court business was first held at this location in the early 1850s, and although a fire destroyed much of the building in 1977, Brown County decided to restore this beautiful historic structure. This postcard came from the family of Mary Nue.

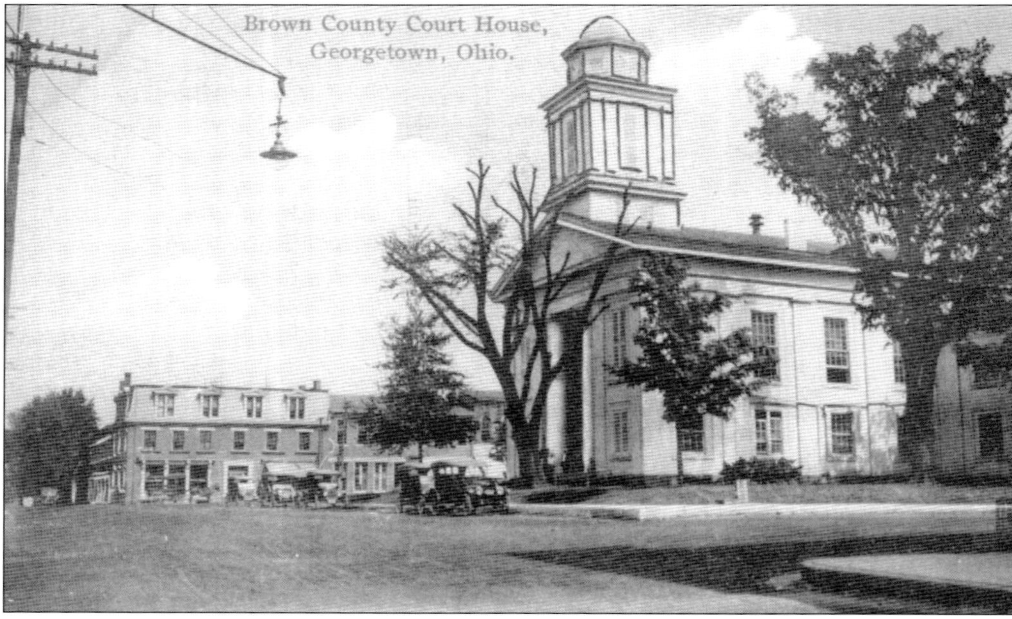

Showing the town square at Georgetown, Ohio, this early-1900s postcard of the Brown County Courthouse was taken by a photographer working for Kraemer Art in Cincinnati, Ohio, and reveals a different view of the courthouse. The wings were added on the sides of the original Greek Revival structure in 1914, so this would have been shortly after the additions.

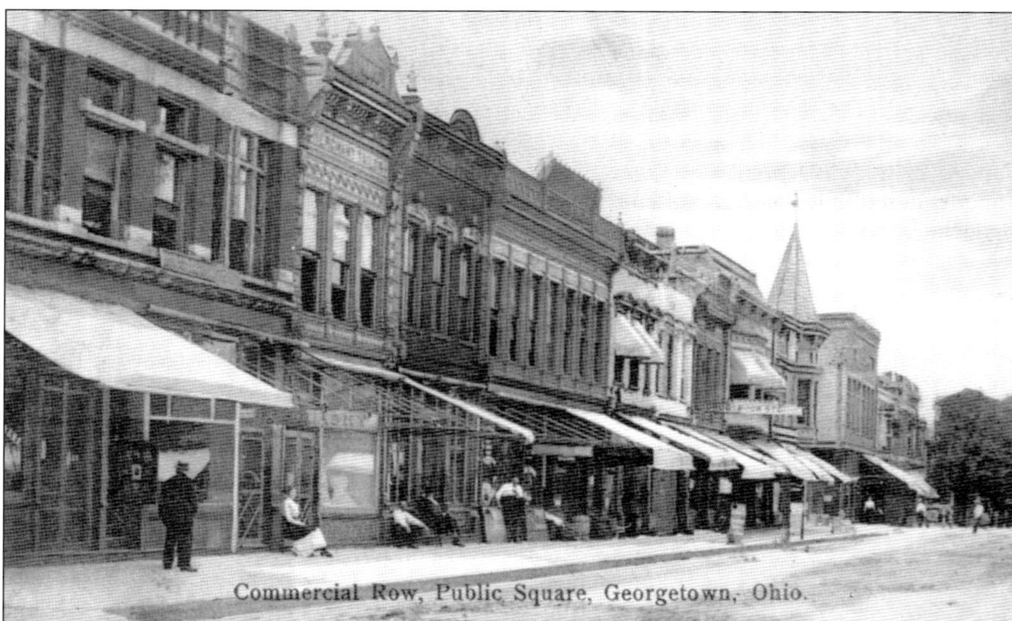

This picture of the early business district area of Georgetown across from the courthouse is dated November 16, 1916. Some of the businesses include a bank, a clothing store, and a combined drug and book store. The card number for this color photograph is 5169, and it was published by Kraemer Art in Cincinnati, Ohio.

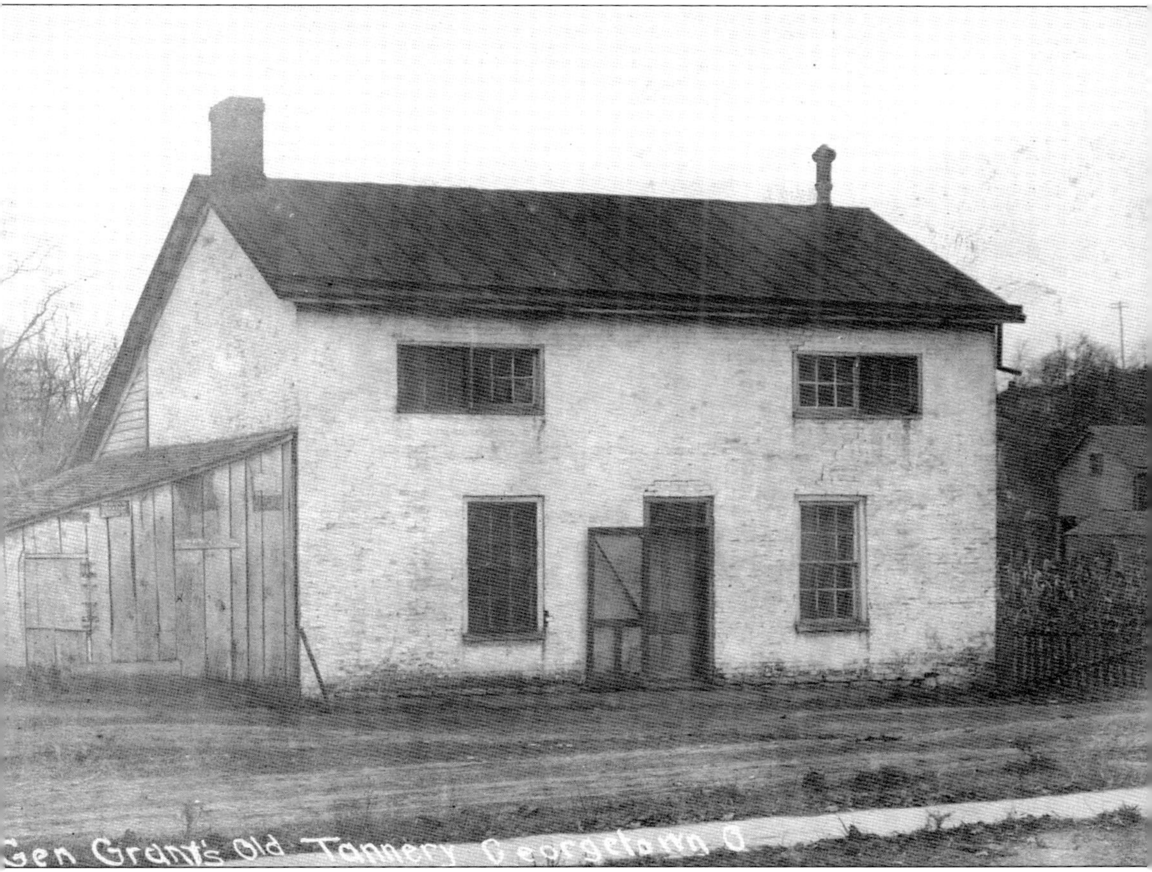

This photograph says, "General Grant's Old Tannery, Georgetown, O," but the tannery was founded by Grant's father, Jesse Grant. The father learned the trade well and had numerous tanneries in multiple states. It is often reported that Ulysses Grant disliked the tannery profession so much, he would do just about anything to get out of working there.

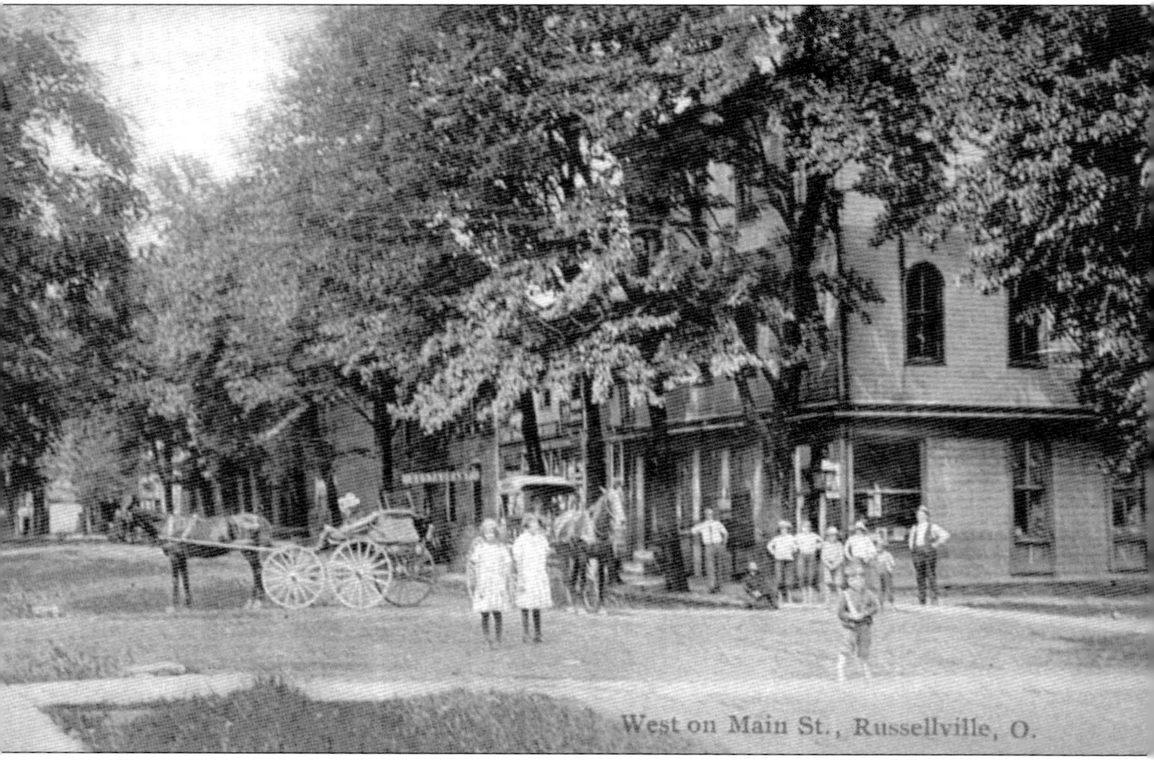

A few miles east of Georgetown on Highway 62 is the town of Russellville, Ohio, named after Russell Shaw. The town was laid out and established in 1817, and this is a view of the heart of the town on Main Street. The town was home to the W.L. Johnson Carriage Factory, built in 1850, and had a public school, Phoenix Flour Mill, and Knights of Pythias Hall.

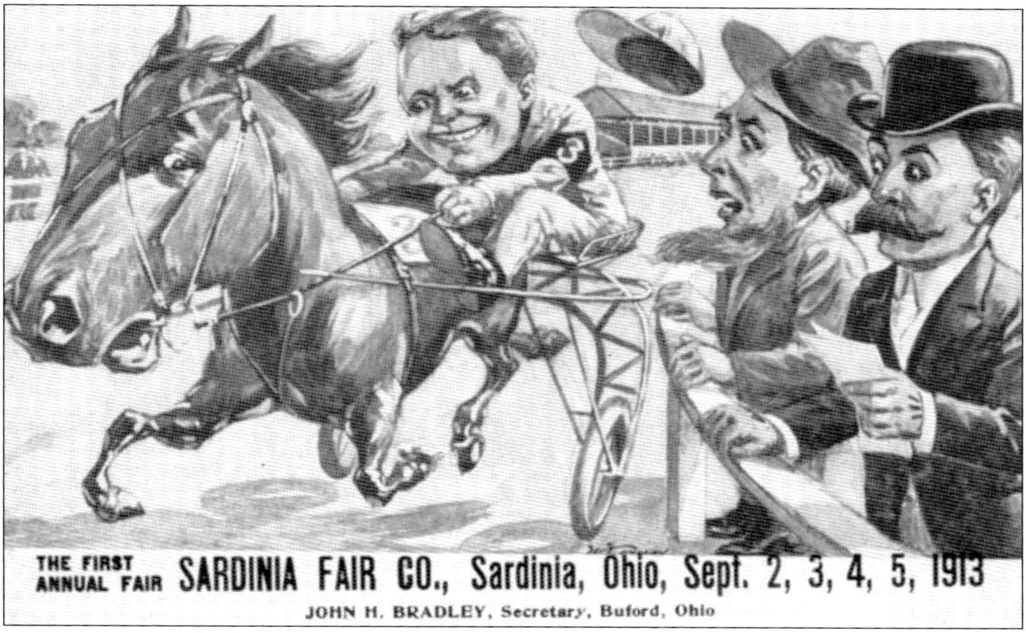

George A. Kennedy donated the land, built the fairgrounds, and held the fair in Sardinia, Ohio, from 1900 to 1911, where people came from Cincinnati, Portsmouth, and Columbus, Ohio. This Sardinia Fair Company advertisement card is promoting the first fair to be held in Sardinia by this company. The original fairground's location is marked by one of two stone gateposts today with George Kennedy's name.

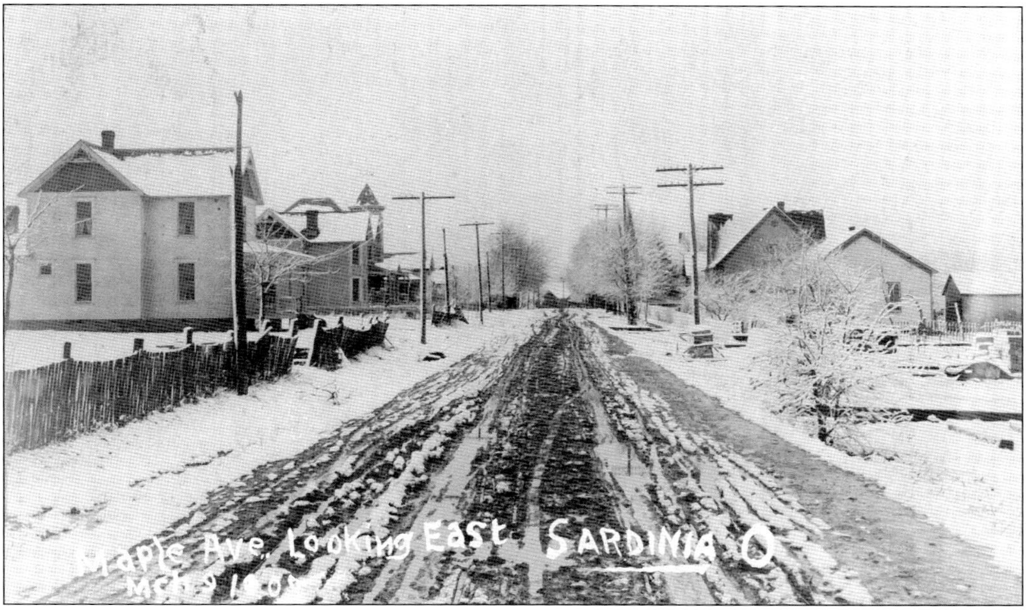

After the early March snow in 1908, the dirt street on Maple Avenue in Sardinia, Ohio, became a slippery place for the narrow tires of the automobiles of the day. Sardinia is located about 44 miles east of Cincinnati, Ohio, on US 32 in Brown County and Highland County. It was named after the Mediterranean island, Sardinia.

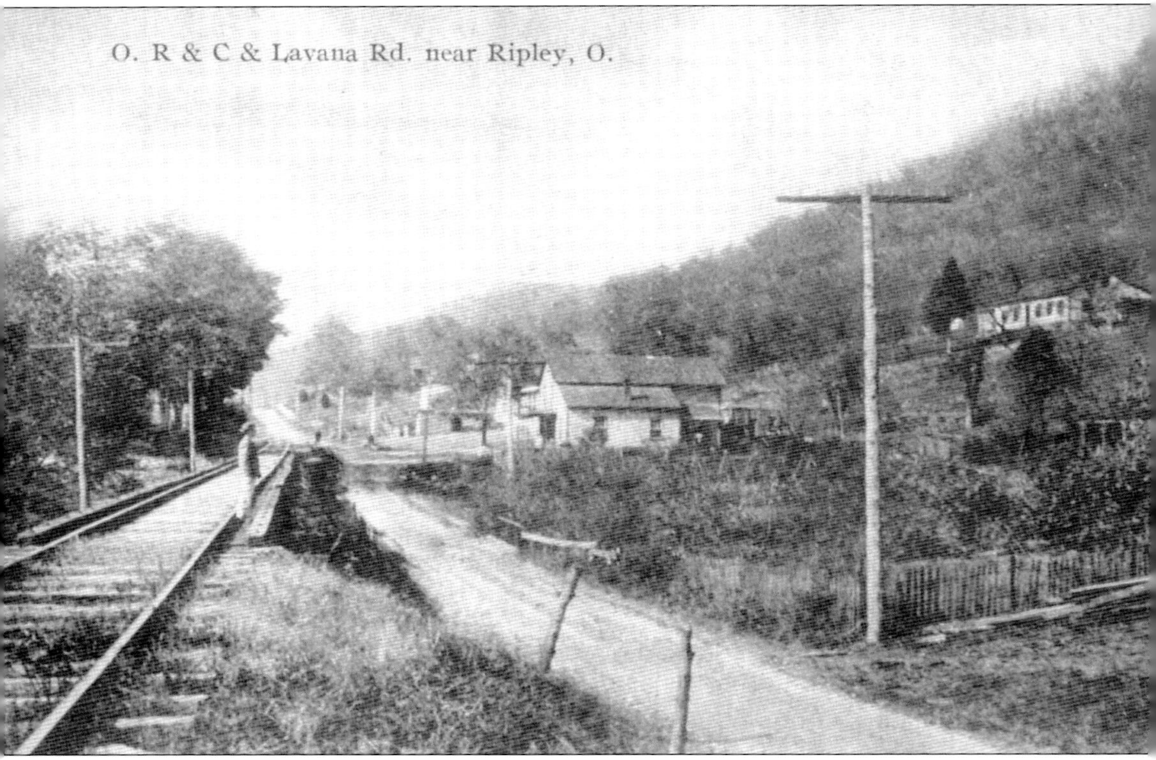

The Ohio River & Charleston Railway (OR&C) ran along highway Route 52 in Levanna, Ohio, a small town settled by John Liggett in 1799, just west of Ripley. At one time, the Ohio Valley & Columbus Railway had a train station there, but it went out of business prior to the 1920s. The building on the hill was a one-room school, Union Township No. 10.

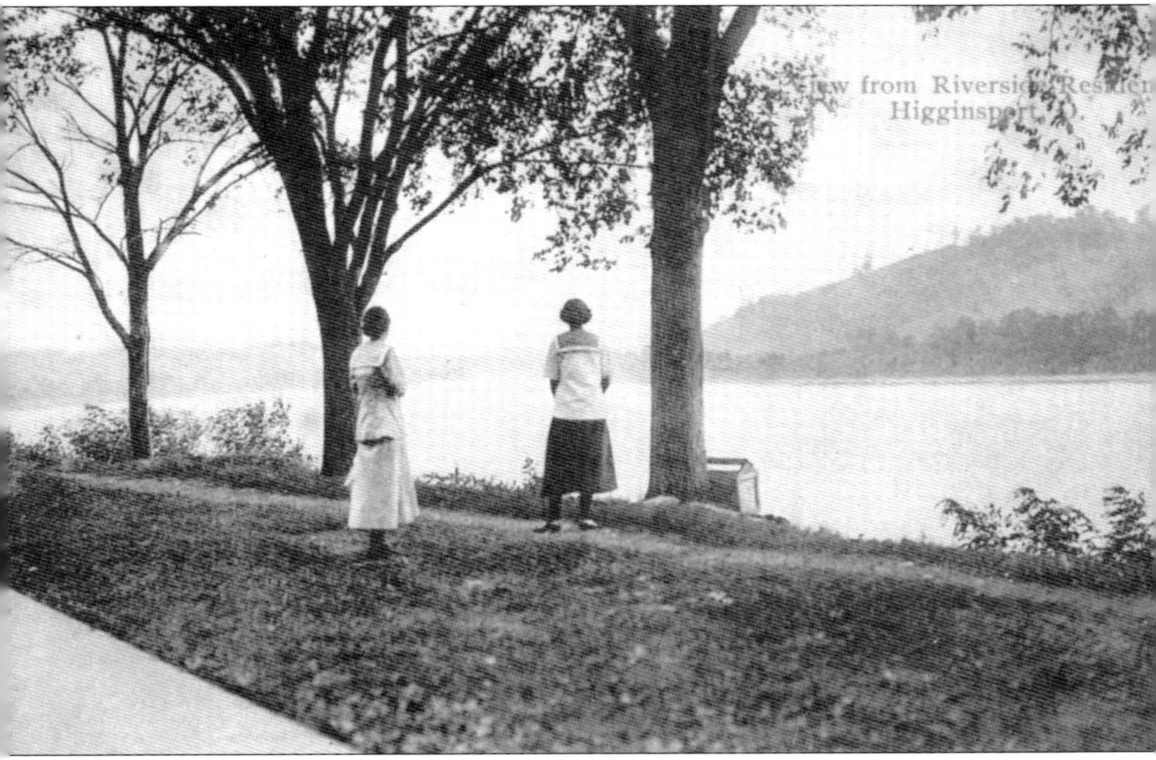

These ladies enjoy the peaceful view along the banks of the Ohio River at Higginsport, Ohio, while looking east upriver towards Ripley and Maysville. Robert and Mary Higgins founded Higginsport in 1816 with 114 plats. Homes along Front Streets in these small towns were blessed with an extraordinary view of the Kentucky hills and the passing steamboats that traveled all along the Ohio.

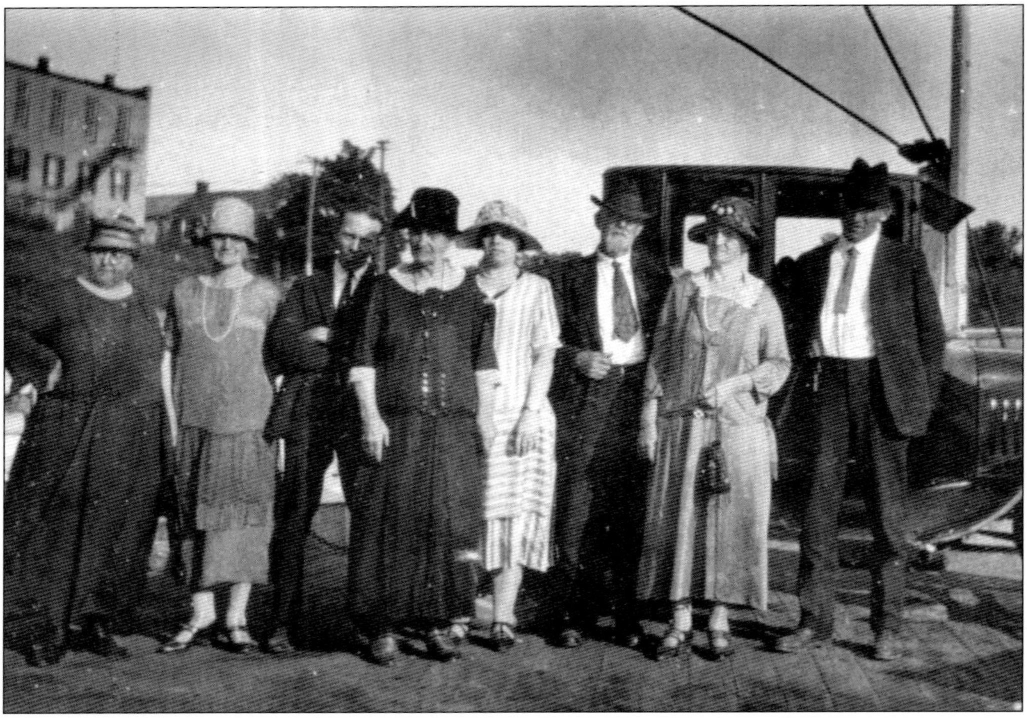

A group of people board the *Proctor K. Smiley* ferry at Ripley, Ohio, near the foot of Main Street, where the local wharf boat was docked. They crossed the Ohio River at this location to enter Route 8 on the Kentucky side. The Model T business coupe behind them dates this photograph to around the mid-1920s.

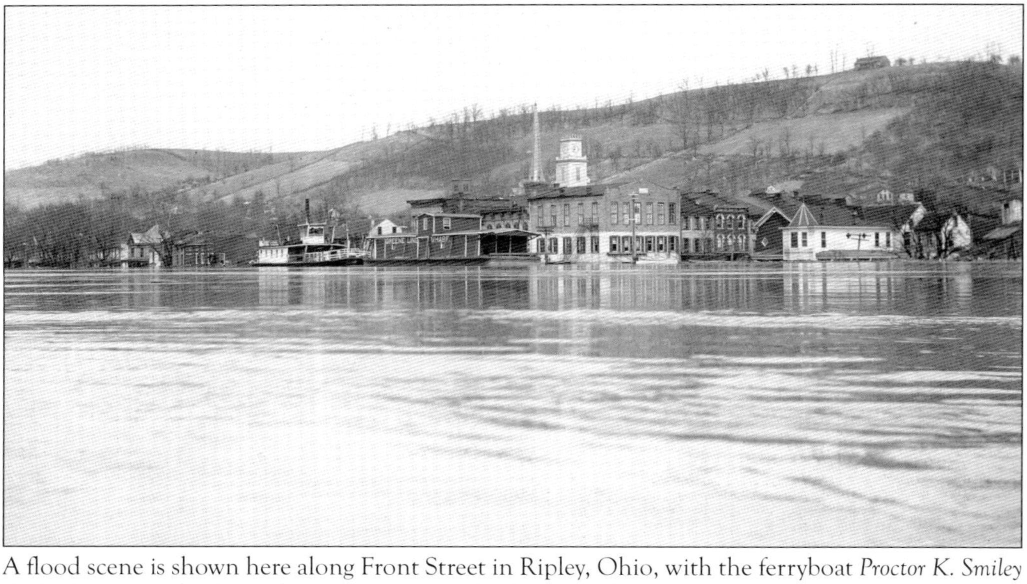

A flood scene is shown here along Front Street in Ripley, Ohio, with the ferryboat *Proctor K. Smiley* docked next to the Greenline wharf boat. The John Rankin home is clearly seen on top of the hill above Ripley, from where Rankin sent signals to enslaved people in South Ripley, Kentucky, letting them know that it was safe to cross the Ohio River to freedom.

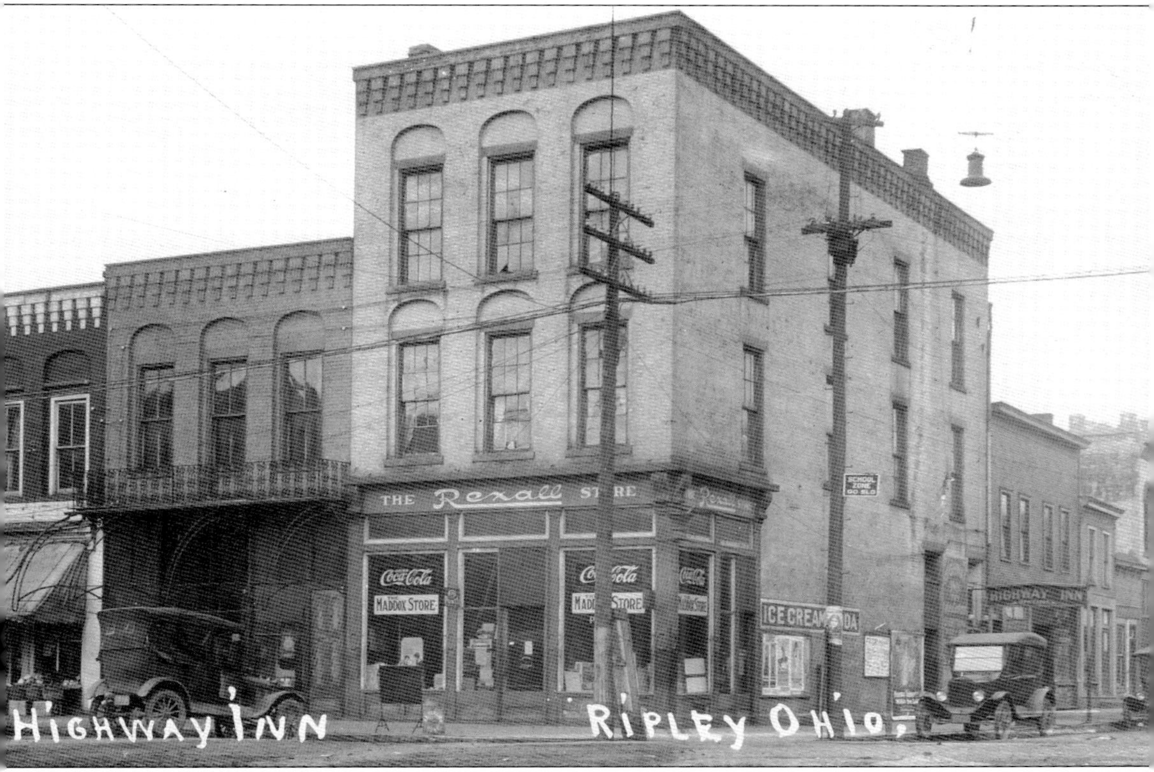

This view of the Maddox Drug Store was taken from Route 52 looking west across Main Street in Ripley, Ohio. According to the sign near the entrance door, patrons could get their medicines, ice-cream sodas, and even house paint here. The Highway Inn Hotel was located on the upper floor of the shorter building just behind the drugstore, facing Route 52. Notice the sign that says, "SCHOOL ZONE GO SLO."

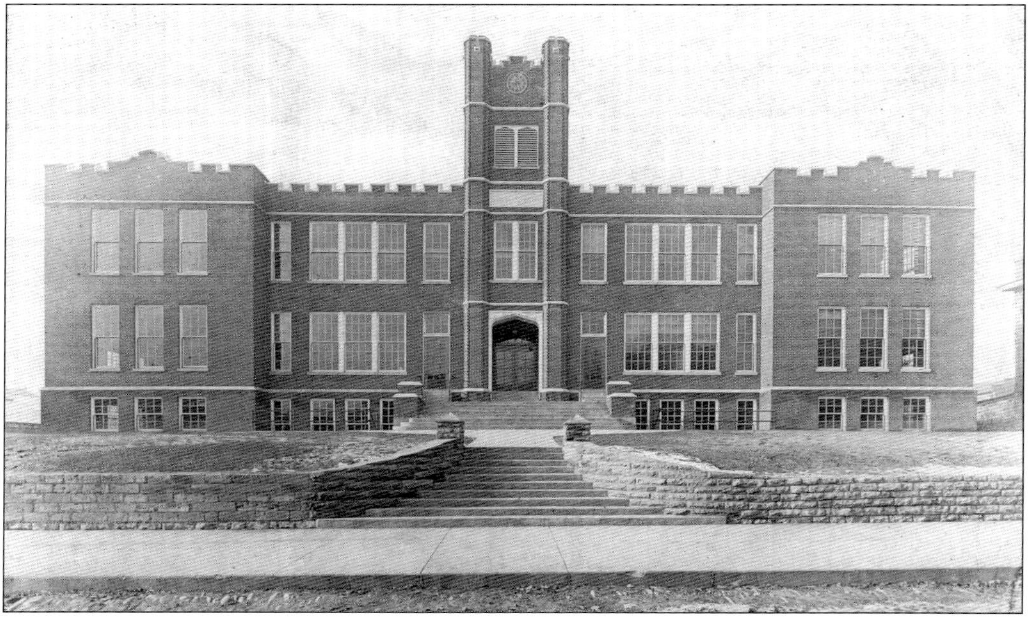

This Union Public School photograph dates to 1916 at Ripley, Ohio, where it was originally an elementary school and later became a high school. Former students at the elementary school said that when the weather was good, the children played in the front yard of the school, and balls often rolled into nearby Second Street. If the weather was bad, they had recess in the basement of the school.

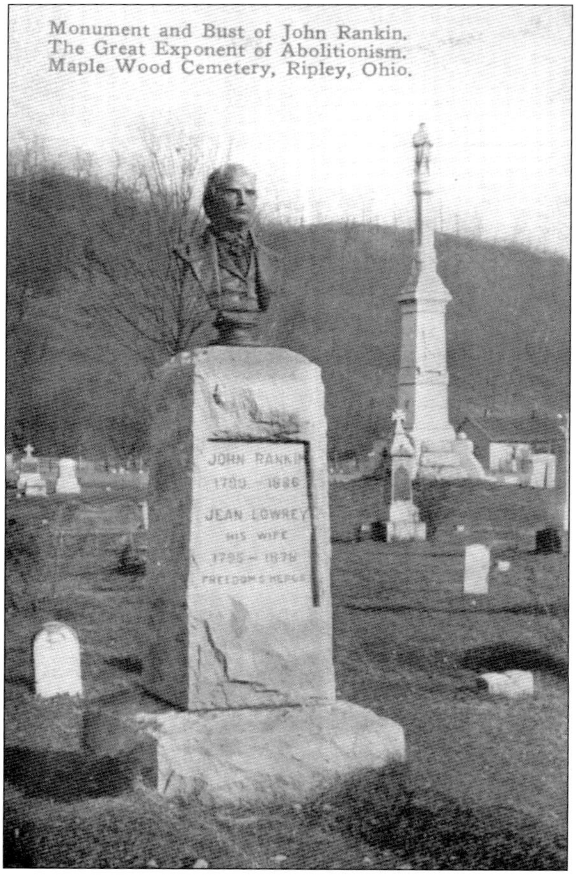

Monument and Bust of John Rankin.
The Great Exponent of Abolitionism.
Maple Wood Cemetery, Ripley, Ohio.

John Rankin was born in Dandridge, Tennessee, on February 5, 1793, and died on March 18, 1886, in Ironton, Ohio. He is buried at Maplewood Cemetery in Ripley, Ohio, where this monument is located. Eliza was a slave who crossed the thin ice of the Ohio River with her two-year-old child near Ripley, Ohio. After hearing of this story Harriet Beecher Stowe referenced her in her book *Uncle Tom's Cabin*. Eliza then met and married a slave by the name of George Harris in Ohio. The two of them went on to help abolitionist John Rankin free as many as 2,000 slaves. Rankin was an Ohio Presbyterian minister and author.

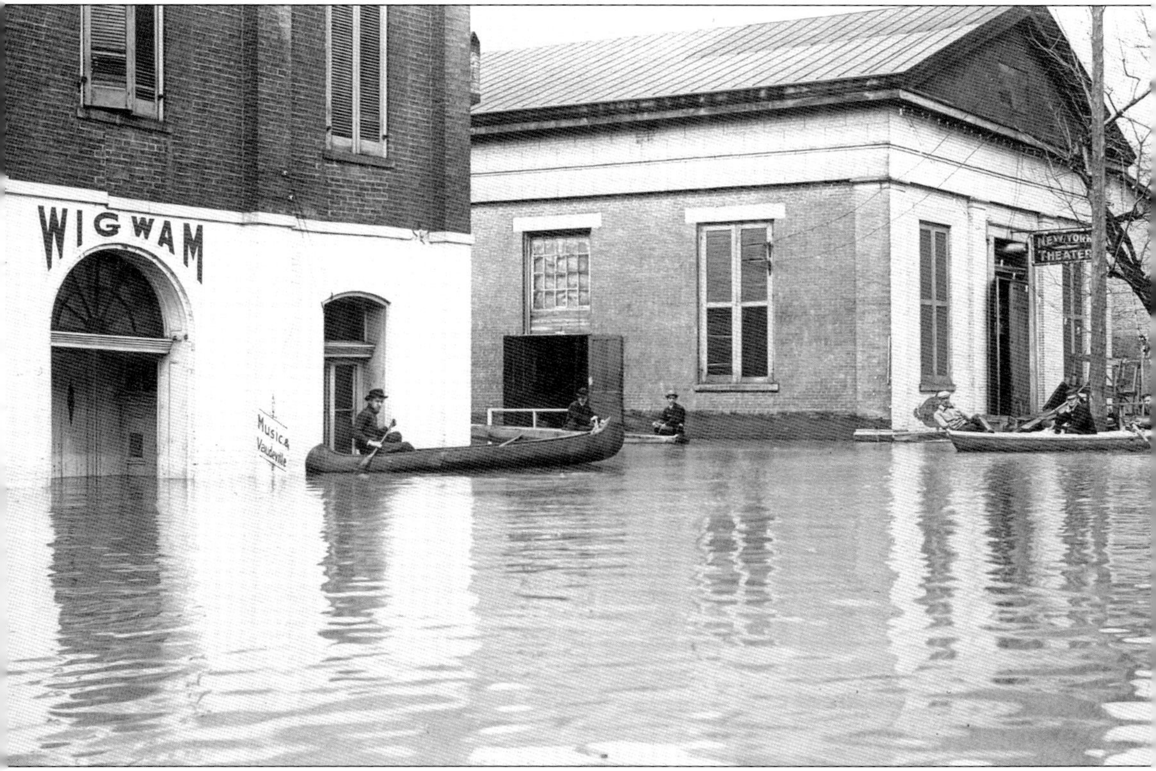

This photograph shows the flood of 1913 on Route 52/Second Street at the corner of Market Street in Ripley, Ohio. The Wigwam Lodge is shown on the left, and the New York Theatre on the right was for silent movies and vaudeville shows in the early 1900s. Originally, the theater was built as a church, but in 1915, it became the Gayety Theatre and remained open until the early 1930s.

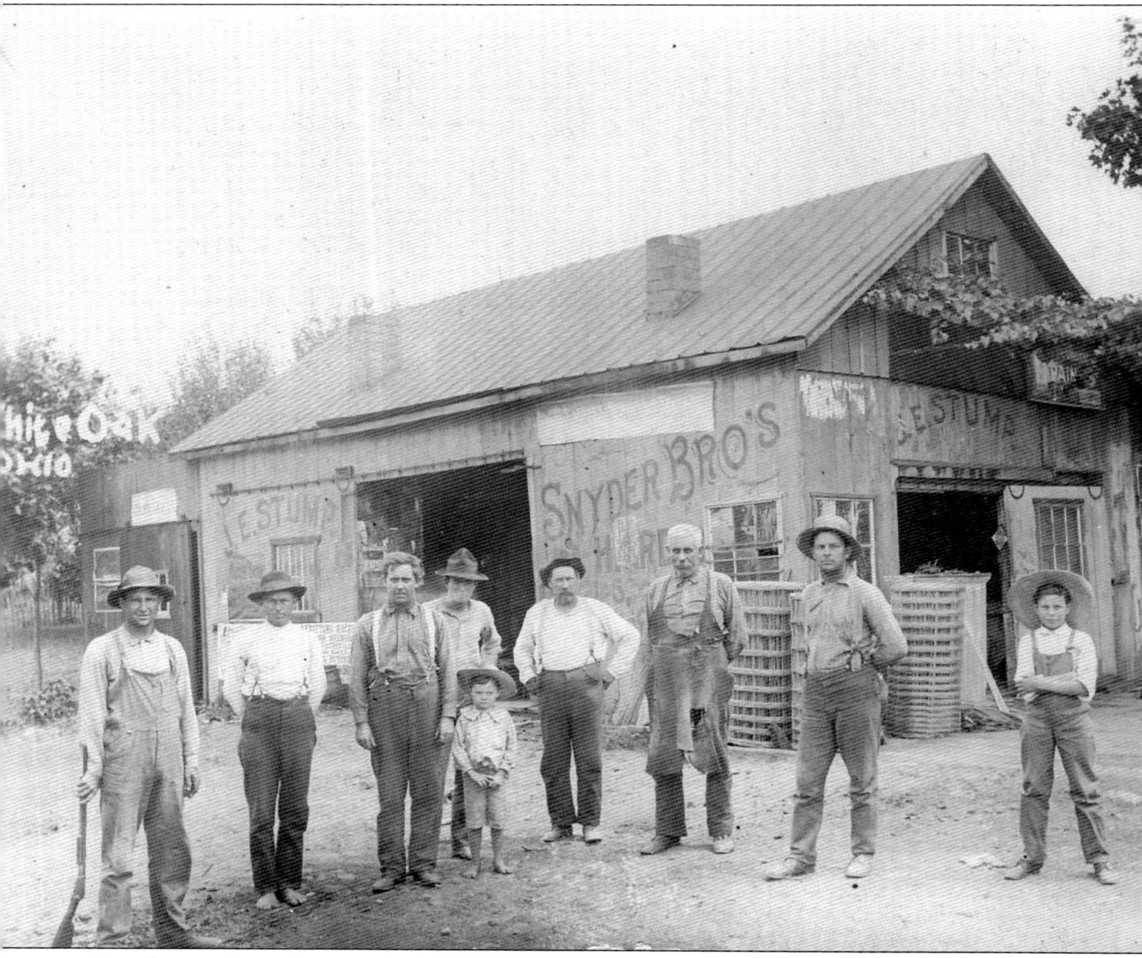

Locals pose for a photograph in front of Snyder Brother's Hardware, located in White Oak, Ohio, near the north fork of White Oak Creek. White Oak is about two and a half miles east of Mount Orab, Ohio, in Brown County. In this rural community, the hardware store was run out of a local farm barn, supplying the whole community.

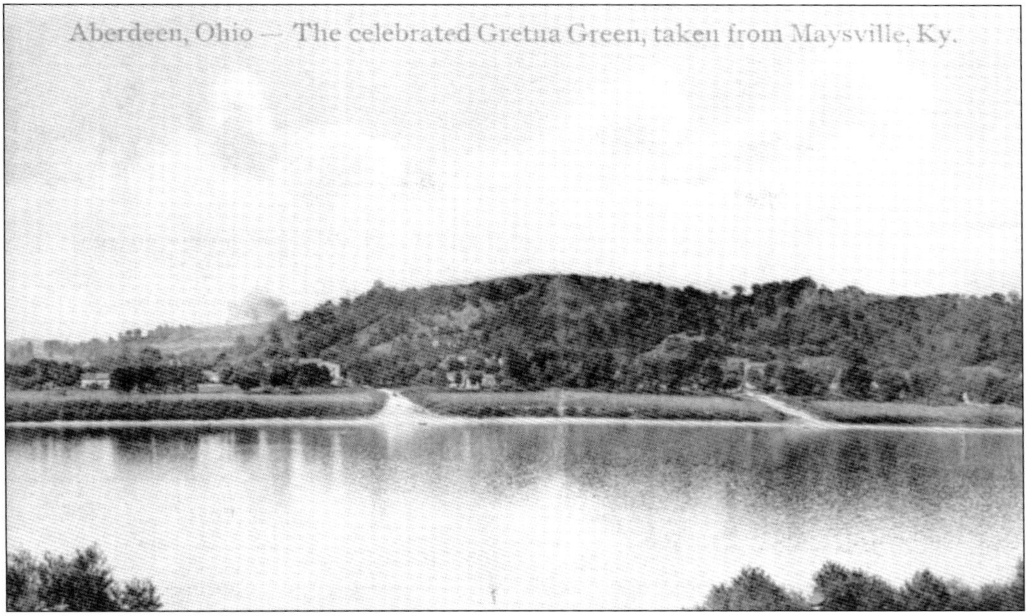

This photograph of Aberdeen, Ohio, was taken from Maysville, Kentucky. The "celebrated Gretna Green" refers to a local service like the Gretna Green in Scotland, a place known to date back to 1754, where young couples underage and in love could get married without permission from their parents. Couples traveled on steamboats up and down the river to the wharf in Maysville and ferried across the Ohio to take their vows.

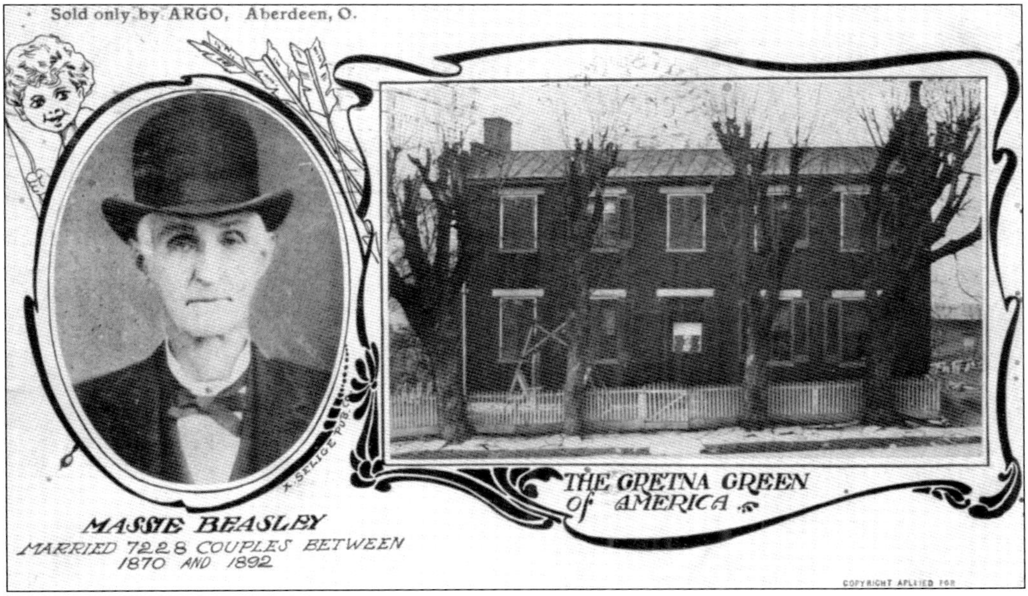

The justice of the peace for Huntington Township in Aberdeen, Ohio, was Massie Beasley, who held that position for 54 years and is thought to have married as many as 20,000 couples. Beasley was married to Jane Cropper in 1832, and they had nine children. His father was a surveyor and helped found the town of Manchester, Ohio, about 10 miles upriver. This card was published by Adolph Selige, St. Louis.

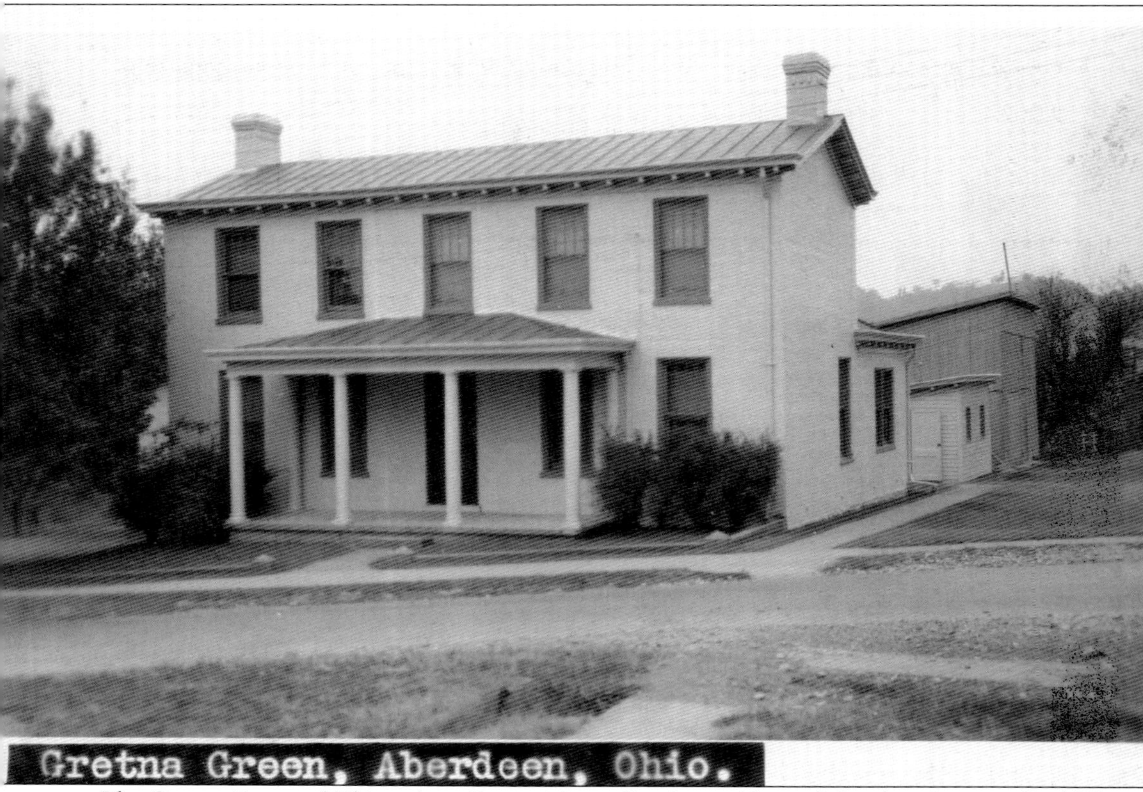

The Gretna Green of Ohio, where Squire Massie Beasley and his wife lived in this pre-Civil War home, is located in Aberdeen, Ohio, and is still standing today. Many couples were married here between 1870 and 1892. Some marriages were even performed on an Ohio River ferryboat piloted by the squire's son Thomas Green Beasley.

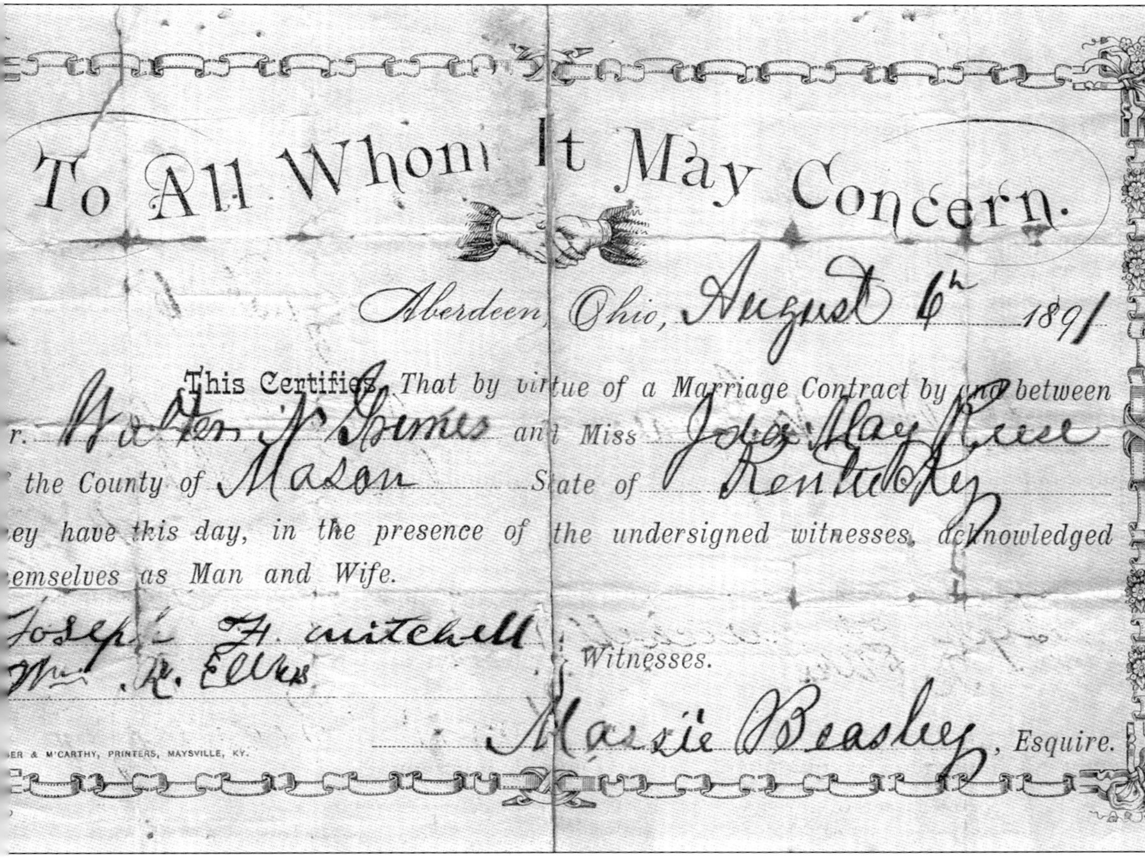

To All Whom It May Concern.

Aberdeen, Ohio, August 6th 1891

This Certifies, That by virtue of a Marriage Contract by and between
r. Walter N. Grimes and Miss Jose May Reese
the County of Mason State of Kentucky
ey have this day, in the presence of the undersigned witnesses, acknowledged
emselves as Man and Wife.

Joseph H. Mitchell
Wm. R. Ellis
Witnesses.

Massie Beasley, Esquire.

ER & M'CARTHY, PRINTERS, MAYSVILLE, KY.

Before Squire Beasley, there was Squire Thomas Shelton, who performed marriages from 1822 until his death in 1870. Squire Shelton did not keep good records and married couples without a license. This is a typical marriage license from 1891, signed by Squire Massie Beasley and two witnesses. Both Shelton and Beasley charged various prices for the weddings, and of course, it had to be cash. This was printed by Rosser and McCarthy in Maysville.